Rights, Religious Pluralism and the Recognition of Difference

Human rights and their principles of interpretation are the leading legal paradigms of our time. Freedom of religion occupies a pivotal position in rights discourses, and the principles supporting its interpretation receive increasing attention from courts and legislative bodies. This book critically evaluates religious pluralism as an emerging legal principle arising from attempts to define the boundaries of freedom of religion. It examines religious pluralism as an underlying aspect of different human rights regimes and constitutional traditions. It is, however, the static and liberal shape religious pluralism has assumed that is taken up critically here. In order to address how difference is vulnerable to elimination rather than recognition, the book takes up a contemporary ethics of alterity. More generally, and through its reconstruction of a more difference-friendly vision of religious pluralism, it tackles the problem of the role of rights in the era of diverse narratives of emancipation.

Dorota Anna Gozdecka is a lecturer in Migration Law at the Australian National University College of Law, Australia.

Rights, Religious Pluralism and the Recognition of Difference

Off the scales of justice

Dorota Anna Gozdecka

Routledge
Taylor & Francis Group

LONDON AND NEW YORK

First published 2016 by Routledge

2 Park Square, Milton Park, Abingdon, Oxon OX14 4RN
711 Third Avenue, New York, NY 10017, USA

Routledge is an imprint of the Taylor & Francis Group, an informa business

First issued in paperback 2017

British Library Cataloguing in Publication Data
A catalogue record for this book is available from the British Library

Library of Congress Cataloguing in Publication data
A catalog record for this book has been requested

ISBN: 978-1-138-79892-2 (hbk)
ISBN: 978-1-138-08433-9 (pbk)

Typeset in Baskerville
by Out of House Publishing

For my father
Dla taty

Contents

Acknowledgements

Acknowledgements always fill the author with dread. The first and primary concern is thanking everyone enough and at the same time avoiding spilling sentimental concerns over a reader who is largely unaware who the people mentioned are. After lengthy and personal acknowledgements written in my dissertation I will opt for a brief and less personal but no less honest or heartfelt note here.

I would like to thank my wonderful former colleagues at the University of Helsinki, including Kimmo Nuotio and Panu Minkkinen, who sincerely encouraged me to write this book. Especially Panu, for offering his time to help me think about what and how to say what I wanted to say. That brainstorming allowed this book to materialise. I am grateful to the members of Law and the Other, the project that I was leading at the time of writing this book, and colleagues at the Centre of Excellence in Foundations of European Law and Polity for their wonderful collegial support and participation in various events that allowed the ideas presented here to crystallise.

I would also like to thank those who warmly welcomed me to the Australian National University (ANU) College of Law. My special thanks go to Marianne Dickie, whose inspiring Migration Law Program has attracted me to this new track in my research and teaching. The participants in the Critical Theory Reading Group who have posed challenging questions on multiple readings referred to here should be able to recognise their influence on the volume, even if they were not aware they might have had one at the time. Particular thanks, too, go to Professor Desmond Manderson for supporting critical legal theory research at the ANU and for his insightful comments on the draft and previous research pieces that have had a heavy influence on the final shape of this volume. On a less formal but no less honest note I am grateful to Professor Oren Ben Dor from the University of Southampton. I still do not know if the sea is just the sea or a sum of its movements, but without our talks the ideas presented here would have not grown to their current shape. I opted for the sum of the movements but I might be completely wrong.

My special thanks go to Christopher Goddard for his careful work with the language. Sometimes it is easy to think that everyone must understand what we mean. I am glad of all the comments that have tested me on that.

And last but not least, no author is a mountain. This book was written at a time of tremendous challenges. Those who have supported me through those obstacles have certainly transformed this book from what I thought was an impossibility to the piece it is now. I will spare readers references to supportive tea-cups and heart-warming conversations. You may not be here by name, but I hope you all trust that your support was in fact the most valuable. And those who have challenged me beyond what I thought was imaginable deserve thanks as well. We find out how rich we are only at times when we think we are left with nothing. And, what goes without saying, big thanks to my parents, because your influence radiates in every word.

Canberra, March 2015

Introduction

Europe has long been considered a secular continent by the majority of scholars looking at religious phenomena there (Keane 2000; Anderson 2004; Casanova 2006; Taylor 2007; Berger, Fokas and Davie 2008; Levey and Modood 2008). Declining church attendance rates have been considered an inevitable indication of that tendency. As a result of this changing social landscape secularism as a legal paradigm has also gained importance (Bader 2007; Joppke 2007; Zucca 2012). Yet, contrary to those who have declared Europe to be a legally secular continent, a lawyer approaching intersections of law and religion in Europe can rather see a legal mosaic of different notions of religious freedom, religious confession, equality, laicism, secularism and state neutrality, or the 'salad bowl' as Katzenstein (Katzenstein 2006) put it. European approaches to freedom of religion vary from one country to another and from region to region. This salad bowl contains regimes as different as French secularism (*laïcité*), Spanish or Polish separation combined with concordat agreements or Maltese and formerly traditionally Scandinavian state churches (Gozdecka 2009; Doe 2011). Taking a deeper look at Europe, we must face an unsolvable puzzle of principles aiming at achieving an increasingly pluralistic liberal democratic standard, mixed with tradition and national religious sentiments often still stemming from the Reformation. Since the Reformation divided Europe's House,[1] diverse historical circumstances have often reinforced identification of national interests with particular religions. Religious wars, struggles for independence or recognition as a distinct national group have on some occasions led to the development of strong national identities based on religions (Rieffer 2003; Friedland 2001).

Due to these historical differences in the European religious landscape, European countries in the process of integration and regional cooperation have avoided open confrontation between their religious or non-religious traditions and newly developing European legal standards. The European Convention on Human Rights did not establish secularism or neutrality. It did not aim to raise a 'wall of separation' analogical to the American concept of neutrality stemming from the First Amendment. Instead, it affirmed the right of everyone to enjoy freedom of

---

[1] I paraphrase the title of MacCulloch's (2003) historical work here.

religion, albeit with 'such limitations as are prescribed by law and are necessary in a democratic society in the interests of public safety, for the protection of public order, health or morals, or the protection of the rights and freedoms of others'.[2] The non-confrontational approach was eventually also affirmed in the process of European Union (EU) integration and included in the declaration accompanying the Treaty of Amsterdam on the status of churches and non-confessional organisations.[3] The EU acknowledged that it respected and did not prejudice the status of churches under national law. This approach has allowed the influence of traditional religions or non-religious approaches to develop independently from each other. Freedom of religion has long continued as a local affair left to particular states instead of as a European matter. Only as late as 1988 in the case of *Kokkinakis* v. *Greece* did a complaint from a Greek Jehovah's Witness challenge national law before a European judicial body, the European Court of Human Rights (ECtHR).[4]

This quietude in the field of law and religion changed into a cacophony of different voices when the cultural and religious diversity of European societies began rapidly growing (Knippenberg 2005). The dynamics of cultural exchange have intensified and confronted the European chaos of multiple and often conflicting standards. Democratic discourse had to face the reality of new religions and cultures arriving in Europe and phrasing their claims in the language of human rights. This not only affected national laws, but due to the omnipresence of rights discourse transcended into international and EU law. EU law was prompted to consider religious difference not as a result of immigration from outside but primarily due to migration occurring within its territory. This internal migration called for strengthening the freedoms foreseen in the European Treaties in the context of religion and culture as well (Vickers 2008; McCrea 2010).

Cultural change has transformed the vague and roughly sketched boundaries of freedom of religion into an increasingly expansive interpretation of standards pertaining to equality of different religious adherents. These interpretative efforts by European legal institutions took a truly dramatic turn especially after the Mohammed caricature controversy. After the Danish newspaper *Jyllands Posten* published a comic strip featuring the prophet Mohammed in 2005 it was nothing but fear of the other that triggered European interest in archaic laws on blasphemy still present in many countries. Laws such as the Greek blasphemy regulation protecting primarily national churches from seditious speech (Temperman 2008) remained unquestioned and without interest from European institutions until the other, the Islamic community, entered the stage of rights. However, the other not only entered the stage but also voiced a claim in the language of rights in the belief that these belonged to 'everybody' in Europe (Gozdecka 2011).

---

[2] Council of Europe, *The European Convention on Human Rights*, Rome, 4 November 1950, Article 9.2.

[3] *Declaration on the Status of Churches and Non-confessional Organisations* (Treaty of Amsterdam), which secures the position of national churches and relations between states and religious communities.

[4] *Kokkinakis* v. *Greece*, European Court of Human Rights, Judgment, Application No. 14307/88, 25 May 1993.

When the other entered the stage of the rights drama, a European obsession with religion and its presence in the public sphere truly began. The Parliamentary Assembly of the Council of Europe (CoE), together with the Venice Commission for Democracy through Law, began active interpretation of the limits of 'necessity in a democratic society'. This interpretation has led to the emergence of a new interpretation principle applicable to freedom of religion – the principle of religious pluralism.

From a non-existing principle, religious pluralism has slowly become a cornerstone of 'necessity in a democratic society'. Whereas *Kokkinakis* made only a modest reference to pluralism as a fact of life, the recent obsessive expansion of interpretative sources concerning religion has slowly impacted the case-law of the ECtHR. The principle of religious pluralism has been declared the underlying value of European democratic societies.[5] It did not take long for the principle to transcend to the EU system of fundamental rights where protection of minorities and pluralism has also begun to play a pivotal role (Ahmed 2011).

At this point the reader may be tempted to ask what is wrong with acknowledging diversity and pluralism as legal principles. After all, this development can be seen as a clear step forward in comparison to blurry boundaries between traditions and freedom of religion in which the position of minorities was not given due attention. But mere acknowledgement may remain wishful thinking if its understanding and application brings contrary effects. Therefore it is important to consider the question differently. Rather than asking 'What is wrong with striving for pluralism?', which this author would most certainly welcome in the religious landscape of Europe, we need to ask: 'How is this principle understood?', 'What is wrong with its construction and why does it have the potential to "cauterise" (Simmons 2011) rather than recognise diverse religiously different others?' In other words: 'What does it mean for the religiously different other?' The next section examines the understanding of the principle in the soft-law documents of the CoE and its subsequent expansion to the case-law of the ECtHR. It evaluates the construction of the principle and discusses the shortcomings of the liberal approach adopted by the Council in these documents before moving in the chapters that follow to examine particular problem areas where others continue appearing on the margins of justice or, worse, become constructed as a threat to the dominant system in question.

In the context of this analysis it is no accident that the cover of this book features Gustave Doré's *War in Heaven*, depicting the banishment of Lucifer and other rebellious angels from heaven. In a different version of this engraving, at the top of his design Doré placed the Archangel Michael surrounded by blinding light and casting lightning from his hand to strike the bodies and wings of the banished. Below the light we see winged creatures writhing in pain and chaos. In the version selected here, we see only the banished as they plunge down, away from the

---

[5] For example, *Hasan and Eylem Zengin* v. *Turkey*, European Court of Human Rights, Judgment, Application No. 1448/04, 9 October 2009, para. 69.

lightning and the blinding light, and fall through a crack into a bottomless pit that will become hell. As they fall the light suddenly changes and enmeshes the world we see, their future world, with darkness. Their feathery wings, even though still feathery, appear dark and spiky, almost as if already undergoing a transformation into the webbed wings we know from later representations of devils and demons. Cast down from heaven they will indeed eventually turn from angels into devils and from the embodiment of good they will eventually symbolise evil unbound. The Bible, probably the most frequently cited religious book in the world, in all its variations used and referred to by different religious creeds, knows no rebellion against God. God's self-righteousness knows no dissent and allows for no revolution. 'The common explanation of Satan's fall is, then, that puffed up with pride and ambition, he sought to equal or surpass the Almighty', observes Arnold Williams in his examination of Milton's *Paradise Lost* (Williams 1945, 256). For the sin of seeking equality Lucifer and his army were shown no mercy and no forgiveness. The heavenly light of Lucifer's world changed for ever into darkness and the crack through which he and his army fell sealed the damned in biblical hell and in the hell of the collective imagination of humanity. Rebellion, a plea for equality and revolution constitute a fundamental biblical sin against God's law. This law and its pre-constituted order has symbolised goodness even if enforced by acts of great violence such as the forceful banishment of the damned angels. Few have asked where God's love is in the process of casting down angels, and those who have, asserting that a God full of wrath is merely a jealous Demiurge who does not represent the true nature of the divine, have filled the records of heretics for centuries (Williams 1992; Read 2007). God, in the act of banishment, knows no altruism and no love but instead enforces obedience to law by brute force. God's law is thus the embodiment of violence and that violence underpins the legal system, as some have argued (Benjamin 1986; Derrida 1992).

The story on the cover is not to be read as a religious apology, as this author herself does not identify with any known religion, but instead as a parabolic illustration accompanying current events in law and religion in Europe. *War in Heaven* illustrates current legal debates through the eyes of those making a plea for equality and hoping to challenge the established order of the law. As in Doré's engraving, which illustrates God's self-righteousness lying at the foundations of the moral order, dissidents challenging the established status quo are frequently cast down for their rebellion against the self-righteousness of established law. In the same way as Lucifer's plea for equality, the appeal of those who challenge the existing legal order in matters of law and religion increasingly results in a battle in which their difference is used to their disadvantage and conceptualised as dissent rather than a legitimate plea. Whether their belief is religious or not, those whose beliefs are different from the dominant religious or non-religious normativity recognised and endorsed by law seem frequently unsuccessful in challenging the established position given to religion in their respective legal orders. Their appeal to rights is futile and turned against them. Instead of recognition they are too often cast down like the biblical angels and frequently become framed into the demonised other, who cannot ever be in an equal position to those being challenged. Human rights increasingly often present religious difference not as a virtue but as a merely antagonistic quality responsible for an egoistic rebellion against a righteous legal order. Human rights law, instead of aiding the plea for equality, reconstructs religiously different individuals and groups into almost mythical challengers of established law and order. As such they become the ultimate other, eventually cast down from Heaven and sealed in the deep pits of the hell of marginalisation. Doré's illustration of this biblical myth focuses the gaze of the viewer not on the law and order of God, but on the consequences of God's wrath for those banished. The viewer sees their faces twisted in pain, their bodies in convulsions and their wings in commotion. Doré's perspective suddenly conjures empathy from the viewer. Lucifer and his army shout out to the viewer and ask her to focus not on their deed framed as diabolical but on their humanity. This book, in analogy to Doré's illustration, analyses recent events on the scene of law, religion and rights through the perspective of those framed as dissidents. It shows the story of their rebellion and appeal to rights and asks the reader to focus on their plea and their attempt to have their religious difference recognised and accommodated. Just like Doré's magnificent illustration it hopes to shift the perspective and ask whether law and rights can focus on their humanity, not their dissent.

Readers sceptical of critical readings might not be convinced that such a perspective is enough to arrive at new findings. They might fear that instead the only value of such an approach lies in pushing the limits of liberal principles to further realisation. Whereas it is true that critical approaches have their limitations, refocusing the debate by viewing it through the perspective of the other illuminates the flaws and insensitivities of liberal approaches to diversity and rights. While encountering the language of politics and ontology, every critique challenges but also inevitably falls into the trap of the language of totalising principles and constructs. As Levinas, who is one of the leading theoretical inspirations for this volume, notes:

> [I]f there were only two people in the world, there would be no need for law courts because I would always be responsible for, and before, the other. As soon as there are three, the ethical relationship with the other becomes political and enters into the totalizing discourse of ontology. We can never completely escape from the language of ontology and politics.
>
> (Cohen 1986, 13–33)

Being aware that ontological traps underpinning liberal theory of rights are not entirely avoidable, this story read and viewed with a focus on the other and the way in which she became the other does not take as its objective outlining new general principles of justice. Instead it hopes to achieve the far more modest objective of challenging and reconstructing approaches to difference in the area of human rights and their interpretational principles. With rights being the new theology of our era (Douzinas 2000, 2007) the influence of rights principles on the wider legal system is vast and reflected in constitutional and international legal regimes. The principle of religious pluralism has slowly, albeit in a different shape, affected law in Europe beyond the strict area of interpretation of the European Convention on Human Rights. Mindful of this enormous power of rights and their principles traversing the boundaries of legal regimes, the book abstains as far as possible from proposing new general principles of justice. Such overarching normative proposals frequently carry more risks than promises and by falling into new ontological traps create new rigidities and injustices. The objective of shifting the perspective to the other and the process of otherisation in the contemporary area of law and religion is thus far more modest than laying down new fundamentals of an ideal system of recognition and distribution. What remains in focus throughout the book is, just as in Doré's engraving, the miscarriage of the justice of rights and the consequences for those affected. Such illumination does not intend to reconstruct the entire system of rights but instead far more modestly seeks to envision anew what Douzinas calls a 'utopian' call of rights for justice (Douzinas 2000, 181) and what is called here their 'emancipatory potential'. Reconstruction of the notion of emancipation requires a shift of analytical perspective from a narrative of construction to one of deconstruction. Without an awareness of the traps of ontology involved in constructing models of justice, a miscarriage of justice cannot be fully exposed. Emancipation, as shown later, cannot be rethought by focusing solely on ontology but must take into account the promises and challenges of the ethics of alterity. As a result of this shift of perspective, this volume addresses the concerns of the disempowered against the concerns of those in power and seeks an answer to the question 'how to prevent the current system from miscarrying justice and disabling the possibility of emancipation' instead of 'how to construct new general principles of justice'. While reading this book it is important to remember that providing a view from a different position is a value of critique as such. Even mere illumination of the position of the marginalised may question existing categories and lay down new normative priorities. The objective of critique does not have to involve a struggle for law reform (Kahn 1999). In a critical reading even a mere challenge to myths existing in the practice of liberalism such as those justifying invisibility and marginalisation is a value added. If as feared by the sceptics it achieves nothing more, it can at least help make liberalism more attentive to minoritarian experiences. In other words, to see current shortcomings in the interpretation of religious pluralism in Europe we need to face the banished, look at their grimaces and their wings and truly comprehend the entirety of *War in Heaven* for all concerned.

This reluctance to engage in an effort to reconstruct a new ideal model of justice is related to the theoretical approach underpinning the book – a critique of Enlightenment discourse. Each attempt at reconstructing a fully liberating and comprehensive system of justice is bound to end in failure. As shown in the part tracing back the evolution of religious pluralism, which ideally aims at guaranteeing genuine 'freedom' in the realm of religion, every attempt to reconstruct its meaning necessarily also marginalises. This is related to ontological traps involved in constructing the notion of freedom (Adorno 1973) and the impossibility of establishing freedom once and for all. Therefore the book favours dislocating the centred and is informed by suspicion towards any totalising accounts. The object- ive of this volume is not to answer the identity crisis of critical theory. It is instead to bring closer the vision of justice of those excluded and construct a culturally informed test of the limits of exclusion. As Matsuda reminds us, alliance with the bottom lends moral force to the project of critical legal studies (Matsuda 1987, 361). Such an alliance may prevent further miscarriages of the justice of rights. Perhaps indeed 'the best' that critical theory can do is to provide useful models for examining injustices in liberal approaches rather than offer 'superior' approaches. The very expectation of 'superiority' of any new approaches implies recreating new forms of exclusion, new mistranslations of the utopian call for justice and new dislocations between an ideally inclusive norm and its legal application. For all these reasons this book does not seek to develop the best system of accommo- dation but instead asks why contemporary systems fall short of their promise. As elaborated further, the critique of pluralism is undertaken having in mind that no system can be entirely free from the possibility of exclusion. Due to the inescap- able traps of the conceptualisation and construction of legal categories, models and systems, all models, whether secular, plural or neutral, cannot entirely escape the problems of ontology involved in creating such workable systems.

Instead of focusing on secularism, the predominant paradigm in studies of law and religion, this volume focuses on the emerging paradigm of religious plural- ism (Requejo and Ungureanu 2014; Sandberg 2015). Despite a growing interest, religious pluralism as a principle remains under-examined in accounts dealing with freedom of religion and is often examined through the prism of secular- ism. Meanwhile as a framework for recognition religious pluralism prima facie appears most promising in terms of its major emphasis on difference. Liberal accounts of pluralism, analysed in the following chapters while introducing the evolution of the principle and its interpretations conducted in a liberal spirit, have not fully embraced the engagement with difference that pluralism promises. It is entirely possible to imagine a pluralism that could engage with difference on a far deeper level than by reducing it to the principles of equality and impartiality. As powerfully argued by Iris Marion Young in her *Justice and the Politics of Difference*, the ideal of impartiality reduces heterogeneity to an imagined unity measuring everything against a standard of 'universal reason' (Young 1990, 99). Pluralism that does not engage with difference and that operates merely with the logic of identity eventually seeks to 'reduce the differently similar to the same' and 'turns the merely different into the absolutely other' (ibid.). Instead of pluralism, this generates a dichotomy resulting in conceptualisations of the other as a dissident and excluding her from the protection of rights. This mechanism, identified and studied by Young and related to ontological problems of defining self by refer- ence to the other, will be encapsulated and examined in selected case studies. The analysis will show that instead of dislocating self-centredness, contemporary interpretations of pluralism frequently result in defining a community in rigid and homogeneous terms and limiting the possibility of creating a heterogeneous community responsive and accepting of difference. Reducing difference to sameness reinforces an understanding of rights as privileges (Levinas 1994) and of individuals as members of a homogenous community. The selected case studies show that pluralism denies difference for a variety of reasons, sometimes too readily repeating assumptions of secularism. The reason the critique is not directed simply at secularism is the assumption that secularism is an unsatisfactory paradigm not solely because of its disengagement with the religious. The book illustrates that secularism is frequently too far from being secular in fact. Instead it is an Enlightenment-inspired fiction, which presents religion as a barbaric function of the unknown other and obscures, if not straightforwardly misinterprets, the role of religion in creating standards of communal homogeneity. The notion of secularism will be elaborated in the parts dealing with the transition from secularism to pluralism. While this volume concurs that in principle the primary problem lies with the inability of European states to cope with diversity (Zucca 2012, 24),[6] it none the less argues that the paradigm of secularism does not adequately reflect what the problem with diversity really is. Rather than being the primary problem, it is just one of many frameworks that might deny difference. Whether envisioning the community in secular or religious terms the primary problem is the reduction to sameness. Secularism is merely one of multiple ways in which such reduction can be done.

Thus this book encourages not so much unconditional acceptance of all religious claims but rather engagement with difference and truly facing the other (Levinas 1994, 1969, 2003), whoever she is in the given circumstances. The book follows the path of those theories that challenge the ontology and assert that not only the self, but also the other cannot be defined in universal terms. It may be an atheist in Italy, a Scientology adherent in Germany, a woman covering her face in France or a woman pleading for abortion in Ireland. This book sets up a challenge for law and human rights to question themselves before a priori excluding those who challenge the status quo.

Taking inspiration from its predecessors such as Costas Douzinas and Paul Simmons, this volume seeks to deconstruct current rights regimes in the context of the justice of the other and reconstruct their emancipatory potential with reference to the ethics of alterity of Emmanuel Levinas and difference as a foundation for community. Mindful that such reconstructions have been made before, among others by authors cited, the book encourages the embracing of a dynamic understanding of difference and a dynamic conceptualisation of the relationship between majority and minority. In the same fashion it encourages an uncemented and dynamic understanding of freedom. This challenge of dynamism could not be embraced without reference to Theodor Adorno and Gilles Deleuze, who challenged the rigidity of ontological structures in relation not only to self but also to freedom. Not forgetting the studies of Jean-François Lyotard, the book illustrates

---

[6] Zucca 2012, 24.

that without escaping the homogenising terms in which pluralism is defined and the static ways in which freedom is interpreted, a principle of pluralism risks remaining no more than another grand narrative. As a result the more talk about pluralism the less pluralism, the more talk about difference, the stronger the othering and the greater the homogeneity.

References

Adorno, Theodor W. 1973. *Negative Dialectics*. Routledge.

Ahmed, Tawhida. 2011. *The Impact of EU Law on Minority Rights*. Hart Publishing.

Anderson, Brian C. 2004. 'Secular Europe, Religious America.' *Public Interest* 155: 143–58.

Bader, Veit. 2007. *Secularism or Democracy? Associational Governance of Religious Diversity*. Amsterdam University Press.

Benjamin, Walter. 1986. *Reflections: Essays, Aphorisms, Autobiographical Writings*, ed. Peter Demetz. Schocken.

Berger, Peter, Effie Fokas and Grace Davie. 2008. *Religious America, Secular Europe? A Theme and Variations*. Ashgate.

Casanova, José 2006. 'Religion, European Secular Identities, and European Integration.' In *Religion in an Expanding Europe*, ed. T. A. Byrnes and P. J. Katzenstein, 65–92. Cambridge University Press.

Cohen, Richard A. 1986. *Face to Face with Levinas*. State University of New York Press.

Derrida, Jacques. 1992. 'Force of Law: The Mystical Foundation of Authority.' In *Deconstruction and the Possibility of Justice*, ed. Drucilla Cornell, Michel Rosenfeld and David Gray Carlson, 3–67. Routledge.

Doe, Norman. 2011. *Law and Religion in Europe: A Comparative Introduction*. Oxford University Press.

Douzinas, Costas. 2000. *The End of Human Rights: Critical Legal Thought at the Turn of the Century*. Hart Publishing.

Douzinas, Costas. 2007. *Human Rights and Empire: The Political Philosophy of Cosmopolitanism*. Routledge.

Friedland, Roger. 2001. 'Religious Nationalism and the Problem of Collective Representation.' *Annual Review of Sociology* 27 (January): 125–52.

Gozdecka, Dorota A. 2009. 'Religions and Legal Boundaries of Democracy in Europe: European Commitment to Democratic Principles.' e-thesis, University of Helsinki.

Gozdecka, Dorota A. 2011. 'Europe's Changing Approach towards Blasphemy: The "Right Not to Be Offended", Sensitive Identities and Relativism.' In *Law and Outsiders: Norms Processes and 'Othering' in the 21st Century*, ed. C.C. Murphy and P. Green, 233–48. Hart Publishing.

Joppke, C. 2007. 'State Neutrality and Islamic Headscarf Laws in France and Germany.' *Theory and Society* 36(4): 313–42.

Kahn, Paul W. 1999. *The Cultural Study of Law*. University of Chicago Press.

Katzenstein, Peter J. 2006. 'Multiple Modernities as Limits to Secular Europeanization?' In *Religion in an Expanding Europe*, 1–33. Cambridge University Press.

Keane, John. 2000. 'Secularism?' In *Religion and Democracy*, ed. David Marquand and Ronald L. Nettler, 5–19. Blackwell.

Knippenberg, Hans. 2005. *The Changing Religious Landscape of Europe*. Het Spinhuis.

Levey, Geoffrey Brahm and Tariq Modood, eds. 2008. *Secularism, Religion and Multicultural Citizenship*. Cambridge University Press.

Levinas, Emmanuel. 1969. *Totality and Infinity: An Essay on Exteriority*. Pittsburgh PA: Duquesne University Press.

Levinas, Emmanuel. 1994. *Outside the Subject*. Stanford University Press.

Levinas, Emmanuel. 2003. *Humanism of the Other*. University of Illinois Press.

McCrea, Ronan. 2010. *Religion and the Public Order of the European Union*. Oxford University Press.

MacCulloch, Diarmaid. 2003. *Reformation: Europe's House Divided 1490–1700*. Allen Lane.

Matsuda, Mari J. 1987. 'Looking to the Bottom: Critical Legal Studies and Reparations.' *Harvard Civil Rights-Civil Liberties Review* 22: 323, 327–8.

Read, Cameron. 2007. 'In Search of Sophia: Origins and Interpretations of the Gnostic Demiurge.' *Chrestomathy: Annual Review of Undergraduate Research, School of Humanities and Social Sciences, School of Languages, Cultures, and World Affairs, College of Charleston* 6: 137–53.

Requejo, Ferran and Camil Ungureanu. 2014. *Democracy, Law and Religious Pluralism in Europe: Secularism and Post-secularism*. Routledge.

Rieffer, Barbara Ann J. 2003. 'Religion and Nationalism: Understanding the Consequences of a Complex Relationship.' *Ethnicities* 3(2): 215–42.

Sandberg, Russell. 2015. *Religion and Legal Pluralism*. Ashgate.

Simmons, William Paul. 2011. *Human Rights Law and the Marginalized Other*. Cambridge University Press.

Taylor, Charles. 2007. *A Secular Age*. Belknap Press of Harvard University Press.

Temperman, Jeroen 2008. 'Blasphemy, Defamation of Religions and Human Rights Law.' *Netherlands Quarterly of Human Rights* 26: 517–45.

Vickers, Lucy. 2008. *Religious Freedom, Religious Discrimination and the Workplace*. Hart Publishing.

Williams, Arnold. 1945. 'The Motivation of Satan's Rebellion in "Paradise Lost".' *Studies in Philology* 42(2): 253–68.

Williams, Michael A. 1992. 'The Demonizing of the Demiurge: The Innovation of Gnostic Myth.' *In Innovation in Religious Traditions: Essays in the Interpretation of Religious Change*, ed. M. A. Williams, C. Cox and M. S. Jaffee, 73–108. Mouton de Gruyter.

Young, Iris Marion. 1990. *Justice and the Politics of Difference*. Princeton University Press.

Zucca, Lorenzo. 2012. *A Secular Europe: Law and Religion in the European Constitutional Landscape*. Oxford University Press.

Part I

From non-confrontation to obsession and back again

Religious pluralism as an emerging legal principle in the European legal sphere

> *No supranational court has any business substituting its own ethical mock-ups for those qualities that history has imprinted on the national identity. On a human rights court falls the function of protecting fundamental rights, but never ignoring that customs are not passing whims. They evolve over time, harden over history into cultural cement. They become defining, all-important badges of identity for nations, tribes, religions, individuals.*
>
> *Lautsi* v. *Italy*, European Court of Human Rights,
> Application no. 30814/06, 18 March 2011,
> Concurring opinion of Judge Bonello, para. 1.1

Chapter I

Council of Europe bodies and soft-law interpretations of religious pluralism

The Council of Europe and its organs were the pioneers in interpreting the limits of freedom of religion and the duties of Member States in securing it. In particular the Parliamentary Assembly of the CoE has become an active interpreter of democratic standards in the area of law and religion. Before religious pluralism became a consideration for the ECtHR it was the Parliamentary Assembly that adopted multiple recommendations and resolutions dealing directly with religious issues. In this active process of interpretation the Assembly created a body of soft law which gave rise to religious pluralism understood as a legal principle in interpreting freedom of religion and necessity in a democratic society (Gozdecka 2009). Even though soft law did not directly refer to any particular theoretical approach, its development reflected liberal theoretical positions concerning diversity and cultural coexistence. It has also mirrored the development of liberal Enlightenment standards – from mere toleration to multicultural adjustment.

In one of its earliest documents dealing with religion, Recommendation 1202 (1993) 'On religious tolerance in a democratic society', the Parliamentary Assembly remained modest in its interpretation and stressed the individual nature of a belief as well as underlined its 'positive impact on the immediate social surroundings'.[1] Following the classic Kantian conception of law and its separation from the moral (Kant 1797), this approach affirmed the liberal division between the private and public spheres and the assumption that religion must always belong to the private (Habermas 2008). At the same time the Recommendation observed the impact of migration on the meeting of different religious groups[2] and put emphasis on religious conflicts stemming from the fundamentalisation of majority religions as well as the growing crisis of values.[3]

Despite the best intentions to respond to the demands of growing diversity, this early Recommendation did not yet speak of 'religious pluralism', but merely of 'religious tolerance'[4] that ought to be fostered in a Western 'secular society'.[5]

---

[1] See Recommendation 1202 (1993), 'On religious tolerance in a democratic society', of the Council of Europe Parliamentary Assembly, para. 13.
[2] *Ibid.*, at para. 4.
[3] *Ibid.*, at paras 7–9.
[4] *Ibid.*, at para. 10.
[5] *Ibid.*, at para. 15.

By adopting tolerance as its starting point, this first approach to religious diversity by definition created the perception of the other. In this neo-colonial approach (Sharma 2009) it is easy to imagine that it was the Christian European male separating the private (religious) and the public (secular) that remained seen as the superior standard (Mancini 2012). Everyone else who did not conform to this standard was to be 'tolerated'. But in the mere conception of tolerance lies a judgment. The one who tolerates does not refrain from passing judgment on the inferiority of the one to be tolerated. But in the enlightened and allegedly superior approach, the one who tolerates knows he must remain righteous and tolerate the presence of the other. He may disapprove of the beliefs of the other but in the name of reason refrains from oppressing that other. In Adorno's words: 'The bourgeois … is tolerant. His love of people as they are stems from his hatred of what they might be' (Adorno 1951). Tolerance as a starting point for diversity offers no more than a precarious peace. A peace based on the hierarchy between the one who is superior and the one who must be tolerated.

But even that precarious peace is not framed with reference to religious pluralism. The Assembly, as if borrowing straight from Locke's *A Letter Concerning Toleration*, sees tolerance as a mere duty of the state to secure every individual's freedom from religious oppression (Locke 1689). Pluralism remained out of the question as a value. It was merely seen as something to be aware of, but not as a goal or an aspiration.[6] Pluralism and the very 'crisis of values' are put close enough to create an illusion that they are but the same thing. Like Locke's 'magistrate', the state in the Recommendation is seen as bearer of the duty of neutrality to all religions in a state of affairs that appears to be no more than an unfortunate turn of history towards pluralism.[7] In the precarious peace of tolerance there is no thought of recognition (Brown 2008).

But the Assembly continued its interpretation with more Enlightenment-inspired documents. In the following Recommendation 1396 (1999), 'Religion and democracy', the Parliamentary Assembly's voice is perhaps a little less archaic but retains a strong liberal democratic tone. It underlines that whereas religion in general impacts democratic society positively,[8] it is also a source of multiple conflicts. To avoid much of the doubt concerning who is the source of the conflict, the Recommendation deals in greater detail with religious extremism, which is seen as a negative and essentially anti-democratic phenomenon.[9] Because of the fear of an extremist other, the vision embedded in the text conceives of a static liberal democratic system based on the idea of a consensus. From Locke's classic understanding of toleration, it evolves towards contemporary liberal democratic models such as proposed by John Rawls or Jürgen Habermas. The Rawlsian conception

---

[6] *Ibid.*, at para. 10.

[7] *Ibid.*, at para. 15.

[8] See Recommendation 1396 (1999), 'Religion and democracy', of the Council of Europe Parliamentary Assembly, para. 5.

[9] *Ibid.*, at para. 9.

of a reasonable consensus resonates throughout the entire text (Rawls 2005). In this model the public sphere is neatly ordered by reasonable citizens, presumably white Christian men rather than emotional 'extremists', such as Muslim women in head-coverings (Mancini 2012). The public good is shaped through negotiation and is reflected in the public sphere, where a static and pre-agreed conception of justice exists. The veil of ignorance, from behind which these just principles are conceived, with utmost certainty in the Assembly's view, must guarantee the equality of all. However, only reasonable citizens are included in the negotiation on the shape of what that public good and justice entail. The Recommendation clearly advocates that governance and religion should not mix and that states should exclude from consultations any religious groups not supporting the fundamental values of democracy. This a priori exclusion from deliberation without a doubt corresponds with the Rawlsian notion of 'unreasonable doctrine'. After all, only reasonable citizens who can surgically separate their religious doctrines and treat them as an individual matter without bringing them into the public sphere of deliberation can join the process of formation of justice:

> It is not up to politicians to decide on religious matters. As for religions, they must not try to take the place of democracy or grasp political power; they must respect the definition of human rights, contained in the European Convention on Human Rights, and the rule of law.[10]

This deliberation on the public good ought to happen through dialogue. In this respect the Recommendation has a distinct flavour of Habermasian discourse theory (Habermas 1998). It underlines the importance of engaging in more regular dialogue with religious and humanist leaders about the major problems facing society. It encourages dialogue between religions and promotion of regular dialogue between theologians, philosophers and historians, as well as with representatives of other branches of knowledge. This dialogue is believed to create harmonious democratic societies through discourses aimed at achieving self-understanding. Through such discourses participants can get a clear understanding of themselves and 'become clear about the kind of society in which they want to live' (Habermas 1998, 282).

This Recommendation is also the first body of soft law which explicitly mentions a link between religious pluralism and democracy, even though it does not yet assign pluralism the value of a principle. It confirms the commitment to a plurality of ethical, moral and ideological conceptions of individual European citizens and casually draws a link between democracy and religious pluralism by placing religious pluralism among certain goals that democracy helps to achieve:

> Democracy and religion need not be incompatible; quite the opposite. Democracy has proved to be the best framework for freedom of conscience,

---

[10] *Ibid.*, at para. 4.

the exercise of faith and religious pluralism. For its part, religion, through its moral and ethical commitment, the values it upholds, its critical approach and its cultural expression, can be a valid partner of democratic society.[11]

But despite this reference to pluralism and its link with democracy the presence of the other is clearly tangible in the Recommendation. It is no longer the 'inferior' newcomer to the traditional religious or non-religious status quo explicitly excluded by the judgment on her inferiority. The other in this text hides in the silence of the margins. She continues to exist in the illusionary assumption that reasonable citizens will separate themselves from their own religious or non-religious majoritarian traditions and refrain from judgment on the 'inferior' other. Instead this conception assumes that they join, without prejudice, in negotiation of the common good and justice. The presence of the other resonates in the a priori exclusion of the 'unreasonable citizen' and 'unreasonable' doctrine concluded by the judgment of none other than the 'reasonable' majority. She lurks in the illusory belief that mere dialogue can solve the problems of society without guaranteeing that truly everyone rather than an elite of experts can participate in shaping the discussion and that the discussion also embraces emancipation. And finally the other lives in the very conception of the consensus so well criticised by Lyotard, who argued that consensus in its dominant understanding is but a component of a system which uses consensus for achieving its real goal – acquisition of power (Lyotard 1984, 60–1).

The tendency to liberal interpretation of pluralism with a development towards multicultural readjustment continues in the subsequent document issued a few years later, even before the Danish cartoon controversy. Recommendation 1720 (2005), 'Education and religion', like earlier documents, neatly separates the public and the private and highlights the importance of seeing religion as a personal matter. But despite retaining its liberal democratic focus the Assembly is evolving into a body more conscious of a communitarian critique (MacIntyre 1981, 1988; Taylor 1979; Sandel 1998; Parekh 2002). For the first time in its interpretative efforts, it attempts to adjust liberalism to a model accommodating both individuals and communities. It discovers the importance of the community in the example of a community that is closest to the individual, the family.[12] In recognising the importance of the family as a community interacting with other communities in a society, it acknowledges possible differences of priorities and attempts to go beyond the narrow understanding of liberalism focusing solely on the individual.

This necessity of acknowledging the community is connected with the observed problem of the disappearing knowledge of religion which, in the Assembly's view, resulted in a lack of 'the necessary bearings' through which young people could fully 'apprehend the societies in which they live and others with which they

[11] Recommendation 1396 (1999), 'Religion and democracy', para. 5.
[12] See Recommendation 1720 (2005), 'Education and religion', of the Council of Europe Parliamentary Assembly, para. 3.

are confronted'.[13] Therefore it has led to emergence of conflicts between different communities, both religious and non-religious.[14] For these reasons the primary focus is on dialogue between religions and learning about diversity. The Recommendation emphasises:

> Knowledge of religions is an integral part of knowledge of the history of mankind and civilisations. It is altogether distinct from belief in a specific religion and its observance. Even countries where one religion predominates should teach about the origins of all religions rather than favour a single one or encourage proselytising.[15]

Whereas religious pluralism is not mentioned verbatim, recommending teaching about the origins of all religions rather than one does acknowledge the *de facto* necessity of recognising and fostering diversity. The Assembly does not view the predominantly mono-religious composition of a society as a sufficient justification for its domination in educational life. It expresses the concern that the beliefs of adherents of other religions must be duly weighed, thus signifying a turning point in the Assembly's approach. It is here that for the first time the differently religious individual is no longer seen as the other that must be barely tolerated and who must tolerate the practices of the majority. It is the other that ought to be recognised. This change of focus acknowledges the concerns of theorists such as Charles Taylor and Amy Guttmann, who observed the impact of non-recognition on personal identity (Taylor and Gutmann 1992), or Bikhu Parekh, who advocated a multicultural society which did not ignore the demands of diversity (Parekh 2002). In this Recommendation liberal and communitarian concerns are for the first time weighed simultaneously.

Yet without a doubt, the Assembly's approach continues to reflect a strong liberalism that should be adjusted to multicultural demands. Key concepts of this text continue focusing on the necessity of keeping religion and politics apart[16] and combating extremism.[17] The body of this Recommendation is built with the help of Rawlsian building blocks rearranged to embrace some who were previously excluded. But despite this readjustment it is still a construction with a strong taste for the other and hesitant to embrace those who are reluctant to accept conditions of discussion void of their own personal beliefs. The one who previously was seen as the other is now to be recognised. Yet she continues to coexist alongside a new other. The accepted One is carefully outlined following the paragon of a 'reasonable' citizen who does not allow private 'irrationality' to affect the 'reasonable consensus' (Rawls 2005). He is neither 'the extremist' nor a proponent of creationism, as Resolution 1580 (2007), 'The dangers of creationism in education', declares.

[13] *Ibid.*, at para. 3.
[14] *Ibid.*, at para. 2.
[15] *Ibid.*, at para. 8.
[16] *Ibid.*, at para. 5.
[17] *Ibid.*, at para. 5.

Indeed, the accepted One is in fact not that different from the one who recognises him. The heart of this recognition continues to lie in similarity rather than in difference, as advocated by Young (Young 1990, 1997).

After these ambitious aspirations of recognition were phrased by the Assembly the discourse on pluralism has taken on a new speed. Pluralism has begun to be seen as the central foundation of a democratic society. The reader develops hope that now at last diverse contexts will be recognised and a broad acceptance of difference will finally become the central focus. So it must come as a surprise, perhaps even as a disappointment, to see that whereas the discourse on pluralism indeed becomes omnipresent, the reading of further recommendations continues to essentialise the other and fix predominant and static paradigms in the area of recognition of religious difference. In order to make sense of these contradictory tendencies we must bear in mind the Mohammed cartoon controversy. The static nature that religious pluralism has taken in subsequent documents stems from the fear of a particular other. The cartoon controversy is the turning point after which collective European Islamophobia truly took off (Esposito and Kalin 2011). After the cartoon controversy the state suddenly became the object of protection from 'the bad Muslim'. In order to secure the foundations of the state, the Assembly moved back to its tried and tested tools – an assumption of the universal nature of European secularism and the fight against extremism. At the same time subsequent documents ever more proudly pronounced the fundamental importance of religious pluralism.

In a desperate effort to include as many options as possible but without abandoning liberal defences against 'extremists', the Assembly put renewed emphasis on state secularity and fixed it as a paradigm in the discussion on law and religion in Europe despite obvious differences in the composition of state-and-religion relations in Europe. In Recommendation 1804 (2007), 'State, religion, secularity and human rights', the separation of state and church is assumed to be one of Europe's shared values 'transcending national differences',[18] even though the Assembly explicitly mentions such differences and must be aware of diverse and sometimes contrary traditions (Ziebertz and Riegel 2008). But the Assembly chooses to homogenise its approach in an effort to affirm that governance and religion are seen as non-overlapping areas,[19] so that matters of religion are seen as strictly private[20] and emphasises that:

> Various situations coexist in Europe. In some countries, one religion still predominates. Religious representatives may play a political role, as in the case of the bishops who sit in the United Kingdom House of Lords. Some countries have banned the wearing of religious symbols in schools. The legislation of

[18] See Recommendation 1804 (2007), 'State, religion, secularity and human rights', of the Council of Europe Parliamentary Assembly, para. 4.
[19] *Ibid.*, at para.10.
[20] *Ibid.*, at para. 4.

several Council of Europe member states still contains anachronisms dating from times when religion played a more important part in our societies.[21]

These anachronisms, however, should not in the Assembly's view prevent Member States from passing on impartial knowledge of all religions in education[22] and fostering intercultural dialogue.[23] Indeed, interculturalism[24] is emphasised strongly for the first time in as many as six separate paragraphs, hand in hand with the necessity of recognising religion 'in all its plurality'.[25] This emphasis indicates a development of pluralism from a mere fact of life, through a necessity for recognition to a value that needs to be fostered through deliberation and dialogue. It is assumed that pluralism is an aim so important that it can indeed transcend differences and be raised to the status of a common good of such a fundamental nature that it must survive democratic deliberation and difference, as Cohen would argue in defence of his deliberative democratic model (Cohen 1997). In fostering this fundamental good the Assembly sees religious communities themselves as important actors and treats them as 'part of civil society' which the Assembly calls on

> to play an active role in the pursuit of peace, co-operation, tolerance, solidarity, intercultural dialogue and the dissemination of the Council of Europe's values.[26]

Because of this role of communities as important actors the Assembly once more emphasises the necessity to recognise different types of cultural groups with potentially different cultural and religious claims. The Recommendation distinguishes a secularised majority,[27] differently established and regulated churches,[28] majority religions[29] and growing Muslim communities,[30] all with potentially different rights claims. Distinguishing between these diverse groups in the religious landscape of Europe the text closely follows models such as that of Will Kymlicka in which he shaped his original group rights model (Kymlicka 2003a).

---

[21] *Ibid.*, at para. 15.
[22] *Ibid.*, at para. 14.
[23] *Ibid.*, at para. 13.
[24] Leaving aside the dispute about whether interculturalism and multiculturalism are interchangeable terms or whether they are used to describe different levels of the same phenomenon, it is necessary to observe the increased significance of the idea of diversity. For more on the difference between interculturalism and multiculturalism, see: Kymlicka 2003b. Kymlicka argues that interculturalism and multiculturalism, although often interchangeable, are in fact two opposite poles of the same phenomenon. While interculturalism refers to individuals, multiculturalism refers to a society.
[25] Recommendation 1804, at para. 3.
[26] *Ibid.*, at para. 23.2.
[27] *Ibid.*, at para. 6.
[28] *Ibid.*, at para. 5.
[29] *Ibid.*, at para. 7.
[30] *Ibid.*, at para. 6.

This affirmation of diversity following an analogical model is fully developed in Recommendation 1805 (2007), 'Blasphemy, religious insults and hate speech against persons on grounds of their religion'. This Recommendation results from the work of the Committee investigating issues of blasphemy led by Finnish Representative Sinikka Hurskainen. The findings of the Committee were initially published on 8 June 2007[31] and subsequently forged into the text of the Recommendation. A similar Report was prepared by the Venice Commission for Democracy through Law and published on 17–18 October 2008. These new documents representing a new European approach towards blasphemy underline that a common European approach is necessary with regard to freedom of expression as a value of vital importance for democracy. It advocates revising and abolishing blasphemy laws as reflecting the historically dominant position of certain religions in certain Member States.[32] The Recommendation expresses a belief that greater understanding between members of different religious groups and greater tolerance towards activities which are critical and even offensive are necessary in Europe.[33] The Assembly encouraged fostering dialogue and critical dispute, being convinced that satire, humour and artistic expression should not be seen as provocation.[34] It also shifted the focus of offensive speech from blasphemy to hate speech. It drew a line between protection of the believer or the non-believer, analogous to protection from discrimination, instead of protection of belief. To distinguish between blasphemy and hate speech, the Report preceding the Recommendation elaborates:

> Hate speech is always directed against persons or a group of persons, but not against a religion or ideas, philosophies, a political party, state organs, a state or nation or mankind as such.[35]

This is the strongest and most decisive common step in a European approach to religions. It not only affirms the multicultural nature of European societies but recognises the necessity of securing equality between adherents of different religions. It is a decisive step towards liberal multiculturalism, which recognises 'democratic religious pluralism'[36] instead of culture- and religion-blind liberalism.

Despite the fact that pluralism is now seen by the Assembly as an inherent feature of a democratic society and the role of authorities is to ensure that various

[31] As Report 11296, 'Blasphemy, religious insults and hate speech against persons on grounds of their religion', the Council of Europe Parliamentary Assembly.

[32] Recommendation 1805 (2007), 'Blasphemy, religious insults and hate speech against persons on grounds of their religion', of the Council of Europe Parliamentary Assembly, 2007, para. 10.

[33] *Ibid.*, at paras 1 and 5.

[34] Report, 'Blasphemy, religious insults and hate speech against persons on grounds of their religion', Doc. 11296, 8 June 2007, Parliamentary Assembly of the Council of Europe, para. 63 recalling Assembly Resolution 1510 (2006) on freedom of expression.

[35] Report, 'Blasphemy, religious insults and hate speech against persons on grounds of their religion', Doc. 11296, para. 9

[36] *Ibid.*, at para. 24.2.

groups in a democratic society stand above religious divisions and strive to ensure diversity,[37] the fundamental approach risks creating even more others than before. On the one hand, the approach openly challenges one of the primary European conditions – inequality between traditional and minority religions. The former, despite being on the wane, often enjoy the protection of national legal systems whereas new and growing religions do not enjoy such protection. On the other hand, though – the solution sought does not enhance inclusion. It is an all-or-nothing approach based on division between the private and public spheres and minimising the influence of religion on the public. It excludes religion in the hope that in European conditions this forceful and uniform expulsion of all religion from the public sphere can bring about inclusion of differently religious individuals. It recognises the religious dynamics between the majority and minorities and hopes that true diversity of religions and non-religions may generate infinite variations, so that protection of this diversity should not be limited only to some recognised beliefs. The assumption is that if not all can be protected effectively then the non-discrimination principle requires that none should be protected at all.

Whereas the emphasis on pluralism is admirable, the true obstacles remain – religious dynamics differ from place to place, from context to context. The division of the private and the public does not always capture the nature of discrimination in the area of belief or non-belief. Moreover, uniform approaches blur the reality of exclusion. A desperate attempt to minimise exclusion by directly and uniformly tackling traditional religions risks no more than agonising those traditions. As illustrated by Judge Bonello's concurring opinion in the case of *Lautsi* quoted above, a direct attack on tradition, rather than on forms of discrimination it may generate in particular contexts, is received defensively. This results in a solidified and strengthened defence of tradition, achieving nothing less than undermining the credibility of the system of international rights protection. States may grow unwilling to accept this expanding definition of rights and begin to see their traditional religious or non-religious tradition as a part of their sovereignty. Religious issues, contrary to the hope of the Recommendation, become a public, not a private matter – a matter of national integrity. Moreover, the documents, even though recognising certain communitarian concerns, risk either essentialising communities as in a model distinguishing between different kinds of community (Kymlicka 2003a) or seeing them merely as conglomerates of various individual interests following the liberal tradition of defining communities and collective rights (Raz 1986). The community understood as a conglomerate will always generate a balancing based on a simple numerical count. It will be the conglomerate of those prevailing in a society. It will be the vast amount of Italian parents who did not protest against the crucifix on the wall and whose interests will remain protected. It will rarely be a community of those who stand out and remain in a numerical minority or are seen as minoritarian (Deleuze and Guattari 1980). Such

---

[37] See Recommendation 1396 (1999), 'Religion and democracy', of the Council of Europe Parliamentary Assembly.

a community risks being seen as a threat, as 'extremists' excluded from deliberation, a community confined to the reality of the other and an existence hidden in the dark corners of society.

Liberalism will forever be caught in a vicious circle perpetuating different forms of exclusion, despite its best intentions. This exclusion will too frequently touch differently religious individuals rather than the majority tradition. Liberalism is condemned to forever correcting its own mistakes, ever further essentialising those it attempts to rescue every time it tries to save them from its own shortcomings.

The rescue effort has already begun and found its expression in the most recent Recommendation, Recommendation 1927 (2010), 'Islam, Islamism and Islamophobia in Europe'. Relying on previously developed principles, this Recommendation notices the negative effects of essentialising and marginalising adherents of Islam in Europe. The Recommendation having observed the spread of Islamophobia once more calls upon European states to strengthen intercultural dialogue[38] and explicitly calls for 'the social and political inclusion of migrants and foreigners, who are often Muslims'.[39] This inclusion is seen as essential for 'democratic cohesion and stability'. The approach attempts to move from recognition to inclusion based on pluralism. The Recommendation calls upon the Member States to end exclusionary practices. In particular, the Assembly calls

> on Switzerland to enact a moratorium on, and to repeal as soon as possible, its general prohibition on the construction of minarets for mosques, which discriminates against Muslim communities under Articles 9 and 14 of the European Convention on Human Rights; the construction of minarets must be possible in the same way as the construction of church towers, subject to the requirements of public security and town planning;
>
> ...
>
> on member states not to establish a general ban of full veiling or other religious or special clothing, but to protect women from all physical and psychological duress as well as to protect their free choice to wear religious or special clothing and ensure equal opportunities for Muslim women to participate in public life and pursue education and professional activities; legal restrictions on this freedom may be justified where necessary in a democratic society, in particular for security purposes or where public or professional functions of individuals require their religious neutrality or that their face can be seen.[40]

But can liberalism ever rescue the other from itself? With its many problems and with the inescapable existence of the self and the other the inclusionary project may never be completed. The struggle for emancipation will eventually

---

[38] See Recommendation 1927 (2010), 'Islam, Islamism and Islamophobia in Europe', of the Council of Europe Parliamentary Assembly, para. 3.10.

[39] *Ibid.*, at para.3.10.

[40] *Ibid.*, at paras 3.12 and 3.13.

result in those initially oppressed becoming the numerical majority. And as Rosa Luxemburg reminds us:

> Freedom only for the supporters of the government, only for the members of one party – however numerous they may be – is no freedom at all. Freedom is always and exclusively freedom for the one who thinks differently. Not because of any fanatical concept of 'justice' but because all that is instructive, wholesome and purifying in political freedom depends on this essential characteristic, and its effectiveness vanishes when 'freedom' becomes a special privilege.
>
> (Luxemburg 1918)

This chapter has illustrated the development of religious pluralism in CoE soft law and its evolution from mere toleration, through recognition to inclusion. It has also tackled the problematic construction of the principle and illustrates its potential to exclude rather than to include. The next chapter briefly analyses how the principle of religious pluralism has been evolving in the case-law of the ECtHR and how soft law has impacted that development. This will be done in the theoretical context before moving further to particular example areas illustrating diverse religious and non-religious dynamics and their divergent forms of generating exclusion and marginalisation.

References

Adorno, Theodor W. 1951. *Minima Moralia: Reflections on a Damaged Life.* Verso.

Brown, Wendy. 2008. *Regulating Aversion: Tolerance in the Age of Identity and Empire.* Princeton University Press.

Cohen, Joshua. 1997. 'Deliberation and Democratic Legitimacy.' In *Deliberative Democracy: Essays on Reason and Politics,* ed. J. Bohman and W. Rehg, 67–92. MIT Press.

Deleuze, Gilles and Felix Guattari. 1980. *A Thousand Plateaus: Capitalism and Schizophrenia.* Continuum.

Esposito, John L. and Ibrahim Kalin. 2011. *Islamophobia: The Challenge of Pluralism in the 21st Century.* Oxford University Press.

Gozdecka, Dorota A. 2009. 'Religions and Legal Boundaries of Democracy in Europe: European Commitment to Democratic Principles.' e-thesis, University of Helsinki.

Habermas, Jürgen. 1998. *Between Facts and Norms: Contributions to a Discourse Theory of Law and Democracy.* MIT Press.

Habermas, Jürgen. 2008. *Between Naturalism and Religion: Philosophical Essays.* Polity.

Kant, Immanuel. 1797. *Groundwork of the Metaphysic of Morals.* Wilder Publications.

Kymlicka, Will. 2003a. *Multicultural Citizenship: A Liberal Theory of Minority Rights.* Oxford University Press.

Kymlicka, Will. 2003b. 'Multicultural States and Intercultural Citizens.' *Theory and Research in Education* 1: 147–69.

Locke, John. 1689. *A Letter Concerning Toleration.* M. Nijhoff.

Luxemburg, Rosa. 1918. *The Russian Revolution and Leninism or Marxism?* University of Michigan Press.

Lyotard, Jean-François. 1984. *The Postmodern Condition: A Report on Knowledge*. Theory and History of Literature 10. Manchester University Press.

MacIntyre, Alasdair. 1981. *After Virtue: A Study in Moral Theory*. Duckworth.

MacIntyre, Alasdair. 1988. *Whose Justice? Which Rationality?* Duckworth.

Mancini, Susanna 2012. 'Patriarchy as the Exclusive Domain of the Other: The Veil Controversy, False Projection and Cultural Racism.' *International Journal of Constitutional Law* 10(2): 411–28.

Parekh, Bhikhu C. 2002. *Rethinking Multiculturalism: Cultural Diversity and Political Theory*. Harvard University Press.

Rawls, John. 2005. *Political Liberalism: Expanded Edition*. Columbia University Press.

Raz, Joseph. 1986. *The Morality of Freedom*. Oxford University Press.

Sandel, Michael J. 1998. *Liberalism and the Limits of Justice*. Cambridge University Press.

Sharma, Ashwani. 2009. 'Postcolonial Racism: White Paranoia and the Terrors of Multiculturalism.' In *Racism, Postcolonialism, Europe*, ed. G. Huggan and I. Law, 119–30. Liverpool University Press.

Taylor, Charles. 1979. *Hegel and Modern Society*. Cambridge University Press.

Taylor, Charles and Amy Gutmann. 1992. *Multiculturalism and 'The Politics of Recognition': An Essay by Charles Taylor*. Fondo de Cultura Económica.

Young, Iris Marion. 1990. *Justice and the Politics of Difference*. Princeton University Press.

Young, Iris Marion. 1997. 'Difference as a Resource for Democratic Communication.' In *Deliberative Democracy: Essays on Reason and Politics*, ed. J. Bohman and W. Rehg, 383–406. MIT Press.

Ziebertz, Hans-Georg and Ulrich Riegel. 2008. *Europe: Secular or Post-secular?* LIT Verlag.

Chapter 2

The European Court of Human Rights and judicial interpretation of the principle of religious pluralism

Despite its richness, the soft law of advisory bodies such as the Parliamentary Assembly frequently risks remaining no more than wishful thinking if it is not followed by judicial practice. In terms of religious pluralism the case-law of the ECtHR incorporated the principle and its application gradually. Similarly to the interpretations included in the recommendations, the case-law slowly modified the interpretation of pluralism from a simple fact of life that ought to be tolerated to seeing it as the cornerstone of a democratic society. Surprisingly, though, the less talk of pluralism, the more engagement with difference displayed by the Court. Meanwhile, when pluralism became indispensable in evaluating the boundaries of 'necessity in a democratic society' embedded in Article 9 of the Convention and used for measuring the lawfulness of limitations on freedom of religion, the engagement with difference weakened, rendering the principle a recurring grand narrative in Lyotardian terms (Lyotard 1984). As such, pluralism became just another large-scale, generally used phrase implying frequently no more than homogenising approaches that fail to represent those appealing for recognition of their difference.

At the outset pluralism was treated by the Court merely as a fact of life. In the first, and one of the most relevant, cases concerning religious freedom before the ECtHR, the case of *Kokkinakis v. Greece*,[1] decided in 1993, the Court for the first time referred to pluralism when dealing with the right of a Jehovah's Witness to teach about religion. Mr Kokkinakis was sentenced multiple times for proselytising, which was at the time banned under Greek law. In pursuance of protection of the dominant position of the Greek Orthodox Church, cemented not only by tradition but also in the 1975 Constitution, Mr Kokkinakis was arrested for proselytism over 60 times and on several occasions imprisoned upon conviction. In 1986 after a discussion with Mrs Kyriakaki, the wife of a cantor at a local Orthodox church, Mr Kokkinakis was arrested once more and this time his case found its way to the ECtHR. In its judgment the Court laid the foundations for interpretation of Article 9 by outlining a few elements crucial for determining the

---

[1] *Kokkinakis v. Greece*, European Court of Human Rights, Judgment, Application No. 14307/88, 25 May 1993.

boundaries of freedom of religion (Evans 2001). For example, the Court expressly linked democracy and pluralism and insisted that 'pluralism [is] indissociable from a democratic society'. Leaving it at that at this point, the Court failed to elaborate and treated pluralism as a simple fact of life and a value that was evident and self-understood. Not going far beyond traditional liberal approaches, religion in the Court's judgment was traditionally confined in the private sphere but supplemented with a right to manifest it in public:

> While religious freedom is primarily a matter of individual conscience, it also implies, inter alia, freedom to 'manifest [one's] religion'. Bearing witness in words and deeds is bound up with the existence of religious convictions.[2]

Despite this unsurprising interpretation *Kokkinakis* stands in contrast to many further judgments. Despite passing silently on the meaning of the phrase 'religious pluralism' the engagement with what pluralism (without being called pluralism) might entail proves extremely affirmative of religious difference. Without emphasising how important pluralism is, the Court instead shows willingness not to 'otherise' but to face otherness created by law. It is one of the few judgments where the Court in fact welcomes a highly pluralistic vision of a society in which protection of dominant religious normativity was not found to be necessary in a democratic society. Quite to the contrary, the Court emphasised the practical possibility of living with one's beliefs despite the existence of a majority and exercising them in practice with a possibility of changing them in the course of a lifetime:

> [F]reedom to manifest one's religion is not only exercisable in community with others, 'in public' and within the circle of those whose faith one shares, but can also be asserted 'alone' and 'in private'; furthermore, it includes in principle the right to try to convince one's neighbour, for example through 'teaching', failing which, moreover, 'freedom to change [one's] religion or belief', enshrined in Article 9 (art. 9), would be likely to remain a dead letter.[3]

By saying that without all these possibilities Article 9 would remain a dead letter the Court implicitly rather than explicitly took an interpretational avenue open to difference and its acceptability in a society. Rather than elaborating on the rigidity of existing law and the cemented nature of its established order, the Court spoke in favour of dynamism in legal interpretation. By focusing on securing possibilities for effective exercise of the right it rejected static approaches accepting dominant tradition and normativity as if they constituted an unquestionable reality. Instead the judgment underlined the necessity for law to change and evolve:

[2] *Ibid.*, para. 31.
[3] *Ibid.*

[The] wording of many statutes is not absolutely precise. The need to avoid excessive rigidity and to keep pace with changing circumstances means that many laws are inevitably couched in terms which, to a greater or lesser extent, are vague.[4]

This progressive and dynamic interpretation instead of merely declaring plural-ism as a principle embraced it broadly and open-mindedly, not only allowing for facing otherness but also by focusing on what Adorno called concrete forms of 'unfreedom' (Adorno 1973, 231).Without excessively referring to difference as if it were a legal mantra, the original shape of pluralism emerging from the findings of *Kokkinakis*, de facto embraced difference. The Court was not convinced that perpetuating dominant traditions that subordinate others to follow them, as Iris Marion Young would say (Young 1990, 60), can suffice as a ground for limiting the freedom of the other. Therefore in circumstances of no obvious harm caused it allowed for the possibility of breaking free from the constraints of the dom-inant normativity. The conceptualisation of freedom lying at the foundation of *Kokkinakis* assumed the necessity of allowing the dynamic movement from unfree-dom towards greater freedom. Without explicit emphasis on the principle, the reading of pluralism was thick, much thicker than in many later cases, where recognising otherness became a risky business. In the cases that followed, acts of balancing 'necessity in a democratic society' and its pluralistic foundations were too frequently interpreted in favour of law-endorsed dominant, majoritarian reli-gious, moral or ethical standards.

It took the Court several more years before the next attempt to put the prin-ciple of pluralism verbatim into its judicial practice. While dealing with cases of religious sensitivity, for a considerable period the Court, rather than expanding the concept of pluralism, abstained from interpreting it and interfering with local traditions and religious morals. In contrast to the broad implications of pluralism stemming from *Kokkinakis* the Court thereafter followed the approach developed much earlier in the 1976 *Handyside*[5] judgment. This approach relied on the less risky concept of the margin of appreciation in regard to local religious traditions. Examining the judgments in *Wingrove* v. *the United Kingdom*[6] or *Otto-Preminger Institut* v. *Austria*[7] the Court showed strong reluctance to upset the established status quo or propose prescriptive solutions challenging established approaches to religious and moral traditions. In the case of *Wingrove*, coming only a few years after *Kokkinakis*, the ECtHR found lawful the decision of the British Board of Film Classification to prevent the distribution of an allegedly blasphemous film. The case concerned

---

[4] *Ibid.*, para. 40.

[5] *Handyside* v. *the United Kingdom*, European Court of Human Rights, Judgment, Application No. 5493/72, 7 December 1976.

[6] *Wingrove* v. *the United Kingdom*, European Court of Human Rights, Judgment, Application No. 17419/90, 25 November 1996.

[7] *Otto-Preminger-Institut* v. *Austria*, European Court of Human Rights, Judgment, Application No. 13470/87, 20 September 1994.

a film, *Visions of Ecstasy*, portraying a woman dressed as a nun accompanied by another naked woman and having erotic experiences with the body of Christ. The argumentation of the producer, namely that the film portrayed the ecstatic visions of St Theresa of Avila, was rejected. Moreover, the decision of the Board preventing the film from being distributed, followed by the argumentation of the state before the Court, emphasised that the state had a right to protect the religious sensitivities of people. Unlike in *Kokkinakis*, in *Wingrove* the ECtHR refused to examine whether provisions sanctioning the existence of the offence of blasphemy were not hindering effective exercise of the right to non-religious belief. Quite the opposite, the judgment affirmed that such an offence is by nature subject to state discretion and the state was in the best position to act on this margin of discretion, which after *Handyside* was termed the 'margin of appreciation'.[8]

This reserved approach was confirmed in the relatively similar case of *Otto-Preminger Institut v. Austria*. As in *Wingrove*, the case concerned a controversial film, *Das Liebeskonzil*, impounded by the Austrian authorities on the grounds of violating section 188 of the Penal Code criminalising the offence of disparaging religious precepts. In this case, the ECtHR, repeating the reasoning of *Wingrove*, referred to Austria's wide margin of appreciation in protecting the religious feelings of Tyrolean Roman Catholics, who instigated the proceedings. The Court decided that the restriction was lawful despite underlining that:

> Those who choose to exercise the freedom to manifest their religion, irrespective of whether they do so as members of a religious majority or a minority, cannot reasonably expect to be exempt from all criticism. They must tolerate and accept the denial by others of their religious beliefs and even the propagation by others of doctrines hostile to their faith. However, the manner in which religious beliefs and doctrines are opposed or denied is a matter which may engage the responsibility of the State, notably its responsibility to ensure the peaceful enjoyment of the right guaranteed under Article 9 (art. 9) to the holders of those beliefs and doctrines. Indeed, in extreme cases the effect of particular methods of opposing or denying religious beliefs can be such as to inhibit those who hold such beliefs from exercising their freedom to hold and express them.[9]

The circumstances of the case, namely a private viewing for members of a film institute, do not directly suggest inhibiting the beliefs of Tyrolean Catholics, but despite this the Court invoked the margin of appreciation in terms of protecting society from 'justified indignation'.[10] In this judgment the concept of pluralism was only vaguely mentioned by underlining that 'in the case of "morals" it is not possible to identify a uniform conception of the significance of religion in

[8] *Handyside v. the United Kingdom*, para 47.
[9] *Otto-Preminger-Institut v. Austria*, para. 47.
[10] *Ibid.*, para. 48.

society'. While at the same time underlining that 'even within a single country such conceptions may vary' the Court did not focus on that internal heterogeneity. Quite conversely, the reading of pluralism privileged pluralism at a horizontal level, assuming the existence of fixed traditions differing from country to country. Despite the reference to vertical religious pluralism and internal heterogeneity within a single country the Court privileged a vision of the existence of homogeneous religious traditions that constitute the foundations of fixed and cemented national communities.

It took another 14 years for the Court to return towards a vertical meaning of pluralism and its interpretation. The most prominent cases explicitly referring to and extensively elaborating on the requirements of pluralism were primarily those concerning religious instruction in schools. In the cases of *Folgerø and Others* v. *Norway*,[11] *Grzelak* v. *Poland*[12] and *Hasan and Eylem Zengin* v. *Turkey*[13] the Court put the existing soft law referring to pluralism into practice. In all three cases the Court relied heavily on the concept of pluralism in determining whether the state had violated Article 2 of Protocol 1 securing the right to education compliant with parental convictions.

In *Folgerø* the Court dealt with the Norwegian model of religious education and a claim by nine parents belonging to the Norwegian Humanist Association who contested the obligation of their children to attend religious education classes (KRL) and the embedding of elements of Christian philosophy in the teaching of other subjects. The Norwegian model included partial exemption from religious classes but it did not allow for exemption from all classes and activities potentially incorporating elements of Christianity and Christian morality. The Court examined the curriculum and its judgment explicitly emphasised that a democratic state is forbidden to pursue the aim of religious indoctrination. In examining the limit of indoctrination the Court underlined that such a limit must never be exceeded and that 'safeguarding the possibility of pluralism in education … is essential for the preservation of a "democratic society"'[14] and that the state must 'take care that information or knowledge included in the Curriculum … be conveyed in an objective, critical and pluralistic manner',[15] not pursuing the aim of indoctrination. While examining the limits of indoctrination, the Court considered the legislative framework of the KRL subject and its impact on non-believers. Upon examination the Court found that:

> [W]hen seen together with the Christian object clause, the description of the contents and the aims of the KRL subject set out in section 2–4 of the

[11] *Folgerø and Others* v. *Norway*, European Court of Human Rights, Judgment, Application No. 15472/02, 29 June 2007.

[12] *Grzelak* v. *Poland*, European Court of Human Rights, Judgment, Application No. 7710/02, 15 June 2010.

[13] *Hasan and Eylem Zengin* v. *Turkey*, European Court of Human Rights, Judgment, Application No. 1448/04, 9 January 2008.

[14] *Folgerø and Others* v. *Norway*, para. 84b.

[15] *Ibid.*, para. 84h.

Education Act 1998 and other texts forming part of the legislative framework suggest that not only quantitative but even qualitative differences are
applied to the teaching of Christianity as compared to that of other religions
and philosophies. In view of these disparities, it is not clear how the further
aim, set out in item (v), to 'promote understanding, respect and the ability to
maintain a dialogue between people with different perceptions of beliefs and
convictions' could be properly attained. In the Court's view, the differences
were such that they could hardly be sufficiently attenuated by the requirement
in section 2–4 that the teaching follow a uniform pedagogical approach in
respect of the different religions and philosophies.[16]

Pluralism was thus defined as proportionality and the ability of non-dominant
beliefs to attain equal access to the educational forum. This interpretation puts
emphasis on something previously unseen in the recommendations, that is, the
aspect of access to the dialogue forum so frequently underlined by theorists
favouring discursive models of pluralism such as Habermas. Going quite deeply
into the core of deliberative models, the Court focused not just on an abstract
model of deliberation but on the practical necessity of securing both qualitative
and quantitative proportionality in access to deliberation. Giving heed to concerns for distribution of power in deliberative models (Knight and Johnson 1997,
307) this approach, like *Kokkinakis*, engaged deeply with pluralism as a principle
and in practice. It examined dominant influences, power distribution between the
majority and minority, conditions of access to deliberation and the ability of the
non-religious other to live a life in accordance with their own beliefs in spite of and
next to the dominant group's religious expressions and the strong dissemination
of those expressions.

Another previously unexamined aspect of the principle was elucidated in a
case concerning issuing final high school certificates which included grades from
religious instruction classes. In the case of *Grzelak v. Poland* agnostic parents complained about inclusion of the final grade from religious instruction classes on
school leaving certificates. While their son was exempted from attending religious
instruction classes, alternative instruction in ethics prescribed by legislation as a
substitute was not available at the school despite multiple requests to organise it.
Since the applicants' son was the only student abstaining from attending religious
instruction the school did not succeed in organising instruction in ethics which
would be graded analogously to religious instruction classes and marked in the
same place on the school leaving certificate. Since their son's certificate featured
a blank space in the slot reserved for the grade in religious instruction or ethics
the applicants complained that leaving the slot blank revealed their religious convictions. The Court examined the claim in the context of Article 14 forbidding
discrimination in conjunction with Article 9. In its approach the Court focused
on the indissociability of pluralism from a democratic society and its crucial

---

[16] *Ibid.*, para. 95.

value for believers, atheists, agnostics and the unconcerned.[17] While focusing on the negative aspect of freedom of religion the Court found the argument of the Government that the lack of a grade reflected a neutral position on the part of the state unconvincing.[18] In this case, the Court took into account the context in which otherness occurred and focused on the analysis in this respect by the Polish Constitutional Court, which rejected the significance of the context as a determining factor:

> The Court notes that the above analysis of the Constitutional Court, while unquestionable in its substance, appears to overlook other situations which may arise in practice. In the present case the pupil had no mark for 'religion/ethics' on his school reports because the school could not organise ethics classes despite repeated requests from his parents. The Court considers that the absence of a mark for 'religion/ethics' would be understood by any reasonable person as an indication that the third applicant did not follow religious education classes, which were widely available, and that he was thus likely to be regarded as a person without religious beliefs. The Government in their submissions indicated that the vast majority of religious education classes concerned Roman Catholicism. The fact of having no mark for 'religion/ethics' inevitably has a specific connotation and distinguishes the persons concerned from those who have a mark for the subject. This finding takes on particular significance in respect of a country like Poland where the great majority of the population owe allegiance to one particular religion.[19]

This case is one of the rare ones when the minoritarian claim was measured against the position and capacity of the majority to influence not only law but also its practice. Despite the strong position of Catholicism as a dominant religious and cultural tradition the Court embraced the possibility of difference and non-religious dissent. Pluralism was seen as securing a chance for the religiously different other for emancipation from dominant normativity and realisation of life objectives. Equality did not simply mean one-size-fits-all treatment but instead implied equity (Douzinas 2004, 212) that creates conditions for empowering the minority and levelling the disadvantage it faces. Difference was not rendered invisible and the judgment took a step against the possibility of stereotyping typically attached by dominant groups to those who do not fall into the dominant structures of meanings and behaviours (Young 1990, 59). The reading of pluralism in *Grzelak* was thicker and broader than the typical reading of neutrality, secularism or equality.

The meaning of religious pluralism discerned by the Court in *Kokkinakis, Folgerø* and *Grzelak* was not based on the idea of creating an all-encompassing static order

---

[17] *Grzelak v. Poland*, para. 85.
[18] *Ibid.*, para. 87.
[19] *Ibid.*, para. 95.

of law serving the preservation of the community centred on an established religious normativity. Instead the meaning of the right to freedom of religion was read as securing a possibility for those who are different to contest the status quo and seek emancipation from the surrounding dominant structures. The concept of a right that the Court endorsed went beyond seeing it as static privileges of either side but instead as a dynamic process allowing the other to move from concrete circumstances of unfreedom towards greater freedom. Since the direction of emancipation from freedom to unfreedom cannot ever be fixed or certain in advance the Court engaged deeply in analysis of the dynamic between the minoritarian and majoritarian experience. Examining that relationship, the Court identified the concrete possibilities of those who are different to live with their belief in circumstances dominated by a particular religious normativity. The Court asked whether the dominant normativity left any room for the other not to be otherised but instead to have her difference embraced and recognised. Such a reading privileged a dynamic vision of pluralism as a force for emancipation and renegotiation rather than a force for ordering. This dynamic reading of pluralism was emphasised by the Court even in a complex case dealing with tensions concerning the coexistence of different religious communities rather than individuals contesting the dominant order. In *Serif* v. *Greece*,[20] concerning the appointment of a new Mufti for the Islamic community of Thrace, the difference was not a characteristic of individuals but instead of communities. Here, too, the Court emphasised not only the importance of pluralism but also highlighted that pluralism does not necessarily mean securing a comfortable and steady order free from contestation. Instead the true possibility of pluralism conveys a possibility of discomfort and a likelihood of conflict. In a thick pluralism of that kind, respect for difference means the necessity to manage conflict rather than removing its source by silencing either side:

> Although the Court recognises that it is possible that tension is created in situations where a religious or any other community becomes divided, it considers that this is one of the unavoidable consequences of pluralism. The role of the authorities in such circumstances is not to remove the cause of tension by eliminating pluralism, but to ensure that the competing groups tolerate each other.[21]

But such a dynamic interpretation of pluralism as a necessary but potentially disruptive force contesting the established order did not prevail for long in the jurisprudence of the Court. Following these thick interpretations of pluralism the approach of the ECtHR mutated into repetitive citation of pluralism as a principle that was first slowly narrowed and then gradually reversed. From a tool of

---

[20] *Serif* v. *Greece*, European Court of Human Rights, Judgment, Application No. 38178/97, 14 December 1999.
[21] *Ibid.*, para. 53.

emancipation of difference, a more rigid interpretation of the principle turned pluralism into a tool for managing difference and outlining the limits of acceptable and unacceptable identities. This slow reversal illustrates Iris Marion Young's point concerning the end destination of the logic of self. When the logic of identity of the self drives the process of inclusion it necessarily ends in the creation of binary oppositions of *a*/*not* signifying exclusive categories of belonging outlined at the expense of the expelled:

> The irony of logic of identity is that by seeking to reduce the differently similar to the same, it turns the merely different into the absolutely other. It inevitably generates dichotomy instead of unity, because the move to bring particulars under a universal category creates a distinction between inside and outside.
>
> (Young 1990, 99)

The emergence of the inside and outside is already visible in the case of *Hasan and Eylem Zengin v. Turkey*. This case concerned a similar situation as in *Folgerø* but in this case dealt with adherents of Alevism who sought an exemption for their daughter from 'religious culture and ethics' classes. According to the applicants the classes were saturated with teaching of Hanafite Islam and thus did not allow them to educate their daughter in conformity with their own beliefs. Just as in *Folgerø* the Court once more examined the teaching and its emphasis on precepts of a specific religion within the course offered. The judgment reiterated the *Folgerø* approach that a course that is designed to teach and preach a specific religion cannot be compulsory and found a violation of the Convention. Interestingly enough, the entire violation was based on infringement of the principle of pluralism itself. While pronouncing that the educational system in question 'does not meet the requirements of objectivity and pluralism and provides no appropriate method for ensuring respect for parents' convictions',[22] the Court also emphasised that the mere fact of teaching Islam is not sufficient to find that the teaching breaches the requirements of objectivity. Therefore it followed a path emphasising the influence of teaching on pupils whose beliefs have acquired a 'certain level of cogency and seriousness':

> [T]he question arises whether the priority given to the teaching of Islam may be considered as remaining within acceptable limits for the purposes of Article 2 of Protocol No. 1. In fact, given the syllabus and textbooks in question, it may reasonably be supposed that attendance at these classes is likely to influence the minds of young children. It is therefore appropriate to examine whether the information or knowledge in the syllabus is disseminated in an objective, critical and pluralist manner.
>
> As to the Alevi faith, it is not disputed between the parties that it is a religious conviction which has deep roots in Turkish society and history and that

---

[22] *Hasan and Eylem Zengin v. Turkey*, para. 84.

it has features which are particular to it …. It is thus distinct from the Sunni understanding of Islam which is taught in schools. It is certainly neither a sect nor a 'belief' which does not attain a certain level of cogency, seriousness, cohesion and importance. In consequence, the expression 'religious convictions', within the meaning of the second sentence of Article 2 of Protocol No. 1, is undoubtedly applicable to this faith.[23]

While the Court placed the burden of securing pluralism on the state and prima facie intensified emphasis on religious pluralism as a principle, the interpretation of pluralism emerging from these findings is thinner and more problematic in terms of recognition of difference. While emphasising diversity, the Court singled out difference, judging it through the prism of the dominant and the recognisable expressed in the moralising discourse of sects and worthiness of a belief. It approached pluralism through the logic of the inside and the outside, pushing the radically different to the outside of the acceptable. Pluralism, despite its prominent position in the reasoning of the Court, was limited to inclusion of that kind of particularity which is carefully outlined by the dominant universality and lies within its acceptable boundaries. The line of argumentation created an otherness that was 'defined from the outside, positioned (and) placed, by a network of dominant meanings' (Young 1990, 59). The dominant universality defined and controlled what kind of difference it found manageable and controllable and what kind breached the boundary of that comfort. Once outside these boundaries the difference would remain unrecognised and the other scorned through classification as a follower of a 'sect', a term that undeniably hides judgment about worthiness. The Alevi applicants were found to be close enough to the comfortable difference and thus could be accommodated. But the image of a truly other lurks behind this interpretation of pluralism. That truly other placed beyond the boundary of a comfort zone becomes a faceless phantom, living in the shadows of the collective equivalent of self that places difference in the comfortable distance from the acceptable image of the 'we'. The meaning of community outlined by this approach relies on the comfort of the familiarity of the 'we' created by its juxtaposition to otherness – otherness defined as that which the imagined community is not. This judgment is the first signpost of the road leading the principle of pluralism away from pluralism. While verbal emphasis on pluralism becomes stronger, its actual meaning mutates towards a recurring but empty grand narrative excluding rather than facing difference.

This tendency towards a thin reading of pluralism despite the strong prima facie endorsement of the principle was also used in a case concerning registration of Jehovah's Witnesses in Austria.[24] The Jehovah's Witnesses Association contested the refusal by the Austrian authorities to grant them legal personality

[23] *Ibid.*, paras 64–6.
[24] *Religionsgemeinschaft der Zeugen Jehovas and Others* v. *Austria*, European Court of Human Rights, Judgment, Application No. 40825/98, 31 July 2008.

and recognise their society under the Recognition Act. In this case, in finding a violation of freedom of religion the Court once more invoked the principle of pluralism, underlining that recognition of difference may be required both for individuals and groups:

> Since religious communities traditionally exist in the form of organised structures, Article 9 must be interpreted in the light of Article 11 of the Convention, which safeguards associative life against unjustified State interference. Indeed, the autonomous existence of religious communities is indispensable for pluralism in a democratic society and is, thus, an issue at the very heart of the protection which Article 9 affords.[25]

Continuing on this note the Court examined whether Jehovah's Witnesses were discriminated against in the context of Article 9 when compared to other religious communities. The careful reader, though, may be surprised that against the backdrop of accepting that multiple shapes of difference may exist, the Court confined difference to the narrow confines of the easily recognisable. While determining whether a lengthy waiting period was required in the case of Jehovah's Witnesses the Court carefully outlined the limits of recognition applicable to the familiar and known religions in contrast to the new and unknown:

> The Court could accept that such a period might be necessary in exceptional circumstances such as would be in the case of newly established and unknown religious groups. But it hardly appears justified in respect of religious groups with a long-standing existence internationally which are also long established in the country and therefore familiar to the competent authorities, as is the case with the Jehovah's Witnesses.[26]

While the Court accepted the argumentation of the well-established association of Jehovah's Witnesses in this interpretation of pluralism it did not dare to extend the application of pluralism to differences less comfortable and more extreme. Those potentially finding themselves on the outside and thus seen as the absolutely other were branded as not truly mature enough for freedom stemming from pluralism and thus subject to control by those in authority, who, as Adorno would put it, were 'mature' enough to administer and control freedom for them (Adorno 1973, 221). This reading of pluralism could not only potentially restrict it, but might also lead to an increase in the control of otherness that could eventually lead to the very annihilation of freedom (Adorno 1973, 222). While disappointing in terms of recognising true difference, these two readings of pluralism did not yet signify a complete reversal of utopian pluralistic ideals but merely a thin, liberal reading of the principle entrenched in the tried and tested tools of neutrality,

---

[25] *Ibid.*, para. 61.
[26] *Ibid.*, para. 98.

equality and reasonableness. Signifying merely the beginning of a transformation of the principle, these two judgments mark a reversal of the principle seen in later cases. While already in this judgment the Court catered to the known and established, the inclusionary goals of the principle were rejected and reversed when pluralism was paired with the margin of appreciation.

As illustrated in the second part of the present book, such pairing rarely puts recognition or inclusion at the forefront. When the margin of appreciation took over the logic of pluralism, it was suddenly reconstructed as a prerogative of the state to protect those wishing not to be affected by a religion or non-religion. Beginning from *Dahlab v. Switzerland*[27] and *Leyla Şahin v. Turkey*,[28] cases analysed frequently in the context of Islamic dress code, the Court began to underline that it 'must have regard to what is at stake, namely the need to protect the rights and freedoms of others, to preserve public order and to secure civil peace and true religious pluralism'.[29] As a consequence of the pairing with the margin of appreciation, the entitlements stemming from the principle of pluralism were shifted (Gozdecka 2015). From a dynamic tool for shaping a diverse community and challenging unfreedom, pluralism changed into a way of establishing and managing order. From the Islamic dress code cases to the case concerning obligatory display of crucifixes in Italy, the interpretation of pluralism mutated from the entitlement of those appealing for recognition of their difference to the quasi right of the state to protect the dominant order and normativity. This reversal fully transformed religious pluralism into a grand myth rather than a tool of recognition. No more than a grand narrative empty of meaning – a recurring phrase hijacked by the forces of power and ordering.

References

Adorno, Theodor W. 1973. *Negative Dialectics*. A&C Black.
Douzinas, Costas. 2004. 'Law and Justice in Postmodernity.' In *The Cambridge Companion to Postmodernism*, ed. Steve Connor, 196–223. Cambridge University Press.
Evans, Carolyn. 2001. *Freedom of Religion under the European Convention on Human Rights*. Oxford University Press.
Gozdecka, Dorota A. 2015. 'Religious Pluralism as a Legal Principle' In *Religion and Legal Pluralism*, ed. Russell Sandberg, 179–195. Ashgate.
Knight, Jack and James Johnson. 1997. 'What Sort of Equality Does Deliberative Democracy Require?' In *Deliberative Democracy: Essays on Reason and Politics*, ed. James Bohman and William Rehg, 279–319. MIT Press.
Lyotard, Jean-François. 1984. *The Postmodern Condition: A Report on Knowledge*. Theory and History of Literature 10. Manchester University Press.
Young, Iris Marion. 1990. *Justice and the Politics of Difference*. Princeton University Press.

[27] *Dahlab v. Switzerland*, European Court of Human Rights, Decision, Application No. 42393/98, 15 February 2001.
[28] *Leyla Şahin v. Turkey*, European Court of Human Rights, Judgment, Application No. 44774/98, 10 November 2005.
[29] *Ibid.*, para.110.

Chapter 3

Relevance of religious pluralism in the EU legal order

Thanks to the expansive force of human rights and their interpretational principles, the question of religious pluralism and religion did not remain confined to the realm of regional human rights treaties such as the European Convention on Human Rights (ECHR). Reinforced by the growing preoccupation with religion, the principle soon also affected European Union law (EU law) and European Union human rights law (EU human rights). Albeit its influence was not as direct as in the case of the soft law of the CoE or the case-law of the ECtHR, the expansion of the ideal of pluralism as a foundational value has led to including pluralism in EU law. The idea of pluralism in EU law and EU human rights was not constructed around the limits of necessity in a democratic society but instead embedded in existing principles of non-discrimination and equality which have shaped the meaning of rights in the EU. Such a construction of pluralism, even if constantly growing in importance, has displayed tendencies of marginalising and controlling the terms on which the other could be recognised. In addition, due to a range of procedural and structural issues, its application has been frequently restricted or even prevented, thus rendering it a legal ornament rather than a recognition principle. Complexities of the relationship between national, European and international law and the importance of citizenship for the execution of rights in EU law successfully minimised the possibilities of the other to appeal to the principle as a tool for recognition. Even if her difference could emerge between the weaknesses of the liberal construction of EU rights, the other in the EU system would have to battle an intricate legal machinery in which her voice frequently disappears among the sounds of procedural concerns that are far from securing a maximally inclusive and religiously plural society. In the intricate machinery of EU legal instruments the principle of pluralism often turns out to be a recurring motif in the background. It is not only a grand narrative, but a grand narrative caricaturised and minimised to such an extent that its employment as an emancipating factor is frequently close to impossible. This chapter analyses the diverse instruments of EU law that engage in discussion of pluralism and illustrates how recognising difference remains but a remote concern of these instruments.

3.1 The Lisbon Treaty and the role of rights and pluralism as underlying legal principles of European integration

The European Community (EC) and later the EU did not rush into including protection of human rights or any form of pluralism, cultural or religious, among its principles. Quite the contrary, the EU, having its origin in the Coal and Steel Community, was founded mainly on the basis of economic cooperation between Western European countries after World War II. Preoccupied with economic concerns, European integration for a long time failed to include fundamental rights as one of its 'founding myths' (Smismans 2010). Developments in recognition of human rights and diversity continued to progress slowly (Craig and Burca 2011, 362–406) and it was in 1969 when the European Court of Justice (ECJ) for the first time referred to human rights in the case of *Stauder*.[1] The first official document other than case-law of the Court that expanded the idea of Europe beyond the idea of economic cooperation was the Declaration on European Identity issued during the 1973 European Community Summit in Copenhagen. Going beyond the concerns of a common market the Declaration expressed a concern about underlying non-economic values of European integration and initiated the discourse of European 'identity'. It was this declaration that listed the principles of representative democracy, the rule of law, social justice and respect for human rights as fundamental elements of that identity.[2] It also affirmed concern for national culture by underlining that:

> The Nine wish to ensure that the cherished values of their legal, political and moral order are respected, and to preserve the rich variety of their national cultures.[3]

In its reserved approach to difference the declaration did not mean automatic recognition of the importance of cultural diversity, particularly within Member States. It took as long as another 20 years from the time of the Copenhagen Declaration before further steps were taken towards recognition of the importance of cultural diversity in European integration. These steps, however, continued to establish the imagery of cemented national cultures and the diversity among them rather than within them. The Treaty of Maastricht founding the EU and later the Treaty of Amsterdam included an explicit article on culture:

> The Community shall contribute to the flowering of the cultures of the Member States, while respecting their national and regional diversity and at the same time bringing the common cultural heritage to the fore.[4]

---

[1] Case C-29/69 *Stauder* v. *City of Ulm* [1969] ECR 149.
[2] *Document on the European Identity*, Nine Foreign Ministers, 14 December 1973, Copenhagen.
[3] *Ibid.*, para.1.
[4] *The Maastricht Treaty*, 7 February 1992, Maastricht, Official Journal of the European Communities C 325/5, para. 128(1).

This reserved approach repeated the concerns of the Copenhagen Declaration and pushed forward the idea of horizontal recognition of diversity of European cultures, albeit not yet directly religion. This turn towards including references to culture remained curtailed and narrow when compared to the first emerging interpretations of the meaning of pluralism slowly issued at the time by CoE bodies. The first step towards recognising the growing vertical diversity within the Member States and prospective Member States was taken as late as in 1993, at the Copenhagen European Council meeting, which prepared criteria for accession of Central and Eastern European countries. Among concerns for stability of institutions guaranteeing democracy, the rule of law and human rights, the summit expressed explicit concern over protection of minorities.[5] Despite applying a narrow concept of minorities, meaning primarily static and established national minorities, the criteria made the first more decisive nod towards recognition of diversity within European countries. In this lengthy process of developing principles leading to recognition of diversity, religion stayed out of the focus of European integration for much longer than culture. Prompted by works of the so-called Kahn Commission and the findings of the Westendorp report encouraging insertion of Articles forbidding discrimination directly into the Treaties (Zanon and Sciortino 2014, 504), explicit mention of religion was for the first time included in the Treaty of Amsterdam in the declaration on the status of churches and non-confessional organisations supplementing the Treaty:

> The European Union respects and does not prejudice the status under national law of churches and religious associations or communities in the Member States.
> The European Union equally respects the status of philosophical and non-confessional organisations.[6]

The approach to religion developed in a similar fashion to the Maastricht approach to culture and was entrenched in a vision of cemented and static horizontal religious diversity between Member States. It was also driven by the idea of preserving appropriate competence and securing non-interference of the EU in this internal sphere. This balancing of competences initiated a twofold approach towards religion as faith and as an 'ethical inheritance' (McCrea 2010, 51–2) of the Member States and the EU as a unity. Although it is not exactly certain what such an 'inheritance' might entail, the struggle over its meaning in the context of religion was particularly vivid in the discourse over the preamble to the Treaty of Lisbon (McCrea 2010, 53–63). The attempt to recognise the Christian heritage of Europe marked the entry point of the discourse of religion into EU law. While the final text of the preamble did not include references to Christianity, the idea

---

[5] Copenhagen European Council, 21–22 June 1993, SN 180/93.
[6] *The Treaty of Amsterdam*, 2 October 1997, Amsterdam, Official Journal of the European Communities C 340/1, Declaration on the status of churches and non-confessional organisations.

of religion as an ethical guideline received new prominence in the current shape of the European Treaties.

Even though religion had entered EU law, its recognition took a slightly different route than within the CoE system. EU law with far more restraint began balancing different interests rather than charging at the unforeseen waters of recognising pluralism as a democratic value. The Treaty of Lisbon indeed underlined the greater importance of pluralism understood as a principle but it expressed concerns to secure both horizontal and vertical diversity. The Treaty of Lisbon[7] combined pluralism with values of equality and non-discrimination. Article 2 of the Treaty of the European Union (TEU) for the first time directly referred to pluralism alongside non-discrimination as a founding value of the Union:

> The Union is founded on the values of respect for human dignity, freedom, democracy, equality, the rule of law and respect for human rights, including the rights of persons belonging to minorities. These values are common to the Member States in a society in which *pluralism*, non-discrimination, tolerance, justice, solidarity and equality between women and men prevail.

These values were supported with Article 3 TEU establishing the obligation to combat social exclusion and discrimination and Article 10 Treaty on the Functioning of the European Union (TFEU) underlining that the Union would combat discrimination based on 'sex, racial or ethnic origin, religion or belief, disability or sexual orientation'. None the less, these references to vertical pluralism within Member States continued to be strongly supplemented with concerns over horizontal pluralism. The text of the declaration concerning the position of national churches which supplemented the Treaty of Amsterdam was incorporated into the text of the current Treaty in Article 17 TFEU.[8] In a similar manner diversity of horizontal religious traditions was also mentioned in the context of the internal market in Article 13 TFEU:

> In formulating and implementing the Union's agriculture, fisheries, transport, internal market, research and technological development and space policies, the Union and the Member States shall, since animals are sentient beings, pay full regard to the welfare requirements of animals, while respecting the legislative or administrative provisions and customs of the Member States relating in particular to religious rites, cultural traditions and regional heritage.

This balancing of the market with religious rites as a part of the European heritage embraced the cultural traditions of religious minorities, but did not go beyond static acceptance of the established shape of the rituals and rites involved.

---

[7]   *Treaty of Lisbon Amending the Treaty on European Union and the Treaty Establishing the European Community*, 13 December 2007, Lisbon, Official Journal of the European Communities 2007/C 306/01.

[8]   *Treaty on the Functioning of the European Union*, 13 December 2007, Lisbon, Official Journal of the European Communities 2008/C 115/01.

All in all, explicit reference to pluralism in EU law is narrow, and the approach to diversity is shaped through principles of non-discrimination and equality. While the reformed Treaties prima facie recognised both dimensions of religious and cultural pluralism – horizontal and vertical – they did so in a constrained and conflicting manner. Basing the approach to diversity in principles of non-discrimination, the Treaties seek to secure pluralism by reference to equal value rather than the importance of preserving difference. But as Young famously elaborated, equality and non-discrimination are frequently too narrow categories for accommodating difference and they do not always adequately respond to primary causes of otherisation, in the shape of marginalisation and oppression:

> Oppression, not discrimination, is the primary concept for naming group-related injustice. While discriminatory policies sometimes cause or reinforce oppression, oppression involves many actions, practices, and structures that have little to do with preferring or excluding members of groups in the awarding of benefits.
>
> (Young 1990, 195)

As further elaborated by Young, in contexts of marginalisation or oppression, absolute equality often results in sameness and fails to address the root causes of exclusion. Ironically, as she insists when law bans discrimination, it frequently becomes impossible to prove discrimination as it is replaced with the appeal to qualifications and preferences for character or similar allegedly neutral grounds (Young 1990, 196). Therefore for difference to be accommodated in an inclusive and participatory manner, differential treatment and equity provide a richer framework for accommodation. In the EU context of balancing between equality and non-discrimination and the need to preserve existing cultural and religious structures of national communities, these narrow principles frequently prove of little help in challenging marginalising practices. Despite the reference to pluralism, issues such as nationality or the practical ability to employ the Treaty mechanism, protection and greater recognition are the main obstacles in making difference more acceptable. These obstacles pile up as soon as we begin the interpretation of Article 6 TEU reforming the system of rights protection in the EU. With the full picture of complexity of the rights regime, even the applicability of non-discrimination and equality appears to harbour a potential for difficulties in application.

3.2 The Charter and the role of equality and pluralism for protection of religious difference

At first glance the Treaty of Lisbon with its Article 6 brought a radical modification of the system of rights. It strengthened their position and introduced what some have called a three-pillared system of human rights protection (Pernice 2008). This system was assumed to have reinforced rights secured by different legal regimes and was intended to create a comprehensive rights protection system. Article 6 TEU reforming a system of rights entrenched them in three legal regimes – domestic, international and European. According to the formulation contained therein, securing fundamental rights happens through their entrenchment in the constitutional traditions of the Member States, the ECHR and the EU's own system of protection, the Charter of Fundamental Rights[9] (the Charter). When it comes to religious pluralism, the Charter, which by virtue of the same Article 6 received value equivalent to that of the Treaties, does not explicitly refer to the principle. Instead it includes Article 22 securing cultural, religious and linguistic diversity.

Additionally in the context of religion, the Charter contains a provision analogous to Article 9 of the ECHR. The first paragraph of Article 10 of the Charter nearly repeats the formulation of Article 9 ECHR:

> Everyone has the right to freedom of thought, conscience and religion. This right includes freedom to change religion or belief and freedom, either alone or in community with others and in public or in private, to manifest religion or belief, in worship, teaching, practice and observance.

The entitlements stemming from the provision regulating freedom of religion in the Charter are even broader than those included in the Convention. They explicitly include freedom to change religion as well as the right to contentious objection recognised in paragraph 2 of Article 10. The provisions of Article 10 are additionally strengthened by the broad definition of non-discrimination contained in Article 21 and forbidding:

> Any discrimination based on any ground such as sex, race, colour, ethnic or social origin, genetic features, language, religion or belief, political or any other opinion, membership of a national minority, property, birth, disability, age or sexual orientation.

Despite these strong safeguards the jurisprudence of the ECJ has been modest in terms of the application and interpretation of discrimination in the context of Article 10. Thus far the judgment in Joined Cases C-71/11 and C-99/11,[10] regarding a preliminary ruling for a German Court in a case concerning the application of refugee qualification, Directive 2004/83, remains the only judgment strongly related to Article 10 and elaborating on the question of religion. More precisely the judgment focuses on the meaning of persecution in the context of religion and deals with a case of members of the religious Ahmadiyyaa minority

---

[9] *Charter of Fundamental Rights of the European Union*, 26 October, Lisbon, Official Journal of the European Communities 2012/C 326/02.

[10] *Y and Z*, Court of Justice of the European Union (Grand Chamber), Judgment, Cases C-71/11 and C-99/11, 5 September 2012.

in Pakistan applying for asylum in Germany. While underlining that a person should not be expected to abandon acts of worship once returned to their country of origin, the judgment at the same time elaborates that not all interference with freedom of religion amounts to persecution:

> Articles 9(1)(a) of Directive [2004/83] … must be interpreted as meaning that not all interference with the right to freedom of religion which infringes Article 10(1) of the Charter of Fundamental Rights of the European Union is capable of constituting an 'act of persecution' within the meaning of that provision of the directive. It is apparent from the wording of Article 9(1) of that directive that there must be a 'severe violation' of freedom of religion having a significant effect on the person concerned in order for it to be possible for the acts in question to be regarded as acts of persecution. Accordingly, acts whose gravity is not equivalent to that of an infringement of the basic human rights from which no derogation can be made by virtue of Article 15(2) of the European Convention on Human Rights cannot be regarded as constituting persecution within the meaning of Article 9(1) of Directive 2004/83 and Article 1A of the Geneva Convention [Relating to the Status of Refugees].[11]

Acceptance of the unchangeable nature of religious worship and denying the expectation that an applicant could perhaps simply change a form of worship might of course be interpreted as a step towards recognising the possibility of radical difference. Prima facie it accepts the importance of belief and its nature and insists that a believer should not be expected to change their belief. Curiously, at the same time, the Court acknowledges and sanctions an approach that is exactly contrary to such a deep engagement with pluralism. The reasoning relies on the traditional interpretation of freedom of religion, assuming that the freedom has two components, a *forum internum* (the core) and a *forum externum* (additional aspects). These interpretations stemming from the approach of the ECHR assume that whereas there can be no interference with the *forum internum*, additional aspects of the freedom can be subject to limitations (Evans 2001). The ECJ in following that approach assumed that even those limitations that violate freedom do not always amount to persecution. The problem with this line of reasoning is of course the risk that the idea of religion or belief and worship can be easily based on an analogy to the known. The very construction of the *forum internum* and the *forum externum* is based on the assumption that religion can after all be interfered with. It remains modelled on Judeo-Christian models of religion informing liberal ideas such as the Rawlsian 'slippage' (Rawls 2005, 160) and a 'reasonable doctrine' (Rawls 2005, 171). The idea of reasonableness and slippage assumes the necessity of adjusting one's own beliefs in situations of conflict between a belief and the public rationale established through the process of reaching a reasonable

---

[11] *Ibid.*, paras 55–61.

consensus. Rawls assumes that no doctrine can ever be fully comprehensive and that each reasonable doctrine includes a margin of 'slippage' allowing for adjustments between the individual conscience and the requirements of public justice. The concept of *forum internum* and *forum externum* reverberates with that understanding of religion, once more taking an approach that reduces possible difference, when it comes to belief, to 'one universal point of view' (Young 1990, 103). It does not conceive of a possibility of difference; quite the contrary, it models the other on the known and the dominant without approaching and engaging with difference. In this particular case, this assumption is disturbing when we keep in mind the context of refuge. Adopting the criterion of reasonableness to examine the circumstances of religious persecution assumes that potentially persecutory interference can be measured as to the degree of 'severity' and that it can be objectively estimated with certainty. The complex circumstances of this case call for much deeper analysis in the context of migration, but in the context of religious persecution Douzinas's words remind one that in the narrow approach of the courts:

> [t]he past pain of the refugee and his fear of future torture have been translated into an interpretable, understandable reality that like all reality is potentially shareable by judge and victim.
>
> (Douzinas and Warrington 1991, 129)

The interpretation that the ECJ took in the cases above erased both the pain and the reality, including feelings and beliefs of the refugee, and translated them with the 'idiom of cognition' in which the 'fear is either reasonable and can be understood by the judge or is unreasonable and therefore non-existent' (Douzinas and Warrington 1991, 130).

Albeit the judgment does not deal with the concept and meaning of religious pluralism it signposts possible problems with the future take on the issue. The reduction to the interpretable and reasonable entails a narrow reading of diversity in which a belief, religion or lack thereof can simply be chiselled to fit the boundaries prepared for it by the dominant and easily recognisable model. Whether that model is religious or secular would remain secondary as long as it can be explained by an appeal to reasonableness.

In the context of Article 22 of the Charter, which protects cultural, religious and linguistic diversity, this analogy to the reasonable and the known risks privileging horizontal pluralism and 'enabling religion to influence law through its role in national cultural identity' (McCrea 2010, 52). While no judgment could currently help with demystifying the concept of religious diversity protected by the Charter it is safe to assume that achieving vertical religious pluralism will be continually weighed simultaneously with the need to preserve horizontal pluralism, which as McCrea calls it is treated as an 'ethical inheritance' (McCrea, 2010). In his words:

[P]ublic morality, and therefore, religion, is well recognised as a permissible basis for legal and policy choices in Community law and as a permissible basis for Member States to derogate from the EU law duties. Individual autonomy is an important principle in the EU legal order and the Union requires that the accommodation of religious influence over law, and the promotion of communal moral standards that this may involve, not be such as to unduly curtail such autonomy. Nevertheless ... the Court of Justice accepts that EU law does, in certain circumstances, permit such moral notions to be invoked to restrict the autonomy of individuals to engage in activities regarded as damaging or sinful for cultural or religious reasons in order to allow Member States to promote their own collective vision of the good life and morality.

(McCrea 2010, 76)

Having in mind the appeal of reasonableness and the tendency towards translation of the unknown by an appeal to common idioms, it is likely that traditional ethical approaches will have a decisive voice in determining the ultimate shape of the 'collective vision of the good life and morality'. The possibility of dissent might not only be limited but additionally subjected to procedural limitations in the application of the Charter. As provided by Article 51, the provisions of the Charter are addressed to the institutions and bodies of the Union. In applying the Charter, these institutions are bound by the principle of subsidiarity. As to the Member States, the provisions of the Charter apply to them only when they are implementing Union law. As provided further in Article 51.2, the Charter establishes no new powers of the Community or the Union. These procedural and structural limitations and their impact on the possibility of recognising difference will be addressed in the following chapters.

3.3 European Directives and non-discrimination on the grounds of religion

Alongside the Directive banning racism,[12] EU law also includes additional documents dealing with religion and based on Article 3(2) of the Treaty. The so-called Employment Equality Directive[13] (2000/78/) was drafted for the purpose of 'combating discrimination on the grounds of religion or belief, disability, age or sexual orientation as regards employment and occupation' (2000/78/EC, Article 1). Similarly to the Charter it does not include direct references to pluralism but instead focuses intensively on the concepts of direct and indirect discrimination

---

[12] Council Directive 2000/43/EC implementing the principle of equal treatment between persons irrespective of racial or ethnic origin, 29 June 2000, Official Journal of the European Communities L 180, 19/07/2000 P. 0022–0026.

[13] Council Directive 2000/78/EC of 27 establishing a general framework for equal treatment in employment and occupation, November 2000, Official Journal of the European Communities L 303, 02/12/2000 P. 0016–0022.

(Vickers 2008, 206–16) as well as harassment (Vickers 2003, 25). Its purpose is to put into effect the principle of equal treatment across the EU. The document underlines that discrimination, among other grounds on the basis of religion or belief, 'may undermine the attainment of a high level of employment, social protection, raising the standard of living and the quality of life, economic and social cohesion and solidarity, and the free movement of persons'.[14] This focus indicates that the protection afforded by the Directive is strongly based on the idea of a free market instead of the idea of pluralism and as such will be evaluated through the prism of the needs of the market, rather than the need to secure pluralism. This ban notwithstanding, Article 4 includes a clause allowing for 'difference in treatment' based, among other factors, on religion, where by 'reason of the nature of the particular occupational activities concerned or of the context in which they are carried out, such a characteristic constitutes a genuine and determining occupational requirement'. This seemingly contradictory provision applies, for instance, to employment of Catholic personnel in a Catholic hospital, or similarly recruitment of clergy. Even if relatively non-controversial, the provision could be used in a discriminatory manner. As explained by Vickers:

> Any discrimination will need genuinely to be for the purposes of preserving the religious ethos of the organisation. Although Christianity is not a white only religion, a requirement that employees be Christian in areas with high Asian Muslim or Hindu populations would be likely to generate a largely white workforce, and so could be used as a cover for race discrimination.
>
> (Vickers 2003, 28)

As a directive the instrument of course requires transposition into domestic law. Indeed, it has been transposed in a variety of forms such as the Employment Equality Regulation 2003 in the UK (Vickers 2003). The Directive has frequently been interpreted by the ECJ, particularly in the context of age (e.g. *Mangold*[15]) and disability (e.g. *Coleman*[16]). Despite prolific ECJ jurisprudence based on the Directive, religion has not yet formed a separate ground for a judgment. In these circumstances it is difficult to tell what the Court would decide for instance in a case of an employee dismissed on the grounds of wearing a demonstrably religious symbol and what approach to pluralism it would take (McCrea 2013).

Even if not directly dealing with freedom of religion, the case of *Coleman* concerning discrimination on the ground of disability brings important insights to the meaning of non-discrimination and the model of pluralism it aspires to foster. While the judgment remains legalistic and modest in terms of further interpretation of the aspirations of the Directive, the opinion of Advocate General

---

[14] *Ibid.*, Preamble, para. 11.

[15] *Werner Mangold* v. *Rüdiger Helm*, Court of Justice of the European Union (Grand Chamber), Case C-144/04, 22 November 2005.

[16] *S. Coleman* v. *Attridge Law and Steve Law*, Court of Justice of the European Union (Grand Chamber), Case C-303/06, 17 July 2008.

Maduro[17] illuminates the principles behind the Directive. While elaborating on forbidden grounds of discrimination, Maduro turns to the notion of autonomy and its connection with equality:

> Equality is not merely a political idea and aspiration but one of the fundamental principles of Community law. As the Court held in *Mangold* the Directive constitutes a practical aspect of the principle of equality. In order to determine what equality requires in any given case it is useful to recall the values underlying equality. These are human dignity and personal autonomy.[18]

Maduro in fact uses the analogy of religion to illustrate discrimination against a person in a relationship with someone being discriminated against on the grounds included in the Directive. Here again he puts extensive emphasis on the principle of autonomy:

> For instance, the autonomy of members of a religious group may be affected (for example, as to whom to marry or where to live) if they know that the person they will marry is likely to suffer discrimination because of the religious affiliation of his spouse.... When the discriminator deprives an individual of valuable options in areas which are of fundamental importance to their lives because that individual is associated with a person having a suspect characteristic then it also deprives that person of valuable options and prevents him from exercising his autonomy.[19]

This concept of pluralism is strongly connected with a model of moral pluralism relying on the assumption that it is only when a person has a variety of morally acceptable choices that they can live an autonomous and good life (Raz 1986). But such a construct can easily lead to erasure of the other and a battle of autonomies (Levinas 1994). Rather than leading to freedom it may result in the encounter of selves being fully focused and concerned with themselves. If every person is equally autonomous then the encounter of two autonomous subjects must necessarily end in minimising and curtailing the autonomy of the other. Law based on the idea of autonomy engages in an abstract balancing void of heteronomic ties, beliefs and origins. But even liberal theorists advocating autonomy admit that, first of all, full autonomy is not possible (Raz 1986, 369–99) and, second, the notion of autonomy runs into difficulty when applied to those who do not value autonomy as a necessary life principle (Raz 1986, 414). When targeting difference, pluralism based on autonomy always risks privileging the autonomy of those stronger and better equipped to ensure that their voice is heard as well as those

---

[17] Poiares Maduro Miguel, *Opinion of Advocate General Poiares Maduro*, Case C-303/06, *S. Coleman v. Attrige Law and Steve Law*, 31 January 2008.

[18] *Ibid.*, para. 8.

[19] *Ibid.*, para. 14.

who neatly fit the boundaries prepared by the model of an autonomous rational agent. The principle of autonomy does not force the law to approach difference. Quite the contrary, it entails modelling each and every person that it encounters on a rational, reasonable and autonomous agent void of the moral, familial and spiritual baggage that they carry. In other words, autonomy itself does not foster difference. Once more the other risks being silenced in favour of those who best fit the clear-cut model of an autonomous rational agent. Focus on autonomy prevents being constituted in relation to otherness and does not conceive of the possibility of a heteronomous relationship to freedom:

> Heteronomy means that freedom is not to be found in autonomy or independence but rather in responsibility – in a sustained ethical posture of 'Here I am.' And while such a notion is admittedly utopian, Levinas says that there is nothing preventing it from investing 'our everyday actions of generosity and goodwill towards the other…. Heteronomy means investing our freedom in the freedom and rights of the other.'
>
> (Chinnery 2003, 14)

Without this alternative, without the possibility of investing in the freedom of others, pluralism based on autonomy cannot prevent marginalisation of religious and non-religious minorities. While those remaining in a minority have the option to voice their grievances, the safeguards securing the positions of majoritarian groups in each Member State (Zanon and Sciortino 2014, 511) may prevent recognition of their autonomy and position. In an abstract act of legal balancing of rights imagined as protection of autonomies, law may marginalise those whose religious or non-religious position renders them 'unfit' for the imagined boundaries of the autonomous rational agent.

3.4 Religious pluralism in the EU or just a recurring shadow?

The construction of rights and pluralism in the EU is primarily informed by the idea of equality, which so often reduces difference to sameness. Rather than liberating and emancipatory, the shape and nature of the principle too frequently privileges the established and the dominant. Its effectiveness is also constrained by larger institutional and systemic concerns underpinning EU law. The position of rights along the complex matrix of EU law reduces the possibilities of the other to voice her claims in the language of rights. While on the surface the Treaty of Lisbon brought a radical modification of the system of rights and was assumed to create a reciprocal reinforcement of rights through different legal regimes (Pernice 2008), their applicability at least in the context of religion is thus far limited. In the context of freedom of religion, protection of equality stemming from the Charter will be applicable only in areas covered by Articles 3 and 4 TFEU determining the scope of EU competences. The applicability of the instrument is also limited territorially through the opt-out protocols signed by the United Kingdom and

Poland (Pernice 2008; Barnard 2008), also potentially diminishing the scope of Charter protection.

But problems of applicability of the Charter form only the tip of the iceberg. Examining the possibility to challenge potentially discriminatory and oppressive actions shows inherent limitations. Due to the design of permissible legal actions before the Court of Justice of the European Union (CJEU), a person claiming violation of freedom of religion is faced with limited possibilities for challenging the legality of EU or national measures (Groussot and Pech 2010; Gozdecka 2010). With a limited *locus standi* of natural persons before the Court, only claims against the actions of a Member State that occur while implementing EU law can be challenged; alternatively, a claim against a discriminatory action by an institution of the EU. Other actions of Member States fall under the scrutiny of the Court only when a court in the Member State applies for a preliminary ruling before the CJEU regarding the relationship between EU law and domestic law. Needless to say, the majority of regulation dealing with religion will remain in the sole competence of the Member States as a matter of domestic rather than EU law.

Difficulties in interpreting the principles might multiply when the Union accedes to the ECHR. While the process is slow, due, among other things, to issues of jurisdiction, should accession be achieved the principles regarding pluralism would also be binding within EU law. Such a formal conjunction, albeit structurally elegant, would not prevent tensions stemming from legal interpretation (Maduro 2009). We have already witnessed the complexities generated by the intersections of EU law and international law. Even though implementation of EU law does not absolve Member States from responsibility for human rights violations under international law,[20] the recent cases of *Kadi*[21] before the ECJ and *Bosphorus Hava*[22] before the ECtHR have illuminated the depth of systemic questions as to who is responsible for protection of rights and what is the meaning of rights when legal orders collide.

For a religious or non-religious other facing a landscape in which many rights and many traditions exist, the collision of legal orders might be a terrifying experience. The rights of the other might become a battlefield between different institutions of the Member States, the EU or other international organisations. On this battlefield, principles aiming to secure religious pluralism risk being just a shadow in a collision of systemic and procedural considerations (Gozdecka 2010; Gozdecka and Jackson 2011). Among these considerations, the other might vanish voiceless, a mere spectator of a grandiose performance that constantly refers to her freedom and equality but fails to see her in the fervour of action. For

---

[20] See also: *Matthews v. UK*, European Court of Human Rights, Judgment, Application No. 24833/94, 18 February 1999.

[21] *Yassin Abdullah Kadi and Al Barakaat International Foundation v. Council of the European Union and Commission of the European Communities*, Court of Justice of the European Union (Grand Chamber), Cases C-402/05 P and C-415/05, 3 September 2008.

[22] *Bosphorus Hava Yollarι Turizm ve Ticaret Anonim Şirketi v. Ireland*, European Court of Human Rights, Judgment, Application No. 45036/98, 30 June 2005.

principles such as pluralism to become more than a shadow, the analysis of trans-national justice systems would have to illuminate the position of the dominated and marginalised:

> [I]f the discussion of principles of transnational justice is to start from an analysis of the present global context of injustice, it needs to see this context as one of a complex system of power and domination with a variety of powerful actors, from international institutions to transnational corporations, local elites and so forth. Shifting perspective to that of the dominated, then, reveals that theirs is a situation of multiple domination.
>
> (Forst 2001, 166)

References

Barnard, Catherine. 2008. 'The "Opt-Out" for the UK and Poland from the Charter of Fundamental Rights: Triumph of Rhetoric over Reality?' In *The Lisbon Treaty. EU Constitutionalism without a Constitutional Treaty?*, ed. Stefan Griller and Jacques Ziller, 257–84. Schriftenreihe der Österreichischen Gesellschaft für Europaforschung (ECSA Austria) / European Community Studies Association of Austria 11. Springer.

Chinnery, Ann. 2003. 'Aesthetics of Surrender: Levinas and the Disruption of Agency in Moral Education.' *Studies in Philosophy and Education* 22(1): 5–17.

Craig, Paul and Grainne de Burca. 2011. *EU Law: Text, Cases, and Materials*, 5th edn. Oxford University Press.

Douzinas, Costas and Ronnie Warrington. 1991. ' "A Well-Founded Fear of Justice": Law and Ethics in Postmodernity.' *Law and Critique* 2 (2): 115–47.

Evans, Carolyn 2001. *Freedom of Religion under the European Convention on Human Rights.* Oxford University Press.

Forst, Rainer. 2001. 'Towards a Critical Theory of Transnational Justice.' *Metaphilosophy* 32(1–2): 160–79.

Gozdecka, Dorota A. 2010. 'Human Rights, Fundamental Rights and the Common Constitutional Traditions in the Protection of Religious Pluralism and Diversity in Europe: A Study in the Democratic Paradox.' *Finnish Yearbook of International Law* 21. Hart Publishing.

Gozdecka, Dorota A. and Amy R. Jackson. 2011. 'Caught between Different Legal Pluralisms: Women Who Wear Islamic Dress as the Religious "Other" in European Rights Discourses.' *Journal of Legal Pluralism and Unofficial Law* 64: 91–120.

Groussot, Xavier and Laurent Pech. 2010. 'Fundamental Rights Protection in the European Union Post Lisbon Treaty'. Fondation Robert Schuman Policy Paper, European Issue 173. Paris and Brussels: Fondation Robert Schuman.

Levinas, Emmanuel. 1994. *Outside the Subject.* Stanford University Press.

Maduro, Miguel Poiares. 2009. 'Courts and Pluralism: Essay on Theory of Judicial Adjudication in the Context of Legal and Constitutional Pluralism.' In *Ruling the World? Constitutionalism, International Law, and Global Governance*, ed. J. L. Dunoff and J. P. Trachtman, 356–80. Cambridge University Press.

McCrea, Ronan. 2010. *Religion and the Public Order of the European Union.* Oxford University Press.

McCrea, Ronan. 2013. 'The Ban on the Veil and European Law.' *Human Rights Law Review* 13(1): 57–97.

Pernice, Ingolf. 2008. 'The Treaty of Lisbon and Fundamental Rights.' In *The Lisbon Treaty. EU Constitutionalism without a Constitutional Treaty?*, ed. Stefan Griller and Jacques Ziller, 235–56. Schriftenreihe der Österreichischen Gesellschaft für Europaforschung (ECSA Austria) / European Community Studies Association of Austria 11. Springer.

Rawls, John. 2005. *Political Liberalism: Expanded Edition*. Columbia University Press.

Raz, Joseph. 1986. *The Morality of Freedom*. Oxford University Press.

Smismans, Stijn. 2010. 'The European Union's Fundamental Rights Myth.' *JCMS: Journal of Common Market Studies* 48(1): 45–66.

Vickers, Lucy. 2003. 'Freedom of Religion and the Workplace: The Draft Employment Equality (Religion or Belief) Regulations 2003.' *Industrial Law Journal* 32(1): 23–36.

Vickers, Lucy. 2008. *Religious Freedom, Religious Discrimination and the Workplace*. Hart Publishing.

Young, Iris Marion. 1990. *Justice and the Politics of Difference*. Princeton University Press.

Zanon, F. and G. Sciortino. 2014. 'The Newest Diversity Is the Oldest: Religious Pluralism and the EU.' *Ethnicities* 14(4): 498–516.

Chapter 4

Relevance of pluralism in European domestic regimes

Despite a strong emerging narrative of religious pluralism, its application within constitutional regimes in Europe is encountering multiple barriers of a legal and social nature. Despite an emerging effort to declare religious pluralism as a common principle, European countries in their constitutional development have established specific legal approaches to religion that render themselves less or more receptive to adoption of the principle. The main recognised models of coexistence of state and church are separation, neutrality, establishment and so-called mixed systems (Gozdecka 2009; Doe 2011). Despite this diversity, these regimes have been analysed primarily through the lens of secularism rather than pluralism (Baines 1996; B. C. Anderson 2004; Freedman 2004; Casanova 2006; Katzenstein 2006; Bader 2007; Berger, Fokas and Davie 2008; Levey and Modood 2008; Calo 2011; Ziebertz and Riegel 2008; Zucca 2012; Combalía and Roca 2014; Requejo and Ungureanu 2014) and critique has usually focused on alleged secularisation.

As has frequently been recalled, the notion of secularism assumes a separation between the public sphere, belonging to the political, and the private sphere, occupied among others by religion, familial ties and other non-public structures. But a heritage of secularism is none other than religious and entrenched in the biblical formulation 'Give to Caesar what is Caesar's, and to God what is God's' (Mark 12:17). This heritage of secularism applies a well-recognised Judaeo-Christian model where the spheres of public and private can be artificially and sometimes strongly divided. At the outset, this heritage poses a problem in terms of claims for recognition by those religions whose heritage is different or those where such separation does not exist. But while this is a well-rehearsed argument related to recognition of the religious, problems involving recognition of claims by atheists or agnostics in societies where, despite formal separation, the influence of the majority religion remains strong fail to be adequately captured by the paradigm of secularism and its critics. Societies that penalise abortion, such as Ireland or Malta, blasphemy against the majority religion, such as Poland or Greece, proselytism, such as Greece before the case of *Kokkinakis*, and legislating other practices aimed at protecting dominant religious normativities might – and frequently do – declare secularism as the underpinning of their legal systems. And it is in those societies that the argument of separation of the private and public spheres fails to examine cases of exclusion. Separation exists formally on the surface level while practice remains bound by recognition of the prevailing normativities. Religious and non-religious difference fails to be captured when such regimes are analysed by reference to secularism and secularisation. In situations of non-religious claims, secularism could in principle be used as a paradigm for embracing difference, but due to its establishment as a formal legal principle it remains powerless and cannot serve as an emancipatory paradigm. In other words, reference to secularism fails to recognise positions of non-religious others, regardless whether secularism is embraced or scorned. Due to the logical paradox in such legal systems, reference to secularism generates situations such as those seen in *Lautsi* v. *Italy*, which will be analysed in the following part of this book. Analogously, the Irish system also serves as an even more straightforward example of a system where analysing problems with recognition of difference cannot be carried out by reference to secularism. Until Amendment 5/1972, which entered into force in 1973, the Irish Constitution[1] acknowledged the privileged position of the Catholic Church. Even after 1973, Article 44 of the Constitution remained embedded therein, confirming that 'The State acknowledges that the homage of public worship is due to Almighty God. It shall hold His Name in reverence, and shall respect and honour religion.' Despite arguments considering it benign (Doe 2011, 34–5) this legal formulation does not reflect a secularist approach despite further constitutional references to the contrary. It not only fails to separate but also obliges the state to honour a particular theistic form of religious worship despite further judicial reiterations of this approach and references to secularism that exist in the Irish system (Doe 2011, 35).

Finally the paradigm of secularism focuses primarily on the state and religion understood in institutional terms (churches). It does not correspond with the quickly evolving reality of less formalised and more individualised forms of contemporary religious belief (Davie 2007). As illustrated, especially by those investigating cases of veiling through the legal pluralistic paradigm (Jackson 2010), the equation of adherents with institutionalised and universalised religions tends to mistranslate the reality of motivations behind minoritarian religious choices. In reality a single worshipper, even one belonging to a larger institutionalised religion, cannot be equated to the sum total of precepts laid down in an institutionalised religion. That approach defies appeal to difference. It not only fails to recognise claims of minority worshippers not following any recognised religion or lacking institutional affiliation, but also ignores difference within religions, presenting them as homogeneous blocks juxtaposed with secularism.

For these reasons legal analysis of the position of religious difference must be expanded beyond appeals or critiques of secularism. As this chapter intends to illustrate, the narrow narrative of religion versus secularism has more often than not failed to capture dominant religious normativities embraced by diverse legal regimes. By erasing social context it has neglected complexities involved in the

---

[1] Constitution of Ireland (last amended June 2004), 1 July 1937.

recognition of those differently religious and shrouded the discussion in a homogenising veil of one versus the other. Meanwhile, when the lens of pluralism is applied, the picture reveals a second bottom. Whereas in strongly secularised legal systems secular normativities prevail and fail to recognise the differently religious other, some legal systems in Europe continue to harbour deeply religious normativites. These normativities, like secular normativities, become paradigms recognised by law and just like secular normativities they can be used for othering. In terms of pluralism, the problem stretches beyond the secular versus the religious and can eventually be encapsulated in the divide between paradigm normativities and their others. Therefore while examining pluralism it is necessary to focus on the potential of legal systems for recognition of difference. The sections that follow try to illustrate how pluralism could be and has been used in some of these contexts and what shape it has taken. They illustrate that the appeal to pluralism is frequently weak or based on established approaches balancing between secularism and religion. The central question posed below is whether pluralism has been used as an emancipatory paradigm and if so what shape it has taken in different socio-legal contexts.

4.1 Established state churches and the idea of pluralism

The institution of an established church dates back historically to the times of the Reformation (MacCulloch 2003) and has over time evolved and diversified, currently standing for different formations influencing societies to a greater or lesser degree. While the United Kingdom, Malta, Denmark, Iceland and Norway feature legally established state churches, their societies display considerable variety in terms of the social influence of those churches and the normativities they generate and maintain. While Iceland, Norway and Denmark display secularist tendencies, the Maltese and Greek systems include legal provisions securing the moral teaching of their churches or banning practices such as abortion or blasphemy. The UK, on the other hand, has grown increasingly diverse despite the establishment of the Church of England, prompting increased discussion on pluralism. Just as the position of the established church differs in these societies, so does the role of the principle of pluralism. In some contexts it has not been widely discussed, while in others it has displayed several problematic tendencies. The analysis below evaluates the position of religious pluralism in the Danish, British, Maltese and Greek systems, illustrating how, depending on the take on difference, pluralism does not always take the shape of an emancipatory paradigm in the discussion on diversity.

The Evangelical Lutheran Church of Denmark is established in Article 4 of the Danish Constitution[2] delegating the responsibility for church matters to the state. Article 6 obliges the king to belong to the Evangelical Lutheran Church, while Article 68 sets an obligation not to impose taxes to any other faith than one's own. In practice the leadership of the church belongs to the church authorities and the

[2] Danmarks Riges Grundlov, 5 June 1953.

church enjoys a high degree of independence. Despite a high level of secularisation the cultural influence of the church cannot be underestimated. Denmark has been a relatively homogeneous society, with four out of five Danes belonging to the state church (Riis 2011, 20). While the teaching of the church does not influence secular law, the established position of the church generates particular socio-religious normativity influencing recognition of difference. While debates on religious pluralism have erupted in the Danish media (Riis 2011, 21), scientific projects (Ahlin *et al.* 2012, 411) and discussions on the separation of state and church,[3] the main focus has remained strongly linked to immigration. Paired with frequent negative images of migrants, including their alleged negative influence on Danish values, the cultural majority has considered religious particularisms as a hindrance to integration (Riis 2011, 22). Instead of becoming a paradigm for recognising difference, the publication of 'Mohammed cartoons' in the newspaper *Jyllands Posten* turned the debate on pluralism into a battle between recognised religious normativity and foreign normativities. Religious otherness became feared as a danger to communal 'Danishness' and a relatively high social level of secularism (Riis 2011, 32). Danish Christianity in its secularist formulation became the dominant normativity in the pluralistic project and the debate on pluralism has not been pushed beyond the stage of infancy (Ahlin *et al.* 2012, 411). In a quasi-colonial discourse pluralism was framed as endangering cultural norms of 'Danishness' paired with secularised Christianity. Defined in opposition to prevailing norms, the discourse of pluralism, rather than embracing difference, became focused on how much 'barbarism' could be accepted in society. Using essentialising images of otherness, pluralism became synonymous with multiculturalism and was seen as a project doomed from the start and undermining 'social cohesion' and security (Riis 2011). In its judgment rejecting a complaint by Muslim associations against publication of the Mohammed cartoons, the Court also framed the complaint as an issue of Danish values. Several organisations with a Muslim background complained against infringement of penal law provisions against libel and defamation. In this famous case in 2008 the High Court (Vestre Landsret Domstole) upheld the judgment of the court of first instance from 2006, referring to the problem in question as a problem of self-censorship. While the organisations argued that the caricatures, especially the one depicting Mohammed with a bomb in his turban, implied that Islam is a religion of terror, gender inequality and oppression, the Court failed to find a direct connection between the images and Islam. Referring to freedom of expression as included in the ECHR the Court questioned whether a link existed between the drawings and the right of the organisations to be protected from libel. While explicitly referring to permitted limitations on freedom of religion based on the text of the ECHR,[4] the Court insisted that limitations on freedom of expression should be interpreted narrowly in order to avoid the danger of self-censorship of the press:

---

[3] 'Når stat og kirke skilles', *Kristeligt Dagblad*, 28 August 2008.

[4] The exercise of freedom of expression may be subject to: 'restrictions or penalties as are prescribed by law and are necessary in a democratic society, in the interests of national security, territorial

Carsten Juste was involved in a journalistic project, the purpose of which was to determine the degree of self-censorship. The purpose was not to provoke, hurt or offend Muslims. The High Court considers there is no proof that *Jyllands-Posten*'s intention was to depict Muslims as aggressive female oppressors, exponents of war or terrorists.[5]

The judgment further underlined that the objective of the drawings was to caricature acts of violence perpetrated in the name of Islam. Despite seemingly speaking in favour of unlimited freedom of expression, the judgment coupled 'objectivity' with forms of expression of the majority. The illusion of objectivity underpinned the depiction of difference presented in the judgment. It is not Muslims but 'unreasonable' Muslims with their 'unreasonable' doctrine of violence that can be judged and caricatured by the 'reasonable' and 'neutral' majority who were merely testing the 'boundaries of self-censorship'. The judgment permeated the paradoxical oppression of the minority by sanctioning stereotypical images. 'Just as everyone knows that gay people are promiscuous, that Indians are alcoholics, and that women are good with children' (Young 1990, 59), so everyone 'knows' that Muslims are terrorists. The application of 'equality for all' resulted in a one-size-fits-all treatment for both the recognised and the marginalised. This approach to pluralism reverberated with the condescending logic of tolerance of 'barbarians' and their barbaric behaviour. While the richness of expression speaks as a strong argument in favour of pluralism, its application fails to live up to the expectation of embracing difference. In the one-size-fits-all model of pluralism the other is unable to challenge the established normativity and the power of what the majority considers normal, ordinary and typical. It disables the other's protest against the majority's essentialising judgment about the other's qualities. The one-size-fits-all model of pluralism fails to meet its promises and serves as a facade unable to challenge the established norms of secularised Christian Danishness. When religion is primarily a cultural tradition of the majority, the minority, despite its protest, can easily be silenced in the name of the freedom of those who are better represented.

The situation looks slightly different in more diverse societies. Despite the establishment of the Church of England in England, recent British debates on freedom of religion feature heightened concern for religious diversity (Bano 2008; Shah 2009; Uberoi and Modood 2013; Jackson 2010; Malik 2013). The Church of England has enjoyed establishment since the Reformation and maintains its strong connection with the Crown. The Act of Supremacy of 1558 and the Bill

---

integrity or public safety, for the prevention of disorder or crime, for the protection of health or morals, for the protection of the reputation or rights of others, for preventing the disclosure of information received in confidence, or for maintaining the authority and impartiality of the judiciary', Vestre Landsret, 5. Afdeling, J.nr. V.L. B-2423-06, 19 June 2008.

[5] Vestre Landsret, 5. Afdeling, J.nr. V.L. B-2423-06, 19 June 2008.

of Rights of 1688[6] established the position of the church and the king or queen in relation to the church. The Act of Supremacy[7] guarantees that all spiritual jurisdiction is united in the Crown. Until the recent constitutional amendment, not only did the monarch have to profess Protestantism but according to the Act of Settlement passed in 1701 could not marry a Catholic. The recent amendment to the Succession to the Crown Act in April 2013 modernised the monarchy in order to adjust it to the demands of an age of diversity (Parpworth 2013). This reform, concerning only royal marriages and succession, did not affect the position of the king or queen as the Supreme Governor of the Church, who continues to approve the appointment of bishops and open meetings of the General Synod of the Church of England. The church continues to be established and constitutional regulations include such concessions to the church as inclusion of 26 so-called Lords Spiritual in the House of Lords. The Anglican Lords Spiritual include the archbishops of Canterbury and York, the bishops of London, Durham and Winchester and 21 bishops in order of appointment to a diocesan see. Dating back to 1878, the Lords Spiritual were supposed to bring a religious ethos to the legislative process. Several plans for reform of the House of Lords have envisioned reducing the number of Lords Spiritual or including Muslim Lords Spiritual in the House. This would not, however, change the position of the Church of England, which 'could continue to be well represented with fewer Bishops' (HM Government 2007, 47). So far these proposals have not gone forward and are under continuous debate, including radically different suggestions such as replacing the House of Lords with a Senate.[8] Despite the atmosphere of reform, the conjunction of church and state is informally present in British political life. During his appointment as prime minister, Tony Blair was expected to avoid changing his religion to that of his wife and family during his term of office due to the traditional expectation that the position be filled by a person connected with the Anglican Church. Thus Blair converted to Catholicism only after his term of office elapsed.[9]

With all the contemporary conundrums and visions of reform, the position of the Church of England has been described as problematic and sitting uneasily with the dominant paradigm of secularism (Sandberg 2011). In what has been branded a British post-Christian era[10] the influence of the church on diversity and pluralism is disputed (Modood 1992; Levey and Modood 2008; Doe 2011; Ahdar and Leigh 2013). Far more religiously diverse than Denmark, the UK population features various Christian denominations including the Church of England, the Church of Scotland, the Church in Wales, Roman Catholics, Protestants and all other Christian denominations, diverse Islamic groups, a sizeable Hindu

---

[6] Bill of Rights, 1688 c.2 1 Will and Mar Sess 2.
[7] Act of Supremacy, 1558 c.1 1 Eliz 1.
[8] Patrick Wintour, 'Miliband calls for second chamber to represent all UK's cities and regions', *Guardian*, 1 November 2014.
[9] Stephen Bates, 'After 30 years as a closet Catholic, Blair finally puts faith before politics', *Guardian*, 22 June 2007.
[10] 'Britain in post-Christian era, says former archbishop of Canterbury', *Guardian*, 27 April 2014.

population as well as Jews, Sikhs, Pagans, Wiccans, Baha'i, Jains and other religious groups.[11]

Despite the growing religious diversity of the British population, the focus on
pluralism appears only to be emerging in scholarship (Mookherjee 2011; Beckford
2014; Requejo and Ungureanu 2014; Sandberg 2015). Since the discussion on
inclusion of religious diversity has been dominated by reference to inclusive multiculturalism in a secularised state, British Anglicanism continues to represent an
important mythical norm against which others can be included. In his fight against
multiculturalism, David Cameron has lately appealed to the Christian heritage of
Britain. Despite the statistically waning influence of the Church of England, the
figure of an Anglican Brit is still seen as a paradigm frequently juxtaposed with
the image of a threatening Muslim (Modood 1998). The influence of Anglican
normativity cannot be underestimated, especially when:

> Identities in this political climate are not implicit and private but are shaped
> through intellectual, cultural and political debates and become a feature of
> public discourse and policies.
>
> (Modood 1998, 386)

Maintenance of a dominant religious normativity, even though symbolic and not
expressed in numbers, or even in the direct influence of the Anglican Church or
its followers on law, reflects how the notion of minority need not be related to
numerical predominance. Indeed, the dominant normativity can be represented
by a numerical minority. When discussion of pluralism continues to be led via a
multicultural lens, it risks ending up in a struggle between an essentialised 'we' and
an essentialised 'them'. Potentially, religious pluralism and religious difference risk
being mere catchphrases used for defining the boundaries of a community. While
some defend a 'mild establishment' (Ahdar and Leigh 2013, 127–54) or argue that
it does not have implications for a religiously plural society (Modood 1992, 59–60)
the importance of dominant symbolism cannot be underestimated (Weller 2000).
When the symbolisation and operationalisation of the state are affected by the
establishment of the church, other traditions risk enjoying a merely second-class
position. It is of course imaginable, as Modood has argued, that the position of
the church is merely symbolic and does not give rise to dominant normativity. But
the mechanism of cementing the imagined religious essence without correlation
to numbers is more likely to occur. In these circumstances, reference to pluralism
becomes fuzzy and its incorporation slow. In contrast, the other continues to be
pushed to the margins despite no longer being in the minority. This approach
risks creating many pressure points, such as the *Begum* case (Sandberg 2011, 197),
and employment of changing narratives, from defence of essence to defence of
secularism. In other words, despite growing religious diversity, pluralism has not

---

[11] Census, April 2011, Office for National Statistics, National Statistics Online: www.statistics.gov.uk

yet evolved into the leading principle of recognising difference even in a society as religiously diverse as the British.

The discourse of pluralism is even more problematic in countries where the religious population remains homogeneous. In these countries pluralism – even if it appears in the discussion – often remains marginal and related to beliefs considered niche. Malta and Greece exemplify countries whose religious identity is closely connected with national values, the historical identity of the nation and the church. In these countries the influence of the church on political and social life is usually stronger and the discourse of pluralism remains marginal. According to Section 2 of the Maltese Constitution from the year 1964,[12] amended in 1994 and 1996, the state church of Malta is the Roman Catholic Church. According to the same section it is endowed with a legal right to determine moral rights and wrongs and is privileged in public education:

1. The religion of Malta is the Roman Catholic Apostolic Religion.
2. The authorities of the Roman Catholic Apostolic Church have the duty and the right to teach which principles are right and which are wrong.
3. Religious teaching of the Roman Catholic Apostolic Faith shall be provided in all State schools as part of compulsory education.

Not only is the church established but the alleged secularist divide between private and public is at best clouded by the established 'duty and the right to teach which principles are right and wrong' vested in the Catholic Church. At the same time this non-secularist establishment is paired with Article 1 of the Constitution proclaiming adherence to democratic values and respect for the human rights and freedoms of the individual. The establishment of the Catholic Church as the state church is connected with Maltese history and the conflict between British and Italian influences over the island (A. S. V. S. 1930). Malta, previously a British colony, has been independent since 1964 with Catholicism forming a part of national identity. Catholicism appears to be professed by as much as 98 per cent of the population with 77 per cent following the teaching of the church.[13] With this particular socio-religious and legal setting, the influence of religion permeates the Maltese legal system. Malta forbids practices such as abortion, which is banned in all circumstances, and penalises both the person administering the procedure and the woman undergoing it. The debate on entrenching the ban in the Constitution has been ongoing,[14] and Malta has successfully protected its legal system from international pressure concerning abortion by including reservations to its international obligations such as Convention on the Elimination of All Forms of

---

[12] Constitution of Malta, 1964.

[13] 'Malta bishops release family synod survey findings', *National Catholic Reporter*, 6 May 2014. http://ncronline.org/news/global/malta-bishops-release-family-synod-survey-findings

[14] J. Ameen, 'Government proposes abortion ban to be included in the Constitution', *Malta Independent*, 7 May 2005; 'Muscat has reservations on proposed Constitutional ban on abortion', *Times of Malta*, 18 September 2008.

Discrimination against Women (CEDAW) Article 16. Moreover, the use of contraceptives has for long been influenced by the dominant religion. Importation of condoms was still prohibited in the 1970s and pharmacies were prohibited from selling them under pain of losing their licence (Milne 1973). Nowadays, the school curriculum includes minimum sexual education and contraception is allowed, but Catholicism appears to have influence on the choice of contraceptive methods and sexual health statistics (Mifsud *et al.* 2009). In addition to issues related to reproduction, Article 163 of the Maltese Criminal Code prohibits vilification of the Roman Catholic Apostolic Religion. This strong influence of religion on law leaves narrow space for otherness:

> The inseparability of religion, politics and ordinary daily life is obvious from the frequency of religious themes and commentary in the media to people's devotion to their village patron saint, expressed most dramatically in annual feasts to honour the saints and celebrate village identity. All social institutions from the family, school and village to national politics, education and law are influenced by Catholicism.
>
> (Rountree 2014, 88)

For these reasons new religions such as Paganism or neo-Paganism enter the Maltese religious scene through renegotiation of Catholicism. Religious diversification happens slowly and hybrid identities such as Christian Pagans are slowly entering the religious landscape (Rountree 2014).

The situation in Greece is comparable. The established church of Greece is the Eastern Orthodox Church and, as in the Maltese Constitution, the Greek Constitution establishes its position in Article 3:[15]

> The prevailing religion in Greece is that of the Eastern Orthodox Church of Christ. The Orthodox Church of Greece, acknowledging our Lord Jesus Christ as its head, is inseparably united in doctrine with the Great Church of Christ in Constantinople and with every other Church of Christ of the same doctrine, observing unwaveringly, as they do, the holy apostolic and synodal canons and sacred traditions.

Moreover, the Constitution deals with certain internal regulations of the church concerning scripture and the ecclesiastical regime. The church enjoys personality in public law and its canons cannot be violated in state courts in terms of doctrine and liturgy (Doe 2011, 31). As in Malta, the influence of the Greek church on Greek life has been extremely strong. This was summarised by Mavrogordatos in the following wording: 'Unless one is willing to bear very substantial costs, one can neither live nor die outside the churches: the Orthodox Church and the few others recognised or tolerated' (Mavrogordatos 2003, 123). This sentiment was expressed

---

[15]   The Constitution of Greece, 18 April 2001.

publicly by Archbishop Christodoulos in a 2000 statement saying that 'For Greeks, to be an Orthodox Christian is a defining attribute of our identity.'[16]

Due to this prevailing understanding of nationality, attempts to separate church and state failed in the constitutional revision of 2001, even though some changes concerning the influence of religion have been introduced, for example those removing religious affiliation from identity cards.[17] Despite this strong identity Greece, like all other European countries, is facing the challenge of converting itself from a monocultural to a religiously diverse society (Alivizatos 1999, 33). This renegotiation, however, is happening with the strong involvement of the church:

> [T]he ID crisis has been part of a broader range of topics that have marked the forceful reappearance of the Church in public life. This list of the various 'hot issues' includes the prohibition of catechism, the public operation of mosques and denominational churches, the issue of cremation and the issue of burial rites and baptism for individuals who have chosen to have a civil wedding ceremony (which the Church does not officially recognize as valid) instead of a religious ceremony. In several of these issues, the Church has to rely on the actions of the State to safeguard its own positions. Therefore, the soft boundary that separates the strictly ecclesiastical issues from those that fall within the realm of state policy and public discourse demands the high clergy's participation and intervention into public debates as a means of shaping public opinion.
>
> (Roudometof 2011, 100)

In the case of Greece and Malta, establishment is reinforced by a religiously homogeneous population. The position of these churches is strong and their views regarding reproductive rights, birth control practices, non-discrimination on the grounds of sexuality (Georges 1996; Paxson 2003) or the position of minorities and internationalisation (Anderson 2002; Payne 2003) is vocal and influential in the legal domain. In these circumstances the thought of diversity is frequently phrased by reference to secularism or multiculturalism rather than pluralism. Each of these narratives, however, is more often than not seen as a threat to religion and national identity (Anderson 2002). Not surprisingly one of the most important judgments concerning violation of freedom of religion was issued against Greece. The *Kokkinakis*[18] case put such strong emphasis on facing the other and recognising difference precisely because of the narrow opportunities to secure religious pluralism in such circumstances. Implementation of the decision, however, encountered difficulties, so that the case was eventually soon followed by *Larissis* v.

---

[16] Athens News Agency, Daily News Bulletin in English, 30 May 2000.
[17] Athens News Agency, Daily News Bulletin in English, 18 May 2000.
[18] *Kokkinakis* v. *Greece*, European Court of Human Rights, Judgment, Application No. 14307/88, 25 May 1993.

Greece.[19] Established churches in countries with a religious population that is relatively homogeneous remain resistant to the idea that freedom of religion could also
belong to religious or non-religious minorities. Legal sanctioning of the 'duty to
teach which principles are right and wrong', like that entrenched in the Maltese
Constitution, are not merely benign statements but an endorsement of recognised
religious normativity. When establishment is constitutional, such statements provide a ground for consolidation of the people around a certain identity principle
which provides a common platform for identification. In these circumstances certain faiths and beliefs are classified as a symbolic other even before talk of rights
begins. The idea of pluralism is overshadowed by a static consensus built around
conceptions of life that are privileged and contrasted with those considered 'other'.
Otherness entrenched constitutionally creates a framework of fear and rejection
that can hardly be challenged by rights or appeal to principles such as pluralism.
Such an appeal in conditions of relative religious homogeneity might be seen not
as a voice for recognition of otherness but as an argument for dismantling national
churches in pursuit of abstract notions that do violence to history and the exigen-
cies of religious life (Ahdar and Leigh 2013). When the discussion is framed in
those terms, difference disappears from the discussion and national churches are
presented as a positive force for national democracy whereas other religions can
easily be framed as non-democratic others. The thought of pluralism remains but
a background image with no potential to be truly actualised.

4.2 Special position of the church without formal establishment

The diagnosis of secularism quite surprisingly also fails in some societies where
religion used to be formally established but has since been formally separated.
Local context and a range of social factors determine the place of difference and
have a significant impact on how the increased effort to achieve a pluralistic standard is phrased in such regimes. Two examples used here show that albeit legally the
church need no longer be established, socially its position may be strong enough to
give rise to a dominant type of recognised normativity contrasted with otherness.
The actual other can be rather different in these different contexts but the mechanisms for exploring difference to create otherness are frequently similar. The analysis below compares the situation of Ireland and Finland, where churches are no
longer established but where social structures perpetuate forms of othering, even
though creating different others in each of these settings.

Throughout most of the twentieth century Ireland was considered one of the
most religious countries in Europe. Like the Maltese, the Irish national identity
developed as a Catholic identity (Inglis 2007), and as mentioned before the Irish

---

[19] *Larissis and Others* v. *Greece*, European Court of Human Rights, Judgment, Application No.
140/1996/759/958-960, 25 February 1998.

Constitution of 1937 ensured the dominant position of the Catholic Church,[20] a situation which lasted until the amendment of 1974. During that period Irish law did not reflect secularist separation but instead was infused with the doctrine of natural law developed in judicial review (Whyte 1996). Catholic doctrine, as in Malta, was primarily reflected in case-law concerning women's reproductive rights and will be briefly discussed in Chapter 7.

As of today, the Irish Constitution in Article 44.1 still prescribes that 'The State acknowledges that the homage of public worship is due to Almighty God. It shall hold His Name in reverence, and shall respect and honour religion.' This quasi-endowment is supplemented with a specific anti-endowment provision embedded in Section 2 of the same Article providing that:

2.1. Freedom of conscience and the free profession and practice of religion are, subject to public order and morality, guaranteed to every citizen.
2.2. The State guarantees not to endow any religion.
2.3. The State shall not impose any disabilities or make any discrimination on the ground of religious profession, belief or status.

While containing almost contradictory provisions, the contemporary Irish system has been characterised by some as a separation system (Doe 2011), while by others as a system of 'inextricable interdependence' (Colton 2006, 97). While Article 44.1, despite its explicitly Catholic heritage, has been interpreted as stretching its benefits to all religious citizens including Protestants, Jews, Muslims, agnostics and atheists,[21] reinterpretation is slow and frequently happens via judicial review. The Irish Constitution continues to forbid practices such as abortion, along with seditious, blasphemous and indecent publications. Both of these prohibitions have been reinterpreted, but the references persist to underpin the system and as shown later are not without an impact on the shape of rights and their application. While in today's Ireland growing diversity has resulted in a change in the traditional religious make-up of the Irish population, the dominant religious normativity has been used as an identity principle limiting the application of rights. This artificial divide has created a dissonance at the heart of law and, as Lyotard would say, a suspicion about the identity of the one who speaks the law and the one to whom the law applies (Lyotard 1988, 99). The divide between these identities might be difficult to maintain in conditions where traditional Catholicism is experiencing a crisis of vocation of the priesthood[22] and plunging numbers of Catholics.[23] New legal initiatives not complying with the traditional teaching of the church, such as the outcome of the referendum on same-sex marriage in May 2015,[24] may

[20] Constitution of Ireland (last amended June 2004), 1 July 1937.
[21] *Conway* v. *Independent Newspapers (Ireland)*, Lts 4 IR 484, 30 July 1999.
[22] 'Catholic Church faces new crisis – Ireland is running out of priests', *The Times*, 27 February 2008.
[23] 'Ireland's changing religious face', BBC News, 11 April 2004.
[24] Chris Johnston, 'Irish voters to decide on same-sex marriage in May referendum', *Guardian*, 20 February 2015.

deepen this dissonance. An appeal to pluralism, even though based on facts, might be rebutted for the sake of imagined homogeneity, capable of recreating 'us' and 'them' and maintaining an illusion of the homogeneity of the constitutional 'we'. Alternatively, a plea for diversity might be discussed by reference to secularism.

In Finland the status of the previously established Lutheran and Orthodox churches is similarly ambiguous. The Finnish Constitution of 2000 does not recognise any state church but in Article 76 refers to specially enacted laws concerning churches previously considered as national. The law on the church[25] and the law on the organisation of the Orthodox Church[26] are the main laws regulating the position and organisation of traditional churches in Finland. The state continues to support these two churches to some degree, for example in the collection of church taxes. In addition, specialised laws issued by the state regulate employment in the Lutheran Church, maintenance of cemeteries, financing and other organisational matters. The Church Council is the main legislative body drafting laws applying to the church, and the state is in the position of either rejecting the law or accepting it, but is not allowed to introduce amendments (Leino 2005). The position of the two traditional churches is supplemented with a law on religious freedom introduced in 2003 allowing any religious association of at least 20 members to register as a religious community.[27]

While Finnish society is highly secularised, participation in national churches in Finland, as in other Nordic countries, is connected to an understanding of nationality and identification with nationality (Sundback 2007). In conditions where the influence of the church on political life remains small and the church often reflects generally secular societal attitudes, the shape of consensus takes the form of neutrality. This neutrality is generally positive towards different religious denominations and on the surface appears to be one of the best-suited models for accommodation of religious pluralism. As the *Halla-aho* case[28] demonstrated, a positive approach towards different denominations was used, for instance, to reinterpret bans such as an archaic law on blasphemy in favour of increased pluralism aiming at protecting religious peace between different denominations. Despite the appeal of neutrality as a way to pluralism, the constructivism of this approach continues to harbour cultural sensitivities having a potential for othering. This becomes visible when those whose position is manifestly religious or manifestly different from recognised and 'reasonable' secularised Christianity vocalise their rights claims. In those circumstances it is not uncommon that such claims are characterised as unreasonable and non-fitting in the narrow brackets of the established consensus:

---

[25] Kirkkolaki (Law on Church) 26.11.1993/1054, 23 November 1993.
[26] Ortodoksisen kirkon kirkkojärjestys (Organisation of the Orthodox Church) 12.12.2006/174 vs. 2007, 12 December 2006.
[27] Uskonnonvapauslaki (Law on freedom of religion) 06.06.2003/453.
[28] KKO:2012:58, R2010/1101, 8 June 2012.

Generally speaking, in Finland, the code of governing and controlling embraces limited pluralism through the discourse on religion. It does not necessarily embrace multi-religiosity, if the religions are not hegemonic in some culture or territory. Multiplicity and plurality relate to 'cultures' or 'communities' whose members share a common origin and history more than non-hegemonic and sometimes relatively new 'religions' do. Mass movements which do not have a leading role in a culture are considered to be dubious and the art of governing in relation to them is to warn or even enlighten consumers and citizens.

(Taira 2010, 385)

Legal amendments removing establishment and replacing it with a somewhat more neutral position, while removing the symbolism of endowment, do not necessarily erase the space for othering. The other still exists among the thin illusions of neutrality. When certain religious conceptions are favoured in practice on the grounds of their traditional position and acquired presumption of 'reasonableness', those visibly different are looked upon as unreasonable and thus threatening the constructivist vision of 'neutral' social justice. In this fiction of recognition, the other is offered a glance at her face, a glance better than outright rejection. Yet, as she is glanced at, she remains in her inferior position, judged and regulated by the community that defined the brackets of consensus a priori and closed them from renegotiation by an 'unreasonable' outsider.

4.3 Concordats: the variety of approaches, diverse effects on pluralism

Concordat agreements are international bilateral agreements signed by a state and the Vatican State (the Holy See). The Roman Catholic Church is the only church that due to the virtue of its Vatican statehood is able to sign international agreements. The position of these bilateral international treaties differs in the respective constitutional systems.[29] Moreover, the texts and provisions of concordats include diverse provisions. Some of them focus on the organisation of the church and its internal regulation by Canon Law, while some grant special legal privileges to Catholics. Currently these special agreements with the Vatican are binding in Italy, Austria, Portugal, Germany, Poland, Luxembourg,[30] Spain and Slovakia. In 2003 the Czech Republic, after reviewing constitutional principles, rejected a proposed concordat, basing its argumentation on the fact that it gave the Catholic Church preferential treatment and violated the state's neutrality in regard to religious matters. As with all previous models of accommodation between state and church, some of the examples below illustrate that countries bound by concordats

---

[29] In some countries, such as Poland or Slovakia, the Constitution guarantees an international agreement's position above ordinary laws.

[30] Luxembourg's concordat applies more broadly to all Benelux countries.

show varying degrees of recognition of difference and varied influence of the Catholic Church over their population.

The original Italian Concordat dating back to 1929 initially privileged the Catholic Church by securing its dominant position.[31] After the amendment of 1984 these provisions were replaced with provisions guaranteeing the sole right of the Catholic Church to provide religious education in state schools, the authority to recognise marriages celebrated in church and the right to establish Catholic schools. The concordat also establishes an obligation to seek solutions to problems in its application by a joint commission appointed by the state and the Vatican.

The Austrian Concordat of 1933 is among Europe's oldest, with the recent amendment dating back to 1962 and its additional protocols dating back to 1971 and 1972.[32] It guarantees, among other rights, that the Catholic Church may enjoy freedom of worship, obliges the state to protect the exercise of spiritual responsibilities by the church and secures the legal personality of the church. It also guarantees compulsory Catholic religious instruction for Catholic students and recognises marriages celebrated in church as well as the right of the church to legally dissolve those marriages in accordance with Canon Law.

The Polish Concordat of 1993 secures certain privileges of the Catholic Church such as the right to provide compulsory Catholic religious education in state schools, a legal personality and the inviolability of religious places as well as recognition of marriages celebrated in church.[33] It also obliges the state to cooperate with the church in 'protecting and respecting the institution of marriage and the family'.

The Portuguese Concordat of 2004, supplementing the concordat of 1940, recognises the legal personality of the church and its right to carry out its religious mission.[34] It also secures the right to teach 'religion and Catholic morality' in state educational institutions and obliges the state to recognise marriages celebrated in church as well as annulments. The state is also required to help with providing religious assistance to members of the armed forces as well as inmates of state prisons. Novelties introduced by the Concordat of 2004 are provisions concerning tax exemptions for the clergy and the church and, most importantly, those incorporating the church into the state system of tax collection, as in Germany or Scandinavia.

---

[31] Agreement between the Holy See and the Italian Republic, Modifications to the Lateran Concordat, 25 March 1985.

[32] Vertrag vom 9. Juli 1962, BGBl. Nr. 273, zwischen dem Heiligen Stuhl und der Republik Österreich zur Regelung von mit dem Schulwesen zusammenhängenden Fragen samt Schlussprotokoll, in der Fassung des Zusatzvertrages vom 8. März 1971, BGBl. Nr. 289/1972 (Treaty of 9 July 1962 BGBl. No. 273, between the Holy See and the Republic of Austria on the regulation of matters related to the school system, including Final Protocol, as amended by the supplementary agreement of 8 March 1971, BGBl. No. 289/1972).

[33] Konkordat między Stolicą Apostolską i Rzecząpospolitą Polską, 28 July 1993 (Concordat between the Holy See and the Republic of Poland).

[34] Concordat with the Holy See and the Portuguese Republic, 18 May 2004.

However, there are also less elaborate concordat texts, like those signed by Belgium, the Netherlands, Luxembourg and Hungary, which provide only basic regulation concerning the appointment of Catholic bishops and communication between the church and the Vatican[35] or the position of the nunciature in the country.[36]

More complicated concordat systems can be found in Germany, where more than one concordat exists. Germany is bound among others by a concordat concluded during the Third Reich[37] and by local concordats with particular states, such as Bavaria or North-Rhine Westphalia. This localisation of concordats is dictated by the tradition of religious coexistence of Catholic and Protestant 'Länder'.

As to recognition of religious difference, concordats – like the state church systems – may pose difficulties in terms of accommodating the principle of pluralism. As with state churches, recognition of religious difference will largely depend on existing normativities and their sources. The factually strong position of a dominant faith being a source of dominant religious normativity might impact on the position of religiously different others. An interesting example from 2004 shows the importance of evaluating the context in examining the possibilities of recognition. The Network of Independent Experts on Fundamental Rights set up by the European Commission examined the issue of the influence of concordats on the right to conscientious objection.[38] The document issued by the Network dealt with the question of adopting another Slovak Concordat on Conscientious Objectors and examined various questions concerning the influence of concordats in general on the international obligations of states, including human rights obligations. The concerns of the experts issuing the document primarily addressed the right of various professionals to object to performing certain services especially in areas concerning health, dignity, family and marriage. An international agreement sanctioning the existence of conscience clauses allowing individuals to refuse to perform certain procedures such as abortion or distributing contraceptives could, according to the experts, in some circumstances endanger human health or life. The experts projected that violations would result from restrictions being imposed on access to counselling in the field of reproductive health and on access to certain medical services, including in particular abortion and contraception, and agreed that such regulation would disproportionately affect women. Such a scenario is naturally less likely in countries where the population is religiously diverse but is not far-fetched in contexts where a dominant religion exists and places non-believers in a disadvantaged position. While not related directly to a concordat, the latest emerging example of conscience clauses introduced to the code of medical ethics in Poland exemplifies

---

[35] Convention and Accord between Pope Leo XII and William I, King of Belgium and the Netherlands, 1827.

[36] Hungary–Vatican Concordat on Diplomatic Relations, 1990.

[37] Concordat between the Holy See and the German Reich with Supplementary Protocol and Secret Supplement, 20 July 1933.

[38] EU Network of Independent Experts on Fundamental Rights, Opinion 4-2005.

the problem. The lack of specialists who profess other faiths and who could reasonably accommodate the wishes of non-believers or followers of other faiths limits access by non-Catholics to legally allowed procedures, like abortion. The recent widely discussed case of Professor Hazan, who refused a legally allowed abortion of a foetus suffering from anencephaly, has become a topical issue in discussions of recognition of religious difference in Poland.[39] While not related to a concordat, arguments in discussions, such as in Poland, concerning the position of the dominant faith and legal privileges granted to it frequently appeal to secularism rather than pluralism.

In these circumstances an appeal to religious pluralism may be associated with granting even more privileges to the already strongly established position of a dominant religion. As a consequence, secularism rather than pluralism becomes a paradigm embraced to challenge the non-privileged position of non-religious others. The appeal to secularism relies on challenging the dominant religious normativity and defending the possibility of holding a different view. When a seemingly pluralistic legal clause such as a conscience clause results in privileging dominant views and disabling others, the appeal of secularism takes over the appeal to pluralism. When the clause is not backed by a mechanism allowing those with different moral and religious views to have their position recognised, a seemingly pluralistic provision risks resulting in non-recognition, in addition to cementing the position of a traditional faith.

Analogously to the effects of establishment, concordats may generate and maintain dominant religious normativities. In such circumstances they risk affecting the beliefs of non-believers and adherents of other religions. Unlike in establishment countries, though, changing a concordat unilaterally might be rather difficult. While countries maintaining state churches maintain the sole competency to regulate relations between state and church through their legislative bodies, amending a concordat takes two parties – the state in question and the Vatican. Since concordats are instruments of international law, unless a concordat agreement has a specific exit clause it might be difficult for the state to denounce it without the agreement of the other side (Helfer 2012). In an era when the religious landscape is rapidly changing, entering into an agreement with a religious state that may potentially be impossible to exit requires a difficult balancing that does not eliminate difference. While again the concordat itself might not be discriminatory, the context and the position of adherents of other faiths are crucial in determining the effects of these agreements and the role they have for the discourse on pluralism and its implementation. An appeal to pluralism on the other hand might be veiled in references to secularism.

---

[39] 'Znany ginekolog odmawia aborcji nieuleczalnie chorego płodu. Powód? Klauzula sumienia' (Known gynaecologist refuses to abort incurably sick foetus. Reason? Conscience clause), *Gazeta Wyborcza*, 9 July 2014.

4.4 A place for pluralism in French *laïcité*?

While the widespread presumption that Europe is 'biased in favour of secularism' (Zucca 2012, 36) is repeated like a mantra, legal reality reveals that only France and Turkey legally embrace the principle. France, following a strong model of separation between the state and religion, has raised a 'wall of separation' akin to the American system. The law of 1905 on the separation of the churches and the state establishes so-called *laïcité*, which could be roughly translated as secularism.[40] Rooted in the French Revolution, *laïcité* emerged as a principle during a violent conflict with the Catholic Church (Gunn 2004, 433). During that period the church's property was first nationalised in 1789 and a year later the Civil Constitution for the Clergy placed the clergy under the control of the government. In 1791 the Legislative Assembly legalised divorce and the state took control of population registers. In the most radical phase of the Revolution, Christianity was replaced by the cult of the Supreme Being, with Robespierre as high priest. In 1789 the National Assembly adopted the – revolutionary at the time – Declaration of the Rights of Man and of the Citizen including Article 10, which forbade disturbing anyone's peace on the grounds of their religious opinions, which bears a resemblance to today's freedom of religion and non-discrimination on religious grounds. After Bonaparte's victory in 1801, France signed a concordat with the Vatican and modified the approach to the church. The law of 1905 ended the concordat era and reinstated *laïcité* in the form we know today.

Laïcité is treated as one of the basic foundations of the French Republic and the source of religious tolerance and understanding. The legal system, according to Article 1 of the law on separation, guarantees everyone freedom of religion, but according to Article 2, the state does not recognise, support or subsidise any faith.[41] Furthermore, Article 1 of the 1958 Constitution declares that:[42]

> France shall be an indivisible, secular, democratic and social Republic. It shall ensure the equality of all citizens before the law, without distinction of origin, race or religion. It shall respect all beliefs.

In addition, the Declaration of the Rights of Man and of the Citizen was recognised by the Constitution of 1958 as a part of the French constitutional system, with Article 10 still binding today. Contemporary French politicians have referred to *laïcité* as the basis for religious respect and tolerance, a foundation of French democracy and a non-negotiable principle. In his address to the nation in 2003, former president Chirac underlined that:

> It is the neutrality of the public sphere which enables the harmonious existence side by side of different religions. Like all freedoms, the freedom to

---

[40] Loi du 9 décembre 1905 concernant la séparation des Églises et de l'État, 9 December 1905.
[41] In French: 'La République ne reconnaît, ne salarie ni ne subventionne aucun culte.'
[42] Constitution of France, 4 October 1958.

express one's faith can only have limits in the freedom of others, and in compliance with the rules of life in society. Religious freedom, which our country respects and protects, must not be abused, it must not call general rules into question, and it must not infringe the freedom of belief of others. This subtle, precious and fragile balance, constructed patiently over decades, is ensured by respect for the principle of secularism.... This is why it is included in Article 1 of our constitution. This is why it is not negotiable.[43]

Similar declarations have been repeated by subsequent presidents and reverberate in the arguments of the government supporting controversial bans on face-covering that were introduced first in state schools then in all public areas.[44] As a utopian founding myth (Gunn 2005), *laïcité* manifested itself as discouragement from developing any cultural or religious group identity. At first glance, complete separation of the institutions of the state from religious influence and no subsidies for religious organisations promises to keep the state out of any possible religious disputes or conflicts. Supporters of the principle argue that it creates a religion-free zone, which separates public issues from religious arguments and places religion in the private sphere where it enjoys full freedom (Hunter-Henin 2012).

But in terms of accommodating religious diversity and truly facing difference, *laïcité* fails to live up to expectations not only of recognition but even of tolerance. When an artificially secular sphere becomes the source of dominant normativity, the individual believer becomes an intruder. As such the believer risks not even being tolerated but instead asked to give up part of their religious identity when present in the so-called public sphere. Unfortunately, the limits of the public sphere appear fluid and expanding, expelling all religious symbols from zones of public interaction. Although the main discussion concerning the topic of the veil will be subject to further scrutiny in later chapters, redefining and stretching the boundaries of the public sphere is one of the most problematic features of *laïcité*. The expulsion of religion from every sphere of visibility eliminates difference and brands it as threatening otherness. Paradoxically, this changing of difference into otherness happens by employing the narrative of religious equality. Meanwhile, the end result is opposite to equality and results in targeting and stigmatising those having a particular religion. This becomes even more problematic when we realise that *laïcité* does not prevent implementation of the remnants of the Napoleonic concordat in relation to consulting the president about the appointment of Catholic bishops (Doe 2011, 34). While it does not prevent the blurring of the lines between the religious and the secular, it prevents an 'uncomfortable' religion from being visible and discomfiting the majority. When *laïcité* begins to target an uncomfortable believer it turns out to be no more than a civil religion aiming at eradicating difference rather than accommodating it and leaving

[43] 'Chirac on the secular society', BBC News, 18 December 2003.
[44] *S.A.S.* v. *France*, European Court of Human Rights, Judgment, Application No. 43835/11, 1 July 2014.

extremely narrow margins for pluralism and renegotiation of dominant normativity (Chelini-Pont 2009).

4.5 Pluralism as neutrality?

Sweden and Norway, which traditionally are among the countries establishing a state church, have recently gone through constitutional debates and changes that placed pluralism at the heart of reform. As in Denmark, Finland and Iceland, the tradition of the state church in Sweden and Norway dates back to the time of the Reformation. And while the results of the reforms were different, they are worth summarising together due their similarities and the aim of achieving neutrality.

As in the majority of Nordic systems, participation in the Church of Sweden was strongly coupled with Swedish national identity. As Gustafsson notes, it was a criminal offence to leave the church until as late as 1858 and even until 1951 it was impossible to exit the church without joining another Christian denomination (Gustafsson 2003). But this traditional place of Christianity was challenged in Sweden on 1 January 2000, when a constitutional reform separated the state from the church. As a result of long preparations and many compromises on the part of both the state and the church (Stegeby 1999; Gustafsson 2003), the state church retained a certain level of support from the state but was officially separated. This historic reform aimed at putting all faiths in a similar position and supplemented the Freedom of Religion Act,[45] with the latest amendment from 1998, and the Religious Denomination Act,[46] also from 1998. Freedom of religion as guaranteed in those acts focuses on religion as an individual matter and allows the individual to freely belong to or resign from a religious community. Religion is treated as a matter between the individual and the religious community. The Religious Denomination Act provides general protection for religious freedom and religious communities and explicitly refers in that aspect to the ECHR[47] by underlining that:

> Provisions on freedom of religion are included in the Constitution and the European Convention for the Protection of Human Rights and Fundamental Freedoms.

It allows a religious denomination to register in order to protect the right to perform religious activities and allow as many religious communities to register as possible.[48] At the same time, the remnants of the establishment live on in the special law governing the status of the Evangelical Lutheran Church. Drafted to preserve the historical continuity of the Church of Sweden and prevent too harsh and too rapid a break between tradition and modernity, the Church of Sweden Act regulates the status of

---

[45] Religionsfrihetslag (1951:680).
[46] Lag (1998:1593) om trossamfund.
[47] Religionsfrihetslag, Section 1.
[48] *Ibid.*, Section 2.

the Church of Sweden (*Folkkyrka*) and organisational aspects of the church. At the same time, to aid the new disestablishment it leaves the right to decide the details of doctrines and teachings solely to the church. The pastors of the Evangelical Lutheran Church are no longer the employees of the state and the state no longer has any influence in the process of choosing bishops. The main remnant of establishment lies in maintaining the requirement that the monarch must belong to the Evangelical Lutheran Church and, as Stegeby reminds us, this was the result of a political compromise which made the reform possible in the first place (Stegeby 1999, 765). The support the church continues to receive from the state is primarily collection of church tax on behalf of the church and administration of graveyards.

Like Sweden, Norway has recently gone through a constitutional reform originally aiming at separation (Plesner 2002, 2006). Traditionally the position of the church was established in Articles 2 and 16 of the Constitution. Article 2 declared the Evangelical Lutheran Church to be the state religion and Article 16 gave the state the responsibility for the Evangelical Lutheran Church. The authority for regulating matters of the church was primarily vested in the monarch, who was also responsible for the organisation of the church and ensuring that the church followed the regulations. The bishops were the employees of the king and the king – as in Sweden – was obliged to belong to the Evangelical Lutheran Church. Inspired by growing religious pluralism, a 2001 committee appointed by the National Council of the state church evaluated the state and church system in Norway and proposed new regulations for relations between state and church. In April 2008, political parties sitting in parliament agreed to introduce a programme of democratic reform of the church.[49] The programme proposed a reform of the Constitution in regard to the relation between state and church. The reform was passed on 21 May 2012 and slightly modified Article 2 and Article 16. While the church remains established, Article 2 refers to a Christian and humanist heritage as well as to democracy, the rule of law and human rights. Article 16 on the other hand reads:

> All inhabitants of the realm shall have the right to free exercise of their religion. The Church of Norway, an Evangelical-Lutheran church, will remain the Established Church of Norway and will as such be supported by the State. Detailed provisions as to its system will be laid down by law. All religious and belief communities should be supported on equal terms.

While the provisions on 'spiritual' leadership of the king, provided previously in Articles 21 and 22, were removed, the monarch continues to be bound by Article 4 expecting the incumbent to be a member of the church.

---

49 Kulturdepartementet, Forslag til endringer i kirkeloven for behandling i Kirkemøtet Staten og Den norske kirke – et tydelig skille 3. mars 2015 (Ministry of Culture, Proposed changes in church law – for consideration by the General Synod. The State and the Norwegian Church – a clear distinction, 3 March 2015).

The radical reform of the Church of Sweden was inspired by growing religious pluralism and was conducted in the spirit of multiculturalism. Similarly, the change in Norway, albeit not entirely disestablishing the church, was motivated in part by growing religious pluralism in Norwegian society and the obligation of a democratic state to safeguard religious equality. Despite differences in the level of disestablishment, pluralism in both of these contexts was understood primarily as neutrality, similar to the Finnish context. The move towards recognising pluralism was motivated by statistical changes in both societies and based on the argument that no denomination should receive preferential treatment above others (Stegeby 1999, 722) and the desire of the churches for greater liberty (Gustafsson 2003). Just as in Finland, while the traditional churches enjoy certain benefits, such as tax collection by the state, the central objective of the constitutional reforms was to secure greater neutrality towards religions. Affirmative of individual belief, the state extended its embrace to both secular and religious beliefs and aimed not to prioritise any doctrine. But, as some assert, the churches did not really change (Gustafsson 2003) and while symbolically the law is friendlier to pluralism it continues to allow room for religious normativity grounded in a specific secular Christian model based on tradition. While being a church member in Norway or Sweden is less a religious and more a civil practice, belonging to the Lutheran Church in the Nordic countries is seen as a natural part of citizenship (Sundback 2007). While neutrality as an approach to pluralism contours the other less clearly and may in practice may be the closest to ensuring pluralism, it aims to treat well-established religions in the same way as minority believers or non-believers. In these circumstances the uneven position of minority adherents and the difficulties they experience in their societies are exacerbated by arguments for the necessity to remain neutral. When this comparison ignores the actual difficulties it also flattens difference and results in perpetuating dominant models, placing those who are different in a position where they are expected to adjust to the dominant consensus.

4.6 Summary: a difficult mosaic for the principle of pluralism

As illustrated above, despite the prominence of religious pluralism in the contemporary discourse of rights, its position in constitutional regimes, where rights ought to be primarily secured, encounters multiple difficulties. The complexity of existing traditions and structures of cultural and religious power more often than law determine the position of religious difference. Not infrequently, existing legal models exacerbate the prominence of dominant religious or secular normativities. When law protects these normativities, the other, whether religious or secular, frequently remains a hypothetical consideration. The other is not seriously faced, but more often marginalised or merely glanced at. In these circumstances the rights of the other, as shown in Part II, risk being interpreted in a way that does not disturb the existing consensus. The principle of pluralism, on the other hand, is too often moulded and shaped to leave the consensus intact and proves powerless. It becomes a powerless myth, full of beauty, but existing only in the realm of legal imagination. The next part uses narratives of traditional myths to illustrate the mythical function of pluralism and debunk fictional and factual elements of that myth.

References

Ahdar, Rex and Ian Leigh. 2013. *Religious Freedom in the Liberal State*, 2nd edn. Oxford University Press.

Ahlin, Lars, Jørn Borup, Marianne Qvortrup Fibiger, Lene Kühle, Viggo Mortensen and René Dybdal Pedersen. 2012. 'Religious Diversity and Pluralism: Empirical Data and Theoretical Reflections from the Danish Pluralism Project.' *Journal of Contemporary Religion* 27(3): 403–18.

Alivizatos, Nikos. 1999. 'A New Role for the Greek Church?' *Journal of Modern Greek Studies* 17(1): 23–40.

Anderson, Brian C. 2004. 'Secular Europe, Religious America.' *Public Interest* 155: 143–58.

Anderson, John. 2002. 'The Treatment of Religious Minorities in South-Eastern Europe: Greece and Bulgaria Compared.' *Religion, State and Society* 30(1): 9–31.

A. S. V. S. 1930. 'Malta: Church and State.' *Foreign Affairs* 9(1): 157–60.

Bader, Veit-Michael. 2007. *Secularism or Democracy? Associational Governance of Religious Diversity*. Amsterdam University Press.

Baines, Cynthia DeBula. 1996. 'L'Affaire des Foulards: Discrimination, or the Price of a Secular Public Education System.' *Vanderbilt Journal of Transnational Law* 29: 303–27.

Bano, Samia. 2008. 'In Pursuit of Religious and Legal Diversity: A Response to the Archbishop of Canterbury and the "Sharia Debate" in Britain.' *Ecclesiastical Law Journal* 10(03): 283–309.

Beckford, James A. 2014. 'Re-thinking Religious Pluralism.' In *Religious Pluralism*, ed. Giuseppe Giordan and Enzo Pace, 15–29. Springer International Publishing.

Berger, Peter, Effie Fokas and Grace Davie. 2008. *Religious America, Secular Europe? A Theme and Variations*. Ashgate.

Calo, Zachary R. 2011. 'Pluralism, Secularism and the European Court of Human Rights.' *Journal of Law and Religion* 26 (February): 101–20.

Casanova, J. 2006. 'Religion, European Secular Identities, and European Integration.' In *Religion in an Expanding Europe*, ed. T. A. Byrnes and P. J. Katzenstein, 65–92, Cambridge University Press.

Chelini-Pont, Blandine. 2009. 'Is Laïcité the Civil Religion of France.' *George Washington International Law Review* 41: 765–813.

Colton, Paul. 2006. 'Religion and Law in Dialogue: Covenantal and Non-covenantal Cooperation of State and Religions in Ireland.' In *Religion and Law in Dialogue: Covenantal and Non-covenantal Cooperation between State and Religion in Europe*, ed. N. Doe and R. Sanberg, 93–115. Peeters.

Combalía, Zoila and María Roca. 2014. 'Religion and the Secular State of Spain'. International Center for Law and Religion Studies, Brigham Young University, Provo, UT.

Davie, Grace. 2007. *The Sociology of Religion*. Sage.

Doe, Norman. 2011. *Law and Religion in Europe: A Comparative Introduction*. Oxford University Press.

Freedman, Jane. 2004. 'Secularism as a Barrier to Integration? The French Dilemma.' *International Migration* 42(3): 5–27.

Georges, Eugenia. 1996. 'Abortion Policy and Practice in Greece.' *Social Science & Medicine* 42(4): 509–19.

Gozdecka, Dorota A. 2009. 'Religions and Legal Boundaries of Democracy in Europe: European Commitment to Democratic Principles.' e-thesis, University of Helsinki.

Gunn, T. Jeremy. 2004. 'Under God but Not the Scarf: The Founding Myths of Religious Freedom in the United States and Laïcité in France.' *Journal of Church and State* 46: 7–24.

Gunn, T. Jeremy. 2005. 'French Secularism as Utopia and Myth.' *Houston Law Review* 42: 81–102.

Gustafsson, Göran. 2003. 'Church–State Separation Swedish-Style.' *West European Politics* 26(1): 51–72.

Helfer, Laurence R. 2012. 'Terminating Treaties.' SSRN Scholarly Paper ID 1937205. Social Science Research Network.

HM Government. 2007. *The House of Lords: Reform*, Cm 7027. The Stationery Office.

Hunter-Henin, Myriam. 2012. 'Why the French Don't Like the Burqa: Laïcité, National Identity and Religious Freedom.' *International & Comparative Law Quarterly* 61(03): 613–39.

Inglis, Tom. 2007. 'Catholic Identity in Contemporary Ireland: Belief and Belonging to Tradition.' *Journal of Contemporary Religion* 22(2): 205–20.

Jackson, Amy. 2010. 'A Critical Legal Pluralist Analysis of the Begum Case.' SSRN Scholarly Paper ID 1696191. Social Science Research Network.

Katzenstein, Peter J. 2006. 'Multiple Modernities as Limits to Secular Europeanization?' In *Religion in an Expanding Europe*, ed. T. A. Byrnes and P. J. Katzenstein, 1–33. Cambridge University Press.

Leino, Pekka. 2005. *Kirkon Oikeudelliset Normit*. Suomalainen Lakimiesyhdistys.

Levey, Geoffrey Brahm and Tariq Modood, eds. 2008. *Secularism, Religion and Multicultural Citizenship*. Cambridge University Press.

Lyotard, Jean François. 1988. *The Differend: Phrases in Dispute*. Theory and History of Literature 46. University of Minnesota Press.

MacCulloch, Diarmaid. 2003. *Reformation: Europe's House Divided 1490–1700*. Allen Lane.

Malik, Maleiha. 2013. *Anti-Muslim Prejudice: Past and Present*. Routledge.

Mavrogordatos, George. 2003. 'Orthodoxy and Nationalism in the Greek Case.' *West European Politics* 26(1): 117–36.

Mifsud, Matthew, George G. Buttigieg, Charles Savona-Ventura and Simon Delicata. 2009. 'Reproductive Health in Malta.' *European Journal of Contraception and Reproductive Health Care* 14(4): 249–57.

Milne, Robin G. 1973. 'Family Planning in Malta.' *Population Studies* 27(2): 373–86.

Modood, Tariq 1992. *Not Easy Being British: Colour, Culture and Citizenship*. Trentham Books.

Modood, Tariq 1998. 'Anti-essentialism, Multiculturalism and the "Recognition" of Religious Groups.' *Journal of Political Philosophy* 6(4): 378–99.

Mookherjee, Monica. 2011. 'Introduction. Liberal Democracy and Religious Pluralism: Accommodating or Resisting the Diversity of a Globalising Age?' In *Democracy, Religious Pluralism and the Liberal Dilemma of Accommodation*, ed. Monica Mookherjee, 1–13. Studies in Global Justice 7. Springer.

Parpworth, Neil. 2013. 'The Succession to the Crown Act 2013: Modernising the Monarchy.' *Modern Law Review* 76(6): 1070–93.

Paxson, Heather. 2003. 'With or against Nature? IVF, Gender and Reproductive Agency in Athens, Greece.' *Social Science & Medicine* 56(9): 1853–66.

Payne, Daniel P. 2003. 'The Clash of Civilisations: The Church of Greece, the European Union and the Question of Human Rights.' *Religion, State and Society* 31(3): 261–71.

Plesner, Ingvill Thorson. 2002. 'State and Religion in Norway in Times of Change.' *European Journal for Church and State Research* 9: 263–70.

Plesner, Ingvill Thorson. 2006. *Skal vi Skilles? Veier Videre for Stat Og Kirke.* Forlaget Press.

Requejo, Ferran and Camil Ungureanu. 2014. *Democracy, Law and Religious Pluralism in Europe: Secularism and Post-secularism.* Routledge.

Riis, Ole. 2011. 'Rejection of Religious Pluralism: The Danish Case.' *Nordic Journal of Religion and Society* 24(1): 19–36.

Roudometof, Victor. 2011. 'Eastern Orthodox Christianity and the Uses of the Past in Contemporary Greece.' *Religions* 2(2): 95–113.

Rountree, Kathryn. 2014. 'Neo-paganism, Native Faith and Indigenous Religion: A Case Study of Malta within the European Context.' *Social Anthropology* 22(1): 81–100.

Sandberg, Russell. 2011. *Law and Religion.* Cambridge University Press.

Sandberg, Russell. 2015. *Religion and Legal Pluralism.* Ashgate.

Shah, Prakash. 2009. 'Coping with Super-Diversity in Law: Thoughts on the British Scene.' SSRN Scholarly Paper ID 1482706. Social Science Research Network.

Stegeby, E. Kenneth. 1999. 'An Analysis of the Impending Disestablishment of the Church of Sweden.' *Brigham Young University Law Review* (1999): 703–76.

Sundback, Susan. 2007. 'Membership of Nordic "National" Churches as a "Civil Religious" Phenomenon.' *Implicit Religion* 10(3): 262–80.

Taira, Teemu. 2010. 'Religion as a Discursive Technique: The Politics of Classifying Wicca.' *Journal of Contemporary Religion* 25(3): 379–94.

Uberoi, Varun and Tariq Modood. 2013. 'Inclusive Britishness: A Multiculturalist Advance.' *Political Studies* 61(1): 23–41.

Weller, Paul. 2000. 'Equity, Inclusivity and Participation in a Plural Society: Challenging the Establishment of the Church of England.' In *Law and Religion in Contemporary Society: Communities, Individualism and the State*, ed. Peter W. Edge and Graham Harvey, 53–69. Ashgate.

Whyte, Gerard. 1996. 'Religion and the Irish Constitution.' *John Marshall Law Review* 30: 725–46.

Young, Iris Marion. 1990. *Justice and the Politics of Difference.* Princeton University Press.

Ziebertz, Hans-Georg and Ulrich Riegel. 2008. *Europe: Secular or Post-secular?* LIT Verlag.

Zucca, Lorenzo. 2012. *A Secular Europe: Law and Religion in the European Constitutional Landscape.* Oxford University Press.

Part II

Three myths of inclusion

...basic to the graph of the traditional literary myth is the notion that there is a common ground to human experience, that man lives in the same universe of matter and motion, and that he functions in typical and recurrent emotional and psychologic patterns. Even as the myth deals with the heroic variation, this variation is seen as existing within 'the deeper sources of common life' which follow the graph of a timeless schema.

The literary myth objectifies man's communal existence. It voices our collective beginnings and our collective goals. It rests on belief in 'the people'. The hero forever revolts against his commune; but he revolts only against its static forms, its 'systematized' stage... But in his very revolt he gets to know the excesses of his own demon, and by recognizing learns to control and tame it.

Slochower, Harry. 'The Function of Myth in Existentialism'.
Yale French Studies 1 (1948): 42–52, 49

Chapter 5

On the way to Elysium

Defining religion and registration of new religious communities

'Night is coming, Aeneas; we waste the hours in weeping. Here is the place, where the road parts: there to the right, as it runs under the walls of great Dis, is our way to Elysium, but the left wreaks the punishment of the wicked, and send them on to pitiless Tartarus.' In reply Deiphobus said: 'Be not angry, great priestess; I will go my way; I will make the count complete and return to the darkness. Go, you who are our glory, go; enjoy a happier fate!'

Virgil, *Aeneid*, Book VI

When Aeneas, the Virgilian counterpart of Odysseus, descends to the underworld to meet great heroes, such as Achilles, it turns out that the underworld is not a place where everyone rests peacefully. The way to Elysium, the place where the greatest heroes rejoice in their eternal glory, is long and treacherous. Charon, the ferryman, warns the travellers that the place is one of shadows. Crossing the Acheron, Aeneas encounters many crossroads, some of which lead straight to Tartarus, where groans and clanking of iron and chains remind him that while some enjoy the delights of eternal rest, others suffer divine torments for their sins. This mythical story reminds us of the journey that law undergoes while defining religions. Like Aeneas, law and rights hope to arrive in the Elysium of pluralism but instead frequently roam in gloomy places meeting suspicious ferrymen and treacherous roads that lead to the Tartarus of rejection. While struggling with what the concept of religion may convey, law encounters many roads that hide traps of exclusion and marginalisation. Instead of an Elysium of pluralism, law's definitional journey too often ends in destinations full of shadows, groans and injustice. This chapter examines the roads and the crossroads that law encounters when attempting to define religions and beliefs.

With inclusion as an objective, law wants to know what it intends to include and thus resorts to its natural tendency to create categories. On its way to the Elysium of pluralism, law may take the path of strict definition or follow a path of loose categorisation. Alternately, law is faced with a path of avoiding definition and facing the phenomenon on a case-to-case basis. Unsurprisingly, each of the paths might turn out to be narrow and dangerous and each risks placing law at the dangerous crossroads where the roads part, leading law not to Elysium but to Tartarus. While religious pluralism with its objective of introducing and shielding greater diversity promises a 'happier fate' primarily to those belonging to religions thus far less known or less numerous, its emphasis on the known and recognisable very often leads it to a crossroads at the very beginning when approaching new religions. And right at this very first crossroads it encounters the basic problem – can law define what religion is?

Whichever way it chooses, the signposts that law uses on its way are multiple and confusing, often even rather enigmatic. The meaning of the word is at best unclear, if not outright obscure. What does it mean to define 'religion' when nearly every branch of science produces an infinite number of questions and inquiries into its nature? As Derrida marvellously pointed out in his description of encounters of philosophers working on religion:

> We met, thus at Capri, we Europeans, assigned to languages (Italian, Spanish, German, French) in which the same word, religion, should mean, or so we thought, the same thing.... But everything remains problematic in this respect.
>
> (Derrida 2013, 70)

The very etymology of the word 'religion', in most European languages[1] derived from the Latin word 'religio', is shadowed with uncertainty. Is it derived from 'relegere', pointing to the role of tradition (to go through again in speech, thought, reading), or from 'religare', pointing to the normative nature of a belief (to bind) (Hoyt 1912; Derrida 2013)? Without even this much being certain, can law can seek signposts in other sciences that could lead it to an accurate definition?

If law on its way to definition took guidance from *anthropological studies* it would perhaps need to focus on the normative nature of religion as a space of human practice and take it as

> a system of symbols which acts to establish powerful, pervasive, and long lasting motivations in men by formulating conceptions of a general order of existence and clothing these conceptions with such an aura of factuality that the moods and motivations seem uniquely realistic.
>
> (Geertz 2004, 4)

But some argue that the focus on symbols is not enough and in such conceptualisations the historically specific relationships of religions with society might be lost. Thus following another approach law perhaps ought also to include historical relations with these symbols and focus on their articulation in social life (Asad 2002). Yet another confusing signpost might lead law to considerations of the supernatural and 'interactions with culturally postulated superhuman beings' (Spiro 2004, 96) or 'fields of social relationships' (Horton 1997, 23). Alternatively

---

[1] Languages where the word describing religion stems from a different core include, among others, Finnish. *Uskonto*, the Finnish equivalent for the word religion, stems from the verb *uskoa* – to believe. Religion thus is etymologically close to a belief.

law might also consider functions of religion in society with its integrating, vesting and cathartic functions in 'a man's attempt to make the supreme, final and unique' and in its search for the 'complete formula for the synthesis of human conduct' (Firth 1996, 44–7).

But if law took another guide on its way to the definition and focused on *psychological accounts* it might see religion as much more private and much more difficult to grasp. It might even dismiss religion as emotion or even an illusion (Freud 2011, 64). In contrast, seeking guidance from *sociological* research would result in the opposite and law would focus on social experience and the role of community in the practice of worship (Durkheim 2012, 47).

Finally, law might also seek guidance from *philosophical and theological* approaches aspiring to reconcile both the social and the individual religious experience (Smart 1992). For some theologians these two aspects are perfectly linked in a religious act where the cultural is formal and the religious is directed towards grasping the Unconditional (Tillich 1973, 59–62). But in theology, just as in other branches of science, nothing is certain about religion:

> The fact that we use a single word does not entail that the definition has to be simple. If it has to be disjunctive – to give alternative conditions for the application of the word in question – this is no tragedy.
>
> (Smart 1992, 26)

But whereas such indeterminacy might be no tragedy for philosophy it might be deadly for law. Thus law tries to retain precision for the sake of certainty. What follows is that both definitions and the lack thereof risk marginalising minoritarian religious experiences and run short of expectations to enhance religious pluralism. While definitions might exclude due to their tendency to totalise, lack of definitions might do so simply by omitting the unknown. The completeness of the account might thus never be possible. The law on its difficult path is thus permanently left with a central question: which way to the Elysium of pluralism?

5.1 The path of exclusive definitions

As with all ontological efforts to describe any form of being or any concept, saying what something is, is frequently easier by saying what something is not and thus drawing exclusive boundaries between subject and object (Adorno 1973, 12; Derrida 1998, 244). Not surprisingly, then, law more often relies on saying why something previously unseen is not a religion instead of saying what it might be. The tempting nature of this path stems from the comfort of analogy to what already exists and juxtaposing it with what appears new, unrecognisable and a poor fit within these previously created confines. Embarking on such a path requires relatively little effort and can easily be achieved by modelling the definition on what has been known as a religion for centuries. But this path, despite promising a quick short-cut, proves treacherous. Adopting such well-tested and familiar models can easily exclude the less desirable and hide a value judgment within.

Such a short-cut was taken in the famous decision of the UK Supreme Court in *Segerdal*[2] in the 1970s, where the Church of Scientology challenged the refusal of the Registrar General to register its chapel as a place of religious worship. In determining the case the opinion of Lord Denning classified Scientology as a 'philosophy of existence' rather than a religion because, as he underlined:

> I think we should take the combined phrase, 'place of meeting for religious worship' as used in the statute of 1855. It connotes to my mind a place of which the principal use is as a place where people come together as a congregation or assembly to do reverence to God. It need not be the God which the Christians worship. It may be another God or unknown God, but it must be reverence to deity.[3]

While Lord Denning also acknowledged there might be exceptions such as Buddhist temples, he emphasised it can only be an exception and for lack of worship of a Supreme Being, Scientology could only be classified as 'a philosophy of the existence of man'. This path was followed several times, including the frequently discussed 1999 decision (Gunn 2003; Edge 2006) of the Charity Commissioners for England and Wales. The decision issued by the Commissioners[4] once more concerned an application by the Church of Scientology, this time for registration as a charity. In their decision the Commissioners concluded that Scientology was not a religion for the purposes of charity law. In a similar type of reasoning that drew analogy to the well-known Judeo-Christian or at least theistic model (Gunn 2003, 194) the Commissioners without difficulty classified Scientology as falling outside of the definition of religion. The decision, referring among others to *Segerdal*,[5] followed the path of an excluding definition and agreed that the definition of 'religion' in English charity law was characterised in addition to a belief in a Supreme Being by an 'expression of that belief through worship'.[6] Scientology in the Commissioners' view missed the element of worship and reverence for a Supreme Being. Similarly to Scientology, this narrow path would exclude some branches of neo-paganism or even less theistic varieties of Buddhism, such as Theravada Buddhism. It does not take much imagination to see that, depending on the perception of worthiness or unworthiness, some beliefs would be classified as 'exceptions' as Lord Denning would have it, while others would be excluded upfront. When constructing the concept with the help of analogy to institutionalised forms

---

[2] *R* v. *Registrar General ex parte Segerdal*, Court of Appeal of England and Wales, [1970] 2 QB 697, 7 July 1970.

[3] *Ibid.*, para. 707.

[4] *Application for Registration as a Charity by the Church of Scientology of England and Wales*, Decision of the Charity Commissioners for England and Wales, 17 November 1999.

[5] *Ibid.*, p.13.

[6] *Ibid.*, p.14.

of organised religions, law creates a definition that conceals the dominant nature of the well-recognised and leaves adherents of minority beliefs on the margins. Under a cloak of analogy, new religions are not classified as a religion when they appear unworthy or less desirable. The list of possible exceptions that Lord Denning referred to is thus driven by the logic of tolerance rather than the logic of inclusion. Resorting to analogy also presupposes what the concept of religion ought to entail before constructing the concept. In such an a priori approach 'the concept hypostatises its own form against the content' (Adorno 1973, 154) and in that hides the identity principle resorting to drawing definitions and boundaries of concepts by reference to the self and its interests.

This identity principle has been frequently summoned when dealing with the Church of Scientology. Measured against the interests of the collective equivalent of the self, Scientology in particular is 'disliked by political and religious officials, treated negatively by the media and viewed with suspicion by many in the general public' (Richardson 2009, 292). It is unknown and ungraspable and due to this more often than not classified with the help of exclusive definitions exemplifying the fear described by Brown:

> We do not tolerate what is outside of our reach, what is irrelevant to us, or what we cannot do anything about. And tolerance is a selected alternative to actions or reactions of a different sort: rejection, quarantine, prohibition, repression, exile, or extermination. If these are not viable, expedient, or morally acceptable responses, if we have little or no choice about living with peoples or practices to which we object, then we cannot properly speak of tolerating what threatens or repels us; rather we are subjected, oppressed, or undone by their presence.
>
> (Brown 2008, 29)

The Church of Scientology defies what is commonly perceived as religion and makes the collective perception of 'us' feeling 'oppressed'. When this unrecognisable presence becomes unbearable for 'us' – the equivalent of the self – the limits of tolerance narrow down and push the threatening presence outside the margins of being tolerated. The examples of legal battles against the Church of Scientology in Germany embody the perception of a threat leading to the rejection of Scientology as a religion and marginalisation of its adherents in terms of privileges stemming from recognition as a religion. Just as in English law, registration of the Church of Scientology spurred discussion on the meaning of the word 'religion' and 'religious' in German law. The Federal Constitutional Court,[7] the Federal Labour Court[8] and the Federal Administrative Court[9] approached

---

[7] Judgment concerning *Weltanschauungsgemeinschaft und Religionsfreiheit*, Bundesverfassungsgericht, BVerfG 1 BvR 632/92, 28 August 1992.

[8] *Religionsgemeinschaftseigenschaft von Scientology*, Bundesarbeitsgericht, 5AZB 21/94, 22 March 1995.

[9] Judgment concerning areas of *Wehrpflicht; Zurückstellung; Berufsausbildung; Ausbildungsgang*, Bundesverwaltungsgericht, 8 C 12/79, 14 November 1980.

religion more openly than *Segerdal* or the Charity Commissioners, but they did not dare step out of law's comfort zone. Religion and religious community, according to the earliest of the judgments, should 'have spiritual content and assign transcendent value to human life'.[10] As if referring to a mix of Durkheimian notions of the religious community combined with some anthropological aspects in definitions such as Spiro's, the Courts expected the Church of Scientology to have presence in public life based on spiritual content.[11] Finally resorting to fear of what was outside their reach, the judges classified the church's commitment as not objectively verifiable and therefore insufficient for the existence of a religious community.[12] The status of the church in Germany remains disputed, with several Land Courts accepting nowadays a broader definition and allowing registration.[13]

The logic of tolerance and its subjective limits involved in definitions by analogy risks coming up with constantly new demands to prove that the threshold of tolerance is satisfied. St Petersburg Church of Scientology in *Church of Scientology of St Petersburg* v. *Russia* challenged the requirements of presenting new proofs in the process of registration by local authorities.[14] The St Petersburg authorities required the church to submit constant new proofs concerning different aspects of the church's existence. Once one aspect was satisfied the next appeared immediately leading to a refusal to register. The ECtHR, testing whether the definition was drawn in a pluralistic spirit, reaffirmed the applicants' assertion that they

> had never engaged in any offensive expressions of their beliefs or otherwise offended religious sensibilities of others. They maintained that the applicable standard should be the one that favours religious pluralism, even where there is religious tension and division within society.[15]

At the same time, however, the Court remained cautious in challenging the legitimacy of definitions by analogy or questioning the logic of tolerance. It affirmed the local authority's mandate to apply and interpret local law and it dismissed the validity of their decision primarily on procedural rather than substantive grounds. The procedural objection concerned the fact that the grounds invoked by the domestic courts for rejecting the confirmation documents and requiring new ones were not based on an accessible and foreseeable interpretation of domestic law. Nor did the ECtHR challenge this underpinning logic in its main substantive consideration on the lengthy waiting period required by legislation:

---

[10] *Ibid.*, para. 18.
[11] *Ibid.*, para. 19.
[12] *Ibid.*, para. 24.
[13] Judgment concerning Church of Scientology, Oberverwaltungsgericht Nordrhein-Westfalen, 5 a 130/05, 12 February 2008.
[14] *Church of Scientology of St Petersburg and Others* v. *Russia*, European Court of Human Rights, Judgment, Application No. 47191/06, 2 October 2014.
[15] *Ibid.*, para. 36.

Where it has been shown that interference was not in accordance with the law, it is not necessary to investigate whether it also pursued a 'legitimate aim' or was 'necessary in a democratic society'. Nevertheless, the Court considers it important to reaffirm its position that the lengthy waiting period which a religious organisation has to endure prior to obtaining legal personality cannot be considered 'necessary in a democratic society'.[16]

This cherry-picking of non-pluralistic elements within a definition, without engaging with the requirements of pluralism in defining religion, did not inject anything new into existing practices determining who can and who cannot enjoy the benefits of recognition as a religion. Quite the contrary, it sustained the logic of tolerance and affirmed that tolerance in a 'democratic society' no longer required lengthy waiting periods. It also hypostatised the content of definition by assuming what form such a definition should take. While not questioning other elements, it found waiting periods no longer to be suitable for construction of a definition.

To be sure, such definitions and constructs exist in multiple legal systems and may affect religions other than Scientology. The approach of the former Dutch Equal Treatment Commission embodied a similarly narrow take on the concept of religion. The Commission was responsible for the enforcement of equality and non-discrimination in Dutch law among others on the grounds of a religion or belief. In 2012 it was replaced by the College of Human Rights, a new independent body deciding among others on matters of anti-discrimination law. In the context of religion the previously existing Commission issued opinions on the definition of a 'religion' and a 'belief'. Opinions CGB 2003-114[17] and CGB 2004-06[18] endeavour to cover a maximally broad spectrum of existing beliefs in the spirit of pluralism. In doing so they draw a dichotomous division between a 'religion' and a 'belief'. Understanding of religion remains extremely narrow and akin to the Charity Commissioners' view signifying 'conviction about life having a Supreme Being as a central point'.[19] This rigidity is relaxed by combining it with a slightly more flexible notion of 'belief'. Belief covers existential conviction that does not necessarily recognise a Supreme Being but is formed into a more or less coherent system of ideas concerning fundamental views on human existence. These definitions, even though mutually supportive, confine religion and belief in the domain of the known and certain and raise artificial divides between what is seen as a religion and what is seen as a belief. While Rastafarianism[20] qualifies as a religion, followers of Osho are classified as believers,[21] falling into two distinct categories. While trying to recognise and

---

[16] *Ibid.*, para. 46.
[17] Commissie gelijke behandeling, CGB 2003-114, 7 November 2006.
[18] Advies Commissie Gelijke Behandeling in zake Arbeid, religie en gelijke behandeling, CGB 2004-06, 12 August 2004.
[19] *Ibid.*, para. 2.4.
[20] Commissie gelijke behandeling, CGB 2005-162, 30 August 2005.
[21] Commissie gelijke behandeling, CGB 2005-67, 15 April 2005.

protect diversity, all such divisions create new boundaries and categories reinforcing known and acceptable models.

These new models of categorising in turn lead to the emergence of stereotyping images and might result in framing new believers into the discourse on 'sects'. The definition of a 'sect' is frequently based on an image of otherness constructed in opposition to what is considered a recognised religion or belief and applied to the new and the unknown. The next step is the unavoidable framing of these beliefs as not only unworthy but also dangerous. This tendency is particularly visible in France, where resistance to new religious movements is strongly embodied in law (Ferrari 2009, 752). The mere name of the law – *Law number 2001-504 of June 12, 2001 intended to reinforce the prevention and repression of sectarian (cultic) movements that infringe on human rights and on fundamental freedoms*,[22] pictures the adherents of certain movements as potential violators of human rights. It equates some religions with danger and operates with a logic of security that allows for framing the adherents of these movements not as subjects of rights but as a danger to them. While it was a subject of Report 9612 of the Committee on Legal Affairs and Human Rights of Europe,[23] the law and its formulations were not found to be in violation of the 'values of the Council of Europe'.[24] But such conceptualisations are only a step away from administering rights and managing pluralism by regulating the frames of worthiness that Butler identified in her *Frames of War* (Butler 2009). Just as lives worth living and protecting are juxtaposed with lives that are damnable, the frame of dangerous and unworthy 'sect' determines which beliefs qualify for access to rights and which can be disciplined with the help of rights. Danièle Hervieu-Léger underlines that this definition of a 'sect' as included in the French law is not neutral but instead relies on majoritarian standards for defining the threshold of worthiness of belief:

> It is as if religious sentiment, when it escapes the major 'organized religions,' *by its very nature* can only degenerate into a 'pathology of belief' that is basically contrary to freedom of thought and individual autonomy.
>
> (Hervieu-Léger 2001, 251)

Such definitions are grounded in fear of the unknown and stray away from the path to the Elysium of pluralism. Treading on a narrow and misleading path of tolerance they 'remain torn between the democratic objective of guaranteeing religious freedom ... and a desire to "tear minds from the influence of beliefs deemed to be in stark contradiction to reason and autonomy"' (Hervieu-Léger

---

[22] Loi no. 2001-504 du 12 juin 2001 tendant à renforcer la prévention et la répression des mouvements sectaires portant atteinte aux droits de l'homme et aux libertés fondamentales, 12 June 2001.

[23] Council of Europe, Report 9612 of the Committee on Legal Affairs and Human Rights of Europe, 14 November 2001.

[24] Recommendation 1309 (2002), 'Freedom of religion and religious minorities in France', of the Council of Europe Parliamentary Assembly, 18 November 2002.

2001, 252). Informed by the identity principle drawing the boundaries of the new by modelling it on the self and fearfully rejecting or merely tolerating everything that falls outside, approaches of this kind come dangerously close to the pitiless Tartarus of 'rejection, quarantine, prohibition, repression, exile, or extermination' (Brown 2008, 29). On such a path rights and the principles underpinning them, such as religious pluralism, reveal their confusing face. Religious difference not only becomes a hindrance in access to rights but also results in constructing the other as a potential violator of rights. This mechanism is becoming rather widespread and, as illustrated in later chapters, clearly visible in cases dealing for instance with religious symbolism. What follows is that the principle of religious pluralism becomes reduced to pluralism based on the identity principle relying on the known and hedging and fencing the unknown by framing it as 'dangerous'. With such underpinning, human rights lose their emancipatory potential and become the rights of the majority that can be used for securing rather than restricting their cultural power. Or, as Young warned, the irony of a logic of identity lies in turning the merely different into the absolutely other (Young 1990, 99).

5.2 Elysium on the horizon? Embracing definitions

With its potential for exclusivity and restraining the unknown, the first of the definitional paths carries little promise for law to embrace the new in a spirit of pluralism. But can law respect both 'the desire for justice and the desire for the unknown' (Lyotard 1988, 67)? If exclusive definitions are flawed and leave those whose religions instigate fear of the unknown on the margins, perhaps more embracing definitions could help? If law follows philosophical guidelines and uses the word 'religion' to describe beliefs characterised by different qualities and inclusive of different aspects, can it be saved from a path leading to exclusion of minority experiences?

Some European countries have attempted to accommodate a wide variety of new religious movements with the help of open-ended definitions. Polish, Finnish and Austrian examples at first glance appear not to limit the definition of what a religion is. They allow for all kinds of movements to apply and be recognised. Against this backdrop, though, laws on registration of religious communities in these countries, while appearing to be broad, exclude new and less numerous beliefs in ways similar to exclusive definitions. Most of the requirements for registration are modelled on traditional understandings of communal aspects of religion. They do not fall far from Durkheim's definition, in which:

> A religion is a unified system of beliefs and practices relative to sacred things, that is to say, things set apart and forbidden – beliefs and practices which unite into one single moral community called a Church, all those who adhere to them.

> (Durkheim 2012, 47)

Such an approach, while not defining what a religion is, accentuates the necessity of forming a church or at least a community. Even though at first glance embracing, the emphasis on the communal core, like narrow definitions, eventually resorts to analogy with existing religious communities and their function in the traditional meaning. The existence of a form less structured or less numerous is frequently rejected despite seeming openness so that new beliefs are met with suspicion and rejection dictated by protecting the recognisable religious normativity from discomfort.

Under Polish law, a community of faith is a 'religious community founded for the purpose of worshipping and propagating a religious faith, which has got its own organisation, doctrine and practices'.[25] While not defining a religious faith as such, the definition none the less requires an application for registration to have a certain form such as information about forms of religious life, methods of functioning and a written statute of the community and signatures and personal data of at least 100 followers. Neither the form of the community nor the methods of worship are pre-defined and the definition appears broad, but the analogy with traditionally recognised religions remains strong. The high requirement as to the number of followers automatically excludes small communities from registering, requiring them to meet numeric criteria based on the notion of religion understood as a large community of believers supported by a certain established tradition bringing together at least 100 people. Similarly, the requirements of having a doctrine, organisation and practices, even though not exclusive *per se*, assume a structure similar to major recognised models. Even though smaller, less organised communities can register in other forms, for instance as public foundations (Borecki 2006), their status remains separate and not recognised as a form of worship. Before the latest amendment to the Law Guaranteeing Freedom of Conscience, the required number of followers was only 15. The change increased the difficulty of the registration process, pushing newly emerging religious movements further to the margins.

But it would be a mistake to think that such a way of defining religions is uncommon or exceptionally restrictive. Quite the contrary, a number of legislators define religion by comparing new movements to traditionally recognised models. In 2001 the Finnish Wicca Association, founded for the purpose of registration, attempted to enrol on a register of religious communities in Finland. While the believers drew open and negotiable boundaries of their religious movement in an attempt to include diverse branches of their belief (Taira 2010, 382–3), their application was rejected by the Ministry of Education, which insisted that:

> The movement is not based on a creed, texts considered sacred or other specified and established foundations considered sacred, but every person or group involved in the movement defines his/her/its view and ritual practice mainly

[25] *Ustawa o gwarancjach wolności sumienia i wyznania* (Law on guarantees of freedom of conscience and faith), Dz.U. 1989 Nr 25 poz. 155, 18 May 1989, para. 31.1.

by him/her/itself by combining influences from different sources. The movement's views and ritual practices are heterogeneous and fluctuating.

(Hjelm 2006, 42; quoted in Taira 2010, 381)

Despite reapplication, the comparison to traditional community persisted and the application was rejected again in 2003 (Taira 2010, 382). The Durkheimian notion of a community based on a creed, text and specific rituals excluded Wiccans, despite the agreement of religious scholars that a movement existed. As demonstrated by Taira, the use of 'religion' in such a definition is a discursive technique and a classifying tool that can channel social and practical interests and is an indiscernible part of power relations (Taira 2010, 391).

Such employment of the term 'religion' is also present in Austrian legislation, which was eventually disputed before the ECtHR specifically in the context of religious pluralism. Like Polish or Finnish legislation, the shape of Austrian legislation on legal personality of religious movements requires new religious movements to meet conditions traditionally associated with communal aspects common in well-recognised religions. Under Austrian law, according to the latest amendments, before being recognised as a religion, a community must first of all have existed in Austria for a minimum of 20 years, including 10 years in an organised form and 5 years in a register of 'confessional communities'. Additionally new grounds allow internationally recognised religions to register but only if they have been recognised for at least 100 years, including 10 years in Austria. Furthermore, a religious community might register if it has been involved in religious teaching internationally for at least 200 years and is represented by at least 2 Austrian residents per 1,000 according to the latest census.[26] In order to be entered into the register as a community, the community must also have a positive attitude towards society and state and cannot interfere with the existence of already established communities.[27] The requirements concerning the high number of followers and existing for many years as a 'confessional community' have persisted for a long time, discriminating against minor and new religions in multiple ways such as exclusion from a range of benefits (Miner 1998). But most importantly the definitional narrative is controlled through reference to the known, in which non-recognised religions are exposed once more to being treated as 'dangerous sects'.

The earlier version of the Austrian legislation was challenged before the ECtHR in a case concerning registration of the Jehovah's Witnesses.[28] The organisation was refused registration despite the elapse of the statutory waiting period. After examining the circumstances the Court found a violation of freedom of religion,

---

[26] Bundeskanzleramt, Rechtspersönlichkeit von religiösen Bekenntnisgemeinschaften, BGBl. I Nr. 19/1998, para. 11.

[27] *Ibid.*

[28] *Religionsgemeinschaft der Zeugen Jehovas and Others* v. *Austria*, European Court of Human Rights, Judgment, Application No. 40825/98, 31 July 2008.

basing their decision on the importance of securing pluralism and the role of religious communities:

> Indeed, the autonomous existence of religious communities is indispensable for pluralism in a democratic society and is, thus, an issue at the very heart of the protection which Article 9 affords.[29]

The judgment found the prolongation of the waiting period set by the Austrian authorities on the Jehovah's Witnesses to be disproportional for achieving the goal of pluralism and thus illegitimate in a democratic society. In addition it found that Jehovah's Witnesses were discriminated against on the grounds of their religion. This seemingly inclusive finding based on the principle of pluralism in the context of defining religion despite its best intention embodied a thin approach to pluralism. The Court even though attempting to recognise diversity reinforced the narrative of the new and the recognised by emphasising that waiting periods might be justified in the case of newly appearing religious movements, but not in the case of religious communities recognised internationally and with a long tradition.[30] Such a distinction not only strengthened the power of the known to define the unknown but also sanctioned the control of otherness and management of difference. Law privileged the collective self to rely on its dominant and recognisable identities to create tools classifying beliefs as more or less worthy based on how strongly they resembled those identities. In this case such resemblance was measured by reference to duration of existence. The envisioned shape of pluralism surrendered recognition of religious difference to an array of analogies that could neither be challenged nor renegotiated.

Yet another, more embracing side path was taken by Lord Toulson in a recent case concerning registration of a church used by the Church of Scientology[31] as a place of religious worship for the purpose of the Places of Religious Worship Registration Act 1855 (PWRA).[32] While reviewing previous approaches, including the changed definition of religion for charity purposes more embracing of different types of beliefs,[33] Lord Toulson agreed that religion should not be confined to religions that recognise a supreme deity. He found that such a formulation would 'form a discrimination unacceptable in today's society'.[34] In his attempt to provide an inclusive definition he described religion as:

[29] *Ibid.*, para. 61.

[30] *Ibid.*, para. 98.

[31] *R (Hodkin) v. Registrar General of Births, Deaths and Marriages* [2013] UKSC 77, Supreme Court of the United Kingdom, 11 December 2013.

[32] Places of Worship Registration Act 1855, 30 July 1855.

[33] The Charities Act 2011, Section 3(2)(a) in addition to monotheistic religions defines religion as a religion which involves belief in more than one god and religion that does not involve a belief in any god.

[34] *R (Hodkin) v. Registrar General of Births, Deaths and Marriages*, para. 51.

[A] spiritual or non-secular belief system, held by a group of adherents, which claims to explain mankind's place in the universe and relationship with the infinite, and to teach its adherents how they are to live their lives in conformity with the spiritual understanding associated with the belief system.[35]

While embracing this definition insisted on the communal and non-secular character of a religion, Lord Toulson explained that such a formulation was not exclusive given the provisions of the Marriage Act that allows for marriages in approved secular premises. When relying on the Marriage Act to supplement this interpretation the definition appears prima facie inclusive. The phrase 'non-secular', though, invites a variety of subjective interpretations of beliefs that do not rely on the existence of a deity. What is the threshold of secularity when the second component relies heavily on theological, anthropological and sociological elements found typically in theistic religions? The invitation to use analogy is strongly signposted and the potential persists for exclusive interpretations and troublesome dichotomies. It is easy to imagine that potential registration of a Wiccan or pagan temple consisting of followers of different branches could still fail under this seemingly open approach due to several factors such as lack of systematic teaching embedded in a variety of more individualistic approaches to contemporary paganism.

Seemingly embracing definitions, even though promising a more successful pathway to pluralism, have on multiple occasions similarly contributed to the emergence of stereotyping images as have strict definitions. As a result they have drawn a distinction between easily recognisable beliefs and those beliefs that cannot meet the thresholds established by majoritarian experiences. Not surprisingly these models, too, could frame new believers into the above-mentioned discourse on 'sects'. Their seemingly open-ended nature has been restricted by modelling the image of difference on the structure of the self. Continuing to present the other as symmetrical to the self (Douzinas and Warrington 1991, 123), these approaches have not really enabled difference to be faced openly or let it be truly different from recognisable and known identities. Instead they have mirrored the tendency of strict definitions to treat religious difference as unrecognisable, often radical and thus impossible to define or include. Ironically that impossibility has stemmed from the impotence of the self to surpass its image of symmetry of the other. Instead of accommodating true difference in the promise of pluralism, this line of definitions has led to arranging society into a structure in which we are concerned about 'living with peoples or practices to which we object' (Brown 2008, 29) and reinforcing the categories of objection.

5.3 Islands of the blessed on the horizon?
Avoidance of definitions

If both exclusive and embracing definitions are likely to lead freedom of religion from the path of pluralism, another obvious path emerges among diverse legal

---

[35] *Ibid.*, at 57.

choices related to defining and classifying as religion. The path of not defining might appear the most promising for accommodating difference. And this path has repeatedly been taken by the ECtHR in matters concerning freedom of religion. The Court has frequently treated 'religion' as a self-understood concept that required no elaboration, especially in the case of well-recognised beliefs. But it has also ruled in favour of recognising multiple new movements as religions or beliefs, including Osho,[36] pacifism[37] or even vegetarianism.[38] But while accepting these as religious movements the Court has often refused to engage in the problematic of defining and has approached concepts of religion or belief by applying analogies similar to those used in cases using stricter definitions. Avoidance has rarely been supported with considerations of religious difference but instead has been informed by the categories of acceptable and unacceptable. Following the definition of acceptable belief elaborated in *Campbell and Cosans* v. *UK*[39] the threshold of acceptable was set at a level of 'cogency and seriousness'. Despite the lack of engagement with the core of faith these judgments approached new religions and beliefs by relying on particular definitional aspects present in narrower definitions. For instance in *Leela Förderkreis E.V.* v. *Germany*, the Court without contestation found Osho to be a belief. None the less, even though the judgment did not engage in defining, it founded the acceptance of Osho as a belief in the traditional elements used both in strict and more open-ended definitions:

> According to their statutes, the applicant associations promote the teachings of Osho. They run Osho meditation centres, organise seminars, celebrate religious events and carry out joint work projects. According to the teachings of their community, the aim of spiritual development is enlightenment. Their conception of the world is based on the idea of achieving transcendence in all essential areas of life and is continuously shared by them and their community. The Court considers that these views can be considered as the manifestation of the applicant associations' belief. Their complaints therefore fall within the ambit of Article 9 of the Convention.[40]

The communal aspects and the theological aspect informed the Court's test of Osho, practically speaking recreating a rather strict definition of what a religion or belief ought to consist of.

[36] *Leela Förderkreis E.V. and Others* v. *Germany*, European Court of Human Rights, Judgment, Application No. 58911/00, 6 November 2008.

[37] *Valsamis* v. *Greece*, European Court of Human Rights, Judgment, Application No. 21787/93, 18 December 1996.

[38] *Jakóbski* v. *Poland*, European Court of Human Rights, Judgment, Application No. 18429/06, 7 December 2010.

[39] *Campbell and Cosans* v. *the United Kingdom*, European Court of Human Rights, Judgment, Application Nos. 7511/76 and 7743/76, 25 February 1982.

[40] *Leela Förderkreis E.V. and Others* v. *Germany*, para. 12.

In contrast, a slightly different path was taken by the Spanish Constitutional Court in its attempt to move the narrative of recognition beyond reinforcing the boundaries between the known and the unknown and therefore between the acceptable and unacceptable. The notion of religion in Spanish law has traditionally been based on the traditional and monotheistic heritage (Martinez-Torron 2001) and frequently characterised by three elements: the belief in a Supreme Being developed into tenets and precepts, external worship and a certain institutional organisation. This traditional approach was challenged in the case concerning registration of the Church of Unification. Upon being refused registration as a religious group the church filed a complaint with the Spanish Constitutional Court.[41] In this case the Court not only ruled in favour of the church but went a step further and rendered the concept of 'religion' inoperative. In an effort to accommodate diversity and prevent the emergence of marginalising discourses the Court simply decided that the administrative authorities had no discretion, or margin of appreciation, to examine the religious nature of any group. Any such examination risked applying analogies and would involve reference to acceptable models. But recognition of the unknown was not unlimited. Arguing that the concept is inoperative and can hinder recognition in practice, the judgment none the less referred the relevant authorities to the Organic Law of Religious Freedom, which in Article 3 stipulates a range of exclusions from being recognised as a religion. It excludes for example the following, stating that:

> [A]ctivities, purposes and entities relating to or engaging in the study of and experimentation with psychic or parapsychological phenomena or the dissemination of humanistic or spiritualistic values or other similar non-religious aims do not qualify for protection.
>
> (Combalía and Roca 2014, 633)

This threshold is not dissimilar to the expectation of seriousness and cogency expressed in *Campbell and Cosans*. While in the majority of circumstance this maximally vague guideline placed the authorities in a position where it became safest to avoid any control and accept a wide range of applications (Martinez-Torron 2001), beliefs such as secular humanism or parapsychological thinking would still be exempted from protection. Yet in the majority of cases the effort of defining religion was shifted from the authorities to the religious community. Consequently recognition as religious relied on self-identification by the community in question and seeing itself as religious. The otherness of the community was no longer to be examined by positioning the unrecognisable in symmetry to oneself and saying what recognisable elements it did not meet. Instead the shift from defining from the outside to internal identification allowed for approaching difference from its core and challenging existing preconceptions of what a religion might be.

---

[41] *Church of Unification*, Spanish Constitutional Court, STC 46/2001, 15 February 2001.

The necessity of putting a threshold even in situations where no definition is formally applied relates to the fear that fictional communities will apply for protection and recognition of their freedom of religion. Whether partly rooted in the fear of mocking traditionally acceptable religions or in the fear of abuse of privileges stemming from freedom of religion, the fictional community is not seen as a part of a pluralistic landscape. Pastafarianism and the Church of the Flying Spaghetti Monster, which recently was refused registration in Poland[42] but has succeeded in having several of its members portrayed wearing a pasta colander on their driving-licence photographs in several other countries, has been a frequently used example of a 'parody religion' (Laycock 2013). While pastafarianism might appear ridiculous to many and offensive to those claiming a religious belief characterised by the expected level of seriousness and cogency, the adherents of the Church of the Flying Spaghetti Monster cannot be straightforwardly dismissed as defying or undermining the goals of pluralism. Even if not considered religious by many, the adherents of pastafarianism are likely to share perhaps not as much a belief considered to be of a religious nature but most certainly a belief about religious beliefs and their position in contemporary societies. A view of that kind can affect the pluralistic dynamic and slowly transform the approach towards religion and belief, its place in society and the protection it deserves when compared with other ideological views on life. It definitely embodies difference unseen before and perhaps unrecognisable when measured with analogies. If pluralism is not to be understood as a force cementing the status quo and preventing societies from evolving and changing, a belief about beliefs veiled in a religious form, like any legitimate religion or critique of religion, deserves a place in shaping the community's views on the place and treatment of a belief. Pluralism in its thickest form is not a principle cementing comfort and safety but instead a dynamic force that allows for constant challenges and creates a space for all forms of renegotiation that can slowly transform and shake the status quo.

5.4 A mirage or paradise: to define or not to define?

In terms of enjoyment of freedom of religion, defining what is and what is not a religion appears to be a natural first step towards securing a religiously plural society in which all religions can coexist. But law, with its tendency to create categories and entitlements stemming from those categories, has an uneasy task when approaching religion. Facing many ways to secure a pluralistic exercise of freedom of religion for as many religions as possible, law faces multiple pathways in terms of defining the threshold of enjoyment of this freedom. As illustrated above, defining what a religion is in a broader or narrower manner frequently risks camouflaging a judgment on the worthiness of a belief and more often than not reinforces the categories of

---

[42] Michal Boni, Minister Administracji i Cyfryzacji (Minister of Administration and Digitalization), 25 February 2015, *Decyja Odmowna* (Refusal), 25 February 2013, available at: www.klps.pl/pliki/decyzja.pdf, accessed 4 March 2015.

acceptable and unacceptable entrenched in the logic of tolerance rather than pluralism. Such an approach stems from the nature of definitions and their reliance on identity. As Adorno observed, the cognition of non-identity is frequently underpinned by thinking of the thresholds of identity that non-identity fails to satisfy:

> But definition also approaches that which the object itself is as non-identical: in placing its mark on the object, definition seeks to be marked by the object. Nonidentity is the secret *telos* of identification. It is the part that can be salvaged; the mistake in traditional thinking is that identity is taken for the goal. The force that shatters the appearance of identity is the force of thinking: the use of 'it is' undermines the form of that appearance, which remains inalienable just the same. Dialectically, cognition of nonidentity lies also in the fact that this very cognition identifies – that it identifies to a greater extent, and in other ways, than identitarian thinking. This cognition seeks to say what something is, while identitarian thinking says what something comes under, what it exemplifies or represents, and what, accordingly, it is not itself. The more relentlessly our identitarian thinking besets its object, the farther will it take us from the identity of the object.
>
> (Adorno 1973, 149)

As illustrated by the variety of approaches to religion, identitarian thinking is not uncommon for law and human rights and gives rise to the logic of tolerance rather than pluralism. While obvious cases have been accepted in a pluralistic spirit, less obvious cases, in both the approaches of authorities and the case-law of domestic courts and the ECtHR, were often imagined as absolute others. Although increasingly many beliefs classify for protection, the discourse of seriousness or worthiness underpins the understanding of pluralism in the context of definition. Pluralism read as maintenance of a consensus reveals its impotence to prevent the totalising consequences of definitions by analogy or the troublesome dichotomies they create. Without tackling such interpretations, pluralism as a principle becomes barely able to prevent exclusion of the less known. When the dichotomy between the self and the other grows in law, human rights might reveal their helplessness in preventing exclusion. Cognitive totality placed against particularity results in creation of a *differend*, a conflict that stems from the gap between the particular and the universal (Lyotard 1988) or in this case between the universally recognised and the new. As Dunn put it, such a differend marks a dissonance at the heart of the dialogue and results in an unbridgeable distance between the subject and the other (Dunn 1993, 196). As illustrated further in the following chapter, when this gap between the universal and the particular becomes unbridgeable the victim becomes a perpetrator and dissonance is placed at the heart of human rights. French law dealing with 'sects' creates such an unbridgeable divide between the self and the other in which she can no longer articulate her claim for recognition. When her claims are presented as unrecognisable for the collective self they symbolise absolute otherness. In such a radical juxtaposition the divide between self and the other becomes impossible to bridge. Guided by such deep dissonance and identitarian thinking, human rights can easily demonise the unrecognised as a grave risk to the collective self. When seen as such, the other becomes the one to be shielded from with the help of human rights. Because of her difference, which has been rejected, she is no longer a beneficiary but instead a violator of human rights. The emancipatory potential of freedom of religion is thus reversed.

Bearing in mind such a grave risk, definitions, as a key component of law, are problematic. Moreover, as Adorno reminds us, they should not be seen as the end of cognition. But nor should they be entirely abandoned (Adorno 1973, 165). To make definitions more inclusive and salvage them from the harmful logic of self-identity, Adorno proposes that the 'idealistic magic circle' of concepts:

> can be transcended only in thoughts still circumscribed by its figure, in thoughts that follow its own deductive procedure, call it by name and demonstrate the disjointness, the untruth, of totality by unfolding its epitome. Pure identity is that which the subject posits and thus brings up from outside. Therefore, paradoxically enough, to criticize it immanently means to criticize it from outside as well. The subject must make up for what it has done to non-identity. This is precisely what liberates it from the semblance of its absolute being for-itself. That semblance in turn is a product of identifying thought – of the thought which depreciates a thing to a mere sample of its kind of species only to convince us that we have the thing as such, without subjective addition.
>
> (Adorno 1973, 145–6)

Not dissimilar to Levinasian thought, this path encourages a definition that could be less totalising and reach outside of the self by facing otherness before facing the self (Levinas 1979, 1981). That is how the subject could make up for what it has done to the other. Without such conceptualisation, mere employment of pluralism in evaluating definitions will always balance on the edge of tolerance without ever becoming truly inclusive. Definitions maintaining the focus on 'being for-itself', by modelling difference on the image of the self, will always risk turning against the other. Without making up for what the centrality of the subject does to non-identity, the roads to Elysium risk remaining mere mirages of pluralism.

References

Adorno, Theodor W. 1973. *Negative Dialectics*. Routledge.
Asad, Talal. 2002. 'The Construction of Religion as an Anthropological Category.' In *A Reader in Anthropology of Religion*, ed. M Lambek, 111–26. Blackwell Publishing.
Borecki, Pawel. 2006. 'Rejestracja Zwiazku Wyznaniowego' [Registration of a Community of Faith]. *Racjonalista* April 2006. www.racjonalista.pl
Brown, Wendy. 2008. *Regulating Aversion: Tolerance in the Age of Identity and Empire*. Princeton University Press.
Butler, Judith. 2009. *Frames of War: When Is Life Grievable?* Verso.

Combalía, Zoila and María Roca. 2014. 'Religion and the Secular State of Spain'. International Center for Law and Religion Studies, Brigham Young University, Provo, UT.

Derrida, Jacques. 1998. *Of Grammatology*. Johns Hopkins University Press.

Derrida, Jacques. 2013. *Acts of Religion*. Routledge.

Douzinas, Costas and Ronnie Warrington. 1991. '"A Well-Founded Fear of Justice": Law and Ethics in Postmodernity.' *Law and Critique* 2(2): 115–47.

Dunn, Allen. 1993. 'A Tyranny of Justice: The Ethics of Lyotard's Differend.' *Boundary 2* 20(1): 192–220.

Durkheim, Émile. 2012. *The Elementary Forms of the Religious Life*. Courier Corporation.

Edge, Peter W. 2006. *Religion and Law: An Introduction*. Ashgate.

Ferrari, Silvio. 2009. 'Civil Religions: Models and Perspectives.' *George Washington International Law Review* 41: 749–63.

Firth, Raymond. 1996. *Religion: A Humanist Interpretation*. Psychology Press.

Freud, Sigmund. 2011. *The Future of an Illusion*. Martino Fine Books.

Geertz, Clifford. 2004. 'Religion as a Cultural System.' In *Anthropological Approaches to the Study of Religion*, ed. Michael Banton, 1–39. Routledge.

Gunn, Jeremy T. 2003. 'The Complexity of Religion and the Definition of Religion in International Law.' *Harvard Human Rights Journal* 16: 189–214.

Hervieu-Léger, Danièle. 2001. 'France's Obsession with the "Sectarian Threat".' *Nova Religio: The Journal of Alternative and Emergent Religions* 4(2): 249–57.

Hjelm, Titus. 2006. 'Between Satan and Harry Potter: Legitimating Wicca in Finland.' *Journal of Contemporary Religion* 21(1): 33–48.

Horton, Robin. 1997. *Patterns of Thought in Africa and the West: Essays on Magic, Religion and Science*. Cambridge University Press.

Hoyt, Sarah F. 1912. 'The Etymology of Religion.' *Journal of the American Oriental Society* 32(2): 126–9.

Laycock, Joseph P. 2013. 'Laughing Matters: "Parody Religions" and the Command to Compare.' *Bulletin for the Study of Religion* 42(3): 19–26.

Levinas, Emmanuel. 1979. *Totality and Infinity: An Essay on Exteriority*. Springer Science & Business Media.

Levinas, Emmanuel. 1981. *Otherwise than Being, or Beyond Essence*. Springer.

Lyotard, Jean-François. 1988. *The Differend: Phrases in Dispute*. Theory and History of Literature 46. University of Minnesota Press.

Martinez-Torron, Javier. 2001. 'Freedom of Religion in the Case Law of the Spanish Constitutional Court.' *Brigham Young University Law Review* (2001): 711–54.

Miner, Christopher J. 1998. 'Losing My Religion: Austria's New Religion Law in Light of International and European Standards of Religious Freedom.' *Brigham Young University Law Review* (1998): 607–47.

Richardson, James T. 2009. 'Scientology in Court: A Look at Some Major Cases from Various Nations.' In *Scientology*, ed. J. Lewis, 283–94. Oxford University Press.

Smart, Ninian. 1992. *Philosophy of Religion*. Oxford University Press.

Spiro, Melford E. 2004. 'Religion: Problems of Definition and Explanation.' In *Anthropological Approaches to the Study of Religion*, ed. Michael Banton, 85–123. Routledge.

Taira, Teemu. 2010. 'Religion as a Discursive Technique: The Politics of Classifying Wicca.' *Journal of Contemporary Religion* 25(3): 379–94.

Tillich, Paul. 1973. *What Is Religion?*, trans. James Luther Adams. Harper & Row.

Young, Iris Marion. 1990. *Justice and the Politics of Difference*. Princeton University Press.

Chapter 6

Regulation of religious symbols

A European Pandora's jar*

For ere this the tribes of men lived on earth remote and free from ills and hard toil and heavy sickness which bring the Fates upon men; for in misery men grow old quickly. But the woman took off the great lid of the jar with her hands and scattered all these and her thought caused sorrow and mischief to men. Only Hope remained there in an unbreakable home within under the rim of the great jar, and did not fly out at the door.

Hesiod, *Works and Days*

In this religiously plural age it may come as a surprise to some that no issue has taken so much space and focus of European legislatures, courts and ballot boxes as religious symbols. Before the age of religious pluralism was declared, the existence of symbols had not attracted much attention. However, within the past decade we have heard of symbols forbidden and symbols permitted, all in the name of neutrality, secularism or even pluralism. Whereas some of these symbols have been deemed threatening and therefore 'fearful' (Gunn 2005a), others have begun to signify a source of a tradition deserving protection and symbolising the local flavour of rights (Weiler 2010). At no other intersection of law and religion has there been as much confusion as to what the law should or should not do in terms of regulating the public sphere. In no other sphere has there been such an active interpretation of boundaries of freedom, nor has any other divided European approaches as much as this. The emergence of legal conflict around religious symbols has opened a pernicious box of legal arguments present in many different rights regimes in Europe. This Pandora's jar, once opened, has freed a strong potential to exclude and marginalise the other. This chapter analyses the main conflict areas in regard to the presence of religious symbols in the public sphere. It questions the expansion of the public sphere and illustrates how the focus on secularism blurs the dynamics of inclusion and exclusion. Whether arguing for a greater presence for religion or greater neutrality of the public sphere, in their struggle to accommodate religious pluralism the dominant discourses fail to situate the claims of the other in an intersectional context (Vakulenko 2007). Against this

---

* The original Greek word, *pithos*, used in the story of Pandora, meant a round ceramic container and has been translated as a jar or a vase rather than a box that we know from the expression 'Pandora's box'.

backdrop, this chapter engages in a critique revealing the mechanism of reversal of the ideal of rights touched upon in the previous chapter. It argues that in the European landscape of rights not only has the majority become protected from the other in the name of pluralism, but individual legal systems have also become subjects of quasi-rights protecting them from the dissident. Legal disputes in cases concerning religious symbols have become the exemplification of Lyotard's *differend*, a dispute that cannot be resolved due to lack of a rule of judgment applicable to both arguments (Lyotard 1988). More than any other area, in encounters between law and religion these cases appear to be those 'where the plaintiff is divested of the means to argue and becomes for that reason a victim' (Lyotard 1988: 9). In parallel to the myth, the other asking for recognition in the name of pluralism has become seen as Pandora opening the jar of sorrow – a sorrow for which she becomes culpable (Phipps 1988).

6.1 The origins of the jar of sorrows

The origins of this contemporary European Pandora's jar can be traced back to the famous 'Affaire du foulard' analysed by multiple scholars over recent years (Freedman 2004; Gey 2005; Gunn 2004, 2005a; Wing and Smith 2006; Benhabib 2010; Joppke 2007; Simmons 2011). The interest of law in religious head-covering was initiated in 1989 when three girls in Creil refused to remove their hijabs at a state school. This refusal eventually led to their expulsion and the heat of legal debate brought the issue before the Conseil d'État. The Conseil was consulted as the body responsible for protecting individual liberties and freedoms. Having examined school regulations banning religious head-covering in schools the Conseil expressed the opinion that *laïcité* in state education ought to be understood so as to allow students to express and manifest their religious beliefs in schools, while respecting pluralism and the freedom of others.[1] But the discussion did not end with the words of the Conseil. On the contrary, it became vivid and more intense and questioned the pluralistic approach of the Conseil (Wing and Smith 2006). In these debates the voice of the other was gradually hushed, made minor (Wing and Smith 2006; Simmons 2011) and eventually nearly eliminated. In rendering her position irrelevant she became no more than a silenced minority. At the same time as becoming irrelevant, recognition of the other was put in opposition to the majority tradition, in this case *laïcité*, a distinct version of French secularism (Saunders 2009). In discussion of religious symbols it also became a substitute for other legal principles, among others equality (Gey 2005) and gender equality (Baines 1996).

Treating *laïcité* as a matter of national interest, President Chirac of France created the Stasi Commission to study the issue. The tasks assigned to the commission were summarised as 'conducting an analysis of the principle of *laïcité* in the Republic'.[2] At the same time French politicians have referred to *laïcité* as the

---

[1] Conseil d'État no. 346893, 27 November 1989.
[2] Decret no. 2003-607, 3 July 2003.

basis for religious respect and tolerance and the foundation of French democracy and a non-negotiable principle. In his address to the nation in 2003, Chirac underlined that:

> It is the neutrality of the public sphere which enables the harmonious existence side by side of different religions. Like all freedoms, the freedom to express one's faith can only have limits in the freedom of others, and in the compliance with rules of life in society. Religious freedom, which our country respects and protects, must not be abused, it must not call general rules into question, and it must not infringe the freedom of belief of others. This subtle, precious and fragile balance, constructed patiently over decades, is ensured by respect for the principle of secularism…. This is why it is included in Article 1 of our constitution. This is why it is not negotiable.[3]

Laïcité as a legal tradition of the majority became a symbol of a consensus equal to religious pluralism. But its content and shape became static and no longer negotiable in the assumption that it was negotiated by the 'reasonable' in their effort to include everyone. Precisely as Lyotard had warned, consensus became synonymous with a component of a system (Lyotard 1984) that is far from the idea of inclusion. The other was not only hushed, denied agency and placed between two dominant male powers trying to control her or rescue her (Simmons 2011). She was first and foremost placed in opposition to the system. She became a dissident seen as no more than a rebel attempting to undermine the hegemonic tradition. Subsequently she became synonymous with Islamic fundamentalism (Gunn 2005a) and thus deemed unreasonable and excluded from processes of negotiating the 'common' good. A woman choosing a religious dress code was equated with 'non-democratic' and structural religion and put against another institutional structure, namely constitutional and 'democratic' *laïcité*. Therefore in balancing between secularism and religion the arguments of women on their religious precepts were simply overturned and considered irrelevant (Wing and Smith 2006). Equal liberty of women to practise their religion placed in opposition to their emancipation (Motha 2007). After the Commission report had been issued, the National Assembly adopted the law on secularity and conspicuous religious symbols in schools.[4] The law banned wearing 'conspicuous religious symbols in schools' and mainly targeted girls wearing various Islamic head-covering garments, usually referred to as 'headscarves'. The findings of the Commission referred primarily to 'Muslim girls' and concentrated on the examples of girls who were forced to wear a headscarf by their religious community.[5] This interpretation

---

[3] 'Chirac on the secular society', BBC News, 18 December 2003.
[4] Loi no. 2004-228 du 15 mars 2004 encadrant, en application du principe de laïcité, le port de signes ou de tenues manifestant une appartenance religieuse dans les écoles, collèges et lycées publics.
[5] French National Assembly, Report no. 1381 fait au nom de la Commission des Lois Constitutionnelles, de la Législation et de l'Administration Générale de la République sur le projet de loi (no. 1378) relatif à l'application du principe de laïcité dans les écoles, collèges et lycées publics, 28 January 2004.

constructed a generalised image of Islam and equated religious perceptions of normativity with intolerance and discrimination.

All of these steps in creating the Pandora's jar of sorrows followed the logic of exclusion and creating the *differend*. First of all, the one who stood in opposition to the tradition was a priori deemed 'extremist'. As an extremist, she was quickly assumed to deny all aspects of the system, including gender equality. And if her concept of gender equality included Islamic modesty, she was presumed to be no more than a victim of 'fundamentalist' force, in accordance with the conviction that no reasonable citizen could dispute the shape of such pre-agreed principles. Through this mechanism of exclusion the state and the other began speaking in different voices. Instead of the question 'Why do you choose to wear religious dress code?', the state began its interrogation with 'Why do you choose to undermine our system?' In excluding the other from the universal, the state in the name of 'we, the French people', authorised its law in the name of a single 'we' concealing heterogeneity (Lyotard 1988). The 'we' and the other became separate in the name of constitutional principles. This separation then authorised creation of norms that obliged 'her', but not 'us'. These norms were not aimed at the universal 'we' but for the repudiated other (Lyotard 1988, 98–9).

6.2 Framing the European Pandora

The 'we' and 'they' logic typical of the traditionally conceived community of a nation state based on homogeneity rather than difference seemed unlikely to become a 'European' matter. Many believed in the potential of human rights to relieve the injustice suffered by the other (Benhabib 2004) and bring back the logic of inclusion. It came as a bitter disappointment when the body frequently believed to be at the service of the justice of the other stood in protection of the hegemonic system in the very same way in which the Stasi Commission did. When Swiss national Lucia Dahlab, Turkish nationals Leyla Şahin and Şefika Köse and French nationals Belgin Dogru and S.A.S. brought claims of infringement of their right to manifest their religion under Article 9 of the European Convention on Human Rights (ECHR),[6] the Court held that institutional policies prohibiting the wearing of hijabs in schools and universities were compliant with democratic principles and met the requirements of proportionality and necessity.

The argumentation of multiple commentators writing on these decisions pointed out, among other matters, the discriminatory nature of secularism (Gunn 2005b), the denial of women's agency (Evans 2006), the homogeneous and narrow

---

[6] *Dahlab* v. *Switzerland*, European Court of Human Rights, Decision, Application No. 42393/98, 15 February 2001; *Leyla Şahin* v. *Turkey*, European Court of Human Rights, Grand Chamber Judgment, Application No. 44774/98, 10 November 2005; *Şefika Köse and 93 Others* v. *Turkey*, European Court of Human Rights, Decision, Application No. 26625/02, 24 January 2006; *Dogru* v. *France*, European Court of Human Rights, Judgment, Application No. 27058/05, 4 March 2009; *S.A.S.* v. *France*, European Court of Human Rights, Judgment, Application No. 43835/11, 1 July 2014.

image of gender equality (Rebouche 2008) and the essentialising image of Islam
(Meerschaut and Gutwirth 2008), in particular in its relations to gender equality
(Marshall 2008). While it may appear that these multiple analyses have exhausted
the potential to criticise the finding of the Court, two mechanisms often remained
overlooked. Rather than simply creating a 'secular sphere' or balancing of conflicting rights (McGoldrick 2006), all of these judgments first and foremost maintained and reinforced the juxtaposition of the other *vis-à-vis* the constitutional
system in question (Gozdecka and Jackson 2011). They also gradually rooted the
legitimacy of rights solely in the respective constitutional systems. Instead of maintaining the distinct quality of human rights as instruments for relieving injustice
and protecting the other from the dominant system, rights became an instrument
of positivised law serving the hegemonic systems in question (Douzinas 2000).
They became preoccupied with legal procedures, political traditions and historical
contingencies losing their critical distance from law (Douzinas 2000, 344). They
became wound up in the 'ugly dealings' of politics and the state revealing the original precariousness of peace based on rights (Levinas 1994).

In all of these cases, just like the national authorities, the ECtHR constructed a negative image of the hijab and similar religious garments as symbols
non-compliant with the values of European democracies. As early as the case of
Dahlab, the other became hushed and disciplined for her allegedly 'fundamentalist' position. The Court framed her as a dissident standing in contravention of
multiple democratic principles and a threat to the rights of the majority:

> [T]he applicant's pupils were aged between four and eight, an age at which
> children wonder about many things and are also more easily influenced than
> older pupils. In those circumstances, it cannot be denied outright that the
> wearing of a headscarf might have some kind of proselytizing effect, seeing
> that it appears to be imposed on women by a precept which is laid down in
> the Koran and which, as the Federal Court noted, is hard to square with the
> principle of gender equality. It therefore appears difficult to reconcile the
> wearing of an Islamic headscarf with the message of tolerance, respect for
> others and, above all, equality and non-discrimination that all teachers in a
> democratic society must convey to their pupils.[7]

Her freedom was limited in the name of protecting the rights and freedoms of
others, recognised by the Convention as a permitted exception. The exception,
however, was justified by abstract rather than actual rights. 'Proper' proselytism had previously been affirmed as an important part of manifestation of religion,[8] so the proselytising effect could hardly be the core reason for the limitation,

---

[7] *Dahlab* v. *Switzerland*, para.13.
[8] *Kokkinakis* v. *Greece*, European Court of Human Rights, Judgment, Application No. 14307/88, 25
May 1993, para. 48.

especially in the absence of any complaint against Lucia Dahlab. It was instead the very understanding of religious pluralism based on the old-fashioned reading of tolerance described earlier that led the Court to uphold the limitation of the applicant's freedom. Tolerance once more became read as no more than maintaining the status quo of the majority who can barely so much as 'tolerate' the dissident. Adopting a generalised image of Islam (Evans 2006) and equating the applicant's religious perceptions of normativity with intolerance and discrimination, the Court framed the applicant's otherness as a universal and radical wrong. In their fear of this wrong, the majority, seen as the guardians and defenders of 'tolerance', were presented as the victims of potential injustice inflicted by the dissident. This reading of tolerance had no roots other than hatred of the inappropriate (Adorno 1951). Stereotypical images of 'inappropriateness' created a strong sense of negative 'otherness'. The Court constructed Islam as static and interventionist and always incompatible with both the Convention and by extension the constitutional values of the Member States (Meerschaut and Gutwirth 2008). Meanwhile religion as part of the identity of the other appealing for recognition was ignored in favour of a perception of religion as a homogeneous organising principle of society (Vakulenko 2007). It became seen as a principle standing in firm opposition to the analogical organising principles of the majority – the respective constitutional systems.

These perspectives adopted in the legal reasoning of the ECtHR led to a simple juxtaposition of Islam versus constitutional principles and invoked a wide margin of appreciation in regulating matters of law and religion. Using two different incommensurable phrases governed by different logic (Lyotard 1988), the Court put them together in creating a *differend*, in which the other could only be silenced in an asymmetric relationship with a powerful and anonymous 'we' standing behind constitutional principles. To create an illusionary common platform for this argument the constitutional system was equated with 'neutrality' in order to 'throw a bridge over the abyss between heterogeneous phrases' (Lyotard 1988). In throwing that bridge, neutrality and pluralism were reduced to the status quo, having little to do with recognition or inclusion of the other. The ECtHR decided that the case of *Dahlab* was manifestly ill-founded and underlined:

> [T]he Court notes that the Federal Court held that the measure by which the applicant was prohibited, purely in the context of her activities as a teacher, from wearing a headscarf was justified by the potential interference with the religious beliefs of her pupils at the school and the pupils' parents, and by the breach of the principle of denominational neutrality in schools.[9]

As mentioned earlier, the lack of any complaint from parents against Lucia Dahlab confirms that the ECtHR's dismissal of the case was primarily based on protecting the denominational neutrality of the state as a constitutional principle.

---

[9] *Dahlab* v. *Switzerland*, para. 12.

It did not aid substantive pluralism or neutrality in any other way than by specu-
lative protection of the potential beliefs of those who 'might be' proselytised – the
anonymous and universal 'we'.

The same logic was followed in *Şahin*, where a prohibition on wearing a hijab
in a Turkish university was found to be in compliance with the constitutional principle of secularism and upheld by the ECtHR. Here the Court referred even less
to the applicant's rights and extensively elaborated on the Turkish constitutional
principle of secularism and the entitlement of local authorities to preserve the
principle:

> Having regard to the above background, it is the principle of secularism, as
> elucidated by the Constitutional Court, which is the paramount consideration
> underlying the ban on the wearing of religious symbols in universities. In such
> context, where the values of pluralism, respect for others and, in particular,
> equality before the law of men and women are being taught and applied in
> practice, it is understandable that the relevant authorities should wish to pre-
> serve the secular nature of the institution concerned and so consider it con-
> trary to such values to allow religious attire, including, as in the present case,
> the Islamic headscarf.[10]

This asymmetry created a quasi-right of the state to preserve its order. Creation of
the quasi-right of the state found its culmination in the case of *Şefika Köse*. In this
case, which is less frequently debated than *Şahin* or *Dahlab*, the ECtHR upheld a
prohibition on wearing headscarves in Turkish Muslim state-funded Imam-Hatip
Secondary Schools. In its decision the Court relied similarly on the domestic constitutional principle of secularism and disregarded the actual beliefs of the pupils,
who were all adherents of Islam:

> In conclusion, the Court finds that the restriction in issue and the related
> measures were justified in principle and proportionate to the pursued aims
> of protecting the rights and freedoms of others, preventing disorder and pre-
> serving the neutrality of secondary education.[11]

In this case recognition of the other played a minor role. The right of the applicant
was asymmetrically positioned against a blanket policy and any act of balancing
between the two was a priori dismissed. This asymmetry was reinforced by the
affirmation of the Court that it was 'sufficient to note that both the parents and the
pupils were informed of the consequences of not obeying the rules'.[12] Analogically
in *Dogru* the Court once more refused to examine compliance of the constitutional
principle of secularism with freedom of religion as entrenched in the Convention

---

[10] *Şahin* v. *Turkey*, para.1.
[11] *Şefika Köse* v. *Turkey*, para.1.
[12] *Ibid.*, para. 1.

and instead emphasised that in the French context when the applicant was forbidden to wear a headscarf while attending physical education classes:

> [T]he purpose of that restriction on manifesting a religious conviction was to adhere to the requirements of secularism in state schools, as interpreted by the Conseil d'État in its opinion of 27 November 1989 and its subsequent case-law and by the various ministerial circulars issued on the subject.[13]

Consequently, the Court referred to its best-known tool used for preserving the legal interests of the state, namely the 'wide margin of appreciation'. In balancing between constitutional principles the arguments of the applicants regarding their religious precepts were simply overturned and considered irrelevant. The state, now equipped with the quasi-right to defend its constitutional principles, was put in the position of one whose rights were infringed by the dissident other. This became particularly evident in *Şefika Köse*, whose claim was not even seriously considered on the ground of her having been warned of the consequences of not respecting the 'rights' of the state. The creation of this problematic asymmetry between the other and the national system prevented the Court from elaborating on the intersectional interaction between gender, religion and identity (Vakulenko 2007). Simmons recalls, paraphrasing Benhabib (2004), that such an asymmetry results in the minority's need to justify itself without an analogous expectation from the system in question to question its own assumptions regarding its approach to minorities (Simmons 2011):

> Those whose fundamental rights are being infringed must justify why they wish to do something different from the majority and must provide an alternative means to meet the state's compelling interests.

The other from these stories can be captured in the metaphor of Pandora. Endowed with a jar promising rights and pluralism, she dares to open it in the hope of seeing pluralism embodied in practice. Sadly, instead of these promised gifts all she receives is blame for her curiosity and the accusation of being the source of 'intolerance', misery and sorrow. The European Pandora and her jar are a result of the flawed logic of the *differend*, where the bridge of 'neutrality' or 'secularism' was thrown to disguise the asymmetry between 'we' and 'her' and between two incompatible legal discourses – that of state interests and that of recognition.

6.3 The jar wide open: expansion of the law's obsession with symbols

The perception of the incompatibility of a religious head-covering with human rights and principles of equality and democracy eventually led to the law's

---

[13] *Dogru* v. *France*, para. 1.

obsession with 'fearful symbols' (Gunn 2005a). The obsession did not stop either at state schools or at secular universities. The expulsion of religious symbols from an extremely broadly conceived public sphere began affecting one group of believers in particular. Growing Islamophobia resulted in two main developments sanctioned by the democratic support of populations of a few European states – the emergence of the minaret ban in Switzerland and the spread of so-called burqua bans first in France, then Belgium and more recently in Italy. The establishment of majoritarian norms excluding the differently religious other disguised the discrepancy between 'we' and 'them' with the paradigm of the 'secular public sphere', which as described in the chapters of Part I examining the principles of religious pluralism eventually became an independent legal paradigm assigned Europe-wide importance.

Although the notion of the public sphere is most frequently understood as the political public sphere (Arendt 1958; Rawls 2005; Habermas 1991), its understanding has been broadened to encompass nearly every aspect of it. It began encompassing not only the sphere of authority but also what Taylor distinguishes as spheres of access and appearance:

> There seem to be two main semantic axes along which the term public is used. The first connects public to what affects the whole community ('public affairs') or the management of these affairs ('public authority'). The second makes publicity a matter of access ('This park is open to the public') or appearance ('The news has been made public').
>
> (Taylor 2003)

And it was primarily the sphere of access from which the other became expelled. In 2009 a Swiss referendum following an Islamophobic campaign democratically sanctioned a ban on the construction of minarets. The referendum changed the supreme legal source of the state – the Constitution of Switzerland itself. Article 72 on church and state nowadays reads under Section 3: 'The building of minarets is prohibited.'[14] Despite the existence of an abundance of church towers present in nearly every city, town and village of Switzerland, the existence of four minarets resulted in a ban on construction dictated by the protection of 'local culture'.[15]

Like minaret bans, the emergence of so-called 'burqua bans' was aimed at targeting the same group of believers. In 2011 France passed a law banning concealment of the face in public.[16] According to the law, wearing clothing concealing one's face in a public space is punishable by either a maximum €150 fine or by an obligation to take a class on the meaning of citizenship. It may also result in both.

---

[14] Constitution of Switzerland, 18 April 1999, Amendment of 29 November 2009.
[15] Cumming-Bruce and Erlanger 2009.
[16] Loi 2010-1192 du 11 octobre 2010 interdisant la dissimulation du visage dans l'espace public (Law 2010-1192 of 11 October 2010 Banning Concealment of the Face in Public Space).

Permitted exceptions include instances where 'clothing is prescribed or authorised by legislative or regulatory provisions, is authorised to protect the anonymity of the person concerned, is justified for health reasons or on professional grounds, or is part of sporting, artistic activity or traditional festivities or events'.[17] The broad scope of exceptions suggests that the ban is strictly aimed at women wearing full face veiling (Nanwani 2011). After entering into force the law was executed by detaining a few women wearing full veiling. Similar bans emerged soon afterwards in Belgium. All laws dealing with concealment of the face include similar provisions and have been passed with the support of democratically elected parliaments.

These developments not only expanded the understanding of the public sphere but clearly positioned the other *vis-à-vis* the dominant axiom of the majority (Deleuze and Guattari 1980) and its legal system. The law's obsession with religious symbols purged the signs of otherness from public view. This purging happened no longer for protection of the rights of the majority but purely with the aim of excluding the other by the will of the majority. In the recent case of *S.A.S. v. France* challenging these developments, the very nature of pluralism was multiple times equated with the government's right to control the conditions of 'living together'.[18] In this latest judgment the Court even more strongly insisted on the necessity of preserving pluralism and revoked its multiple previous findings for instance on the necessity of protecting gender equality, considering them deeply flawed. It even explicitly defined pluralism as the necessity for preventing abuse of the dominant position of the majority.[19] Against this seemingly open pluralistic framework it disappointingly found that:

> [H]aving regard in particular to the breadth of the margin of appreciation afforded to the respondent State in the present case, the Court finds that the ban imposed by the Law of 11 October 2010 can be regarded as proportionate to the aim pursued, namely the preservation of the conditions of 'living together' as an element of the 'protection of the rights and freedoms of others'.[20]

The judgment equated majoritarian will with the 'rights and freedoms of others' without specifying what element other than perceived discomfort in social relations caused by the face-covering infringed these rights and what rights those were.[21] This continuing line of judicial reasoning appears to be repeatedly balancing between the rights of the majority and minority by positioning the other as an element foreign to the status quo. In this status quo she has no place and is not

---

[17] *Ibid.*, at Article 2.2.
[18] *S.A.S. v. France*, para. 141.
[19] *Ibid.*, para. 128.
[20] *Ibid.*, para. 157.
[21] *Ibid.*, para. 122.

seen as a believer or the co-creator of pluralism but as an enigmatic 'extremist' who poses a danger or at least causes discomfort to the majoritarian consensus. Instead of asking how the rights of the other can change the conditions of 'living together', a broad, abstract notion of the 'public sphere' sweeps the rights of the other under cover of a blanket of an undefined freedom of the majority entrenched in the constitutional axiom or the right to create social order. This approach not only silences the minority (Simmons 2011) but exemplifies Luxemburg's fear that freedom of the majority has no liberating potential at all. Quite the contrary, it has a potential for enslaving those in a minority (Luxemburg 1918) by equating freedom with creating order. Expulsion of the other from public view relieved the threat to majoritarian axioms but at the same time widened the gap between the majority and the minority. The modest demand of the minority to express and define itself was hampered by the 'impotence' of the dominant axiom to accommodate the particular rather than the universal (Deleuze and Guattari 1980, 471). The fixed and static axiom of the majority became embedded in the notion of a 'neutral' or 'secular', or in the latest judgment 'comfortable', public sphere that the other was prevented from defining. The law's obsession with symbols not only silenced her. It rendered her invisible and standing not simply in opposition to the dominant system, but in its darkest shadow. She became a dissident, a contestant, a harbinger of social discomfort even when her claims were assessed without instant dismissal.

And the body designed for protection of the other, the ECtHR, more than once disappointed those hoping for recognition of discrimination. The Court dismissed not only the *S.A.S.* claim but also claims brought against the minaret ban by the Islamic community in Switzerland. Basing it on procedural grounds the Court found the complaint against the discriminatory nature of the provision inadmissible due to the fact that neither of the applicants in the two cases lodged against Switzerland envisaged building minarets in the near future.[22] Whereas the abstract interests of the majority, such as creating comfortable conditions for living together, sufficed for purging the other from public view, the others' abstract claim of discrimination, albeit more directly related to their circumstances, was not sufficient for recognition.

6.4 Did any hope remain? Not simply secularism but the 'other' truly other

In his telling of Pandora's tale, Hesiod insists that one element was left after the jar of sorrows had been opened – hope. In response to the latest developments in the area of law and religion in Europe many have hoped that the law's preoccupation with religious symbols signifies no more than an Islamophobia that

---

22 *Oudri v. Switzerland*, European Court of Human Rights, Decision, Application No. 65840/09, 28 June 2011; *Ligue des Musulmans de Suisse and Others v. Switzerland*, Application No. 66274/09, 28 June 2011.

can be curtailed and reversed. After all, as Habermas has attempted to convince us, liberalism, if properly understood, protects rather than curtails everybody's rights (Habermas 2000). A misinterpretation amounting to exclusion of a certain group could therefore be targeted and prevented. It is precisely that hope that is envisioned in Recommendation 1927 (2010), 'Islam, Islamism and Islamophobia in Europe'. It hopes to save liberalism from totalising and universalising discourses focusing on one more group facing discrimination and intolerance.

There was a hope that this discrimination is no more than a result of the spread of secularism as a dominant legal paradigm in the sphere of law and religion. Thus it came as a surprise to many that the revised case of *Lautsi* concerning another instance of display of religious symbols further confused the picture of the relationship of law and religion with symbols. Disguised in the paradigm of 'a secular public sphere', which after the cases concerning religious dress codes became a dominant axiom of its own, the revised *Lautsi* attempted to rescue this sphere from forceful 'secularisation'. In that desperate attempt to maintain the discourse within the paradigms of secularism, the crucifix, which this time was the subject of legal debate, became defined as an 'essentially passive' and 'secular' symbol. This artificial classification of a clearly religious symbol as 'secular' reveals the highly problematic nature of 'secularism' as a universal paradigm in the examination of issues surrounding law and religion.

The question of crucifixes in state schools received wide publicity after the revised decision of the ECtHR in the case of *Lautsi* v. *Italy*.[23] The case was introduced to the Court in 2008 and questioned the mandatory display of crucifixes in Italian schools prescribed by Royal Decree no. 1297 of 1928 listing crucifixes as a necessary item of classroom equipment. The Decree was issued 20 years before adoption of the 1948 Constitution establishing the separation of the state and the Catholic Church and amending the force of Lateran Pacts originally securing a privileged position for the Catholic Church. In the legal dispute that emerged around the obligatory display, Ms Soile Lautsi, an atheist of Finnish origin, argued that the obligatory display of a crucifix violated the right to freedom of religion of her non-religious children under Article 9 of the ECHR and her right as a parent to guarantee education of her children in conformity with their own convictions under Article 2 of Protocol 1 to the ECHR.[24] The government, on the other hand, caught up in defence of the paradigm of secularism, asserted that the display of crucifixes did not undermine the secular foundations of the state.[25]

In the first instance the Chamber of the ECtHR found, similarly to the reasoning in *Dahlab*, that the presence of a crucifix may easily be interpreted as a

[23] *Lautsi* v. *Italy*, European Court of Human Rights, Grand Chamber Judgment, Application No. 30814/06, 18 March 2011.
[24] *Lautsi* v. *Italy*, Chamber Judgment, 3 November 2009, paras 30–3.
[25] *Ibid.*, at paras 34–44.

religious sign marking the school environment with a particular religion[26] and found a violation of Article 9 in conjunction with Article 2 Protocol 1.

But the response to the judgment brought first of all criticism focusing on similar aspects as had criticism of the judgments concerning Islamic religious dress. The Court was criticised for pairing religious pluralism with neutrality and removal of religion from the public sphere and public expression (Calo 2011). Additionally, as if following criticism of the emerging rights empire (Douzinas 2007), the ECtHR was also reproached for acting as an apodictic 'Oracle'. It was described as disrespectful to the constitutional system of Italy and refusing to be a dialogical partner with the Member States (Weiler 2010). Unsettlingly, while embracing these two emancipatory discourses the Court came to a conclusion that strengthened the distinction between the private and the public, reinforced the dominant paradigms in analyses of freedom of religion and pushed the other even deeper into her private sphere, leaving her this time not only voiceless but ridiculed. With no attention paid to the dynamic between the dominant axiom and the minoritarian position, the judgment fossilised previous deconstruction and critique into a new form of totalising grand narrative.

In its hope to escape three major accusations: that of spreading secularism, that of judicial activism and that of being no more than an agent of a globalised rights empire, the Grand Chamber overturned the previous findings on 18 March 2011 by deciding that Ms Lautsi's rights were not violated by the presence of crucifixes in Italian schools.

Embarking on an analysis from the middle of the bridge of 'secularism' thrown over the abyss between the arguments of majority and minority, the bridge itself became the key argument. The Court focused on the 'duty of neutrality and impartiality', retaining a stringent division between the private and public spheres and this time underlining considerable differences in European regulation of the presence of religious symbols in the public sphere. At the same time, it focused little on interpretation of the limitations stemming from the demands of the public sphere allowed under the Convention and their impact on the very freedom of the applicant and its so-called *forum internum* (Evans 2001). It is almost shocking that while embracing the narrative of 'religious pluralism', the Court made so little effort to ensure that the goals of pluralism understood as the equal right of religious and non-religious individuals to public religious or non-religious expression (Calo 2011) were met. Instead the focus remained one-sided and elaborated in great detail on abstractly and generally understood concepts of 'secularism' and 'neutrality'. The judgment attempted to respond to the critique of secularism by bringing religious symbols back into the public sphere and making an explicitly religious tradition appear secular.

To the disillusionment of those arguing for greater recognition of difference, the Court, while declaring public religious expression to be 'secular', did little to positively endorse the personal beliefs of the applicant (Annicchino 2011). Instead

[26] *Ibid.*, at para. 55.

some of the judges expressed hostility to them. Judge Bonello explicitly referred to Ms Lautsi as a dissident aiming at destruction of the system:

> May it please Ms Lautsi, in her own name and on behalf of secularism, not to enlist the services of this Court to ensure the suppression of the Italian school calendar, another Christian-cultural heritage that has survived the centuries without any evidence of irreparable harm to the progress of freedom, emancipation, democracy and civilisation.[27]

Read together with the religious head-covering cases, the revised *Lautsi* pushed the religious other deeper into her private sphere. In an acrobatic effort to make secularism more 'religion friendly' and religion more 'secular', it forced a differently religious other to adjust his or her religious or non-religious expression to the dominant symbolism of public institutions. Reading the cases on religious symbols together, it becomes evident that the differently religious other is either required to adjust to a religiously aseptic environment or to a public sphere heavily influenced by the symbolism of the dominant faith. As the judgment underlines, the other is confined to the private sphere:

> [T]he ... applicant retained in full her right as a parent to enlighten and advise her children, to exercise in their regard her natural functions as educator and to guide them on path in line with her own philosophical convictions.[28]

The interpretation applied in *Dahlab* and *Lautsi* reversed the entitlement of human rights holders and human rights duty bearers. While religious and non-religious persons seem to have duties to adjust to institutions, at the same time keeping to their personal beliefs in private, institutions seem to have freedom to express their religious or secular tradition, almost as if they were human rights holders themselves.

The objective of responding to the critique of secularisation of the public sphere in combination with the objective of avoiding an imperialistic tone (Weiler 2010) resulted in the focus of the ECtHR's argument on problems of sovereignty and competences leading to even further reinforcement of the privileges of the state. It diminished the importance of the voice of the other, positioned her in opposition to the constitutional system and fossilised a non-negotiable 'tradition'. As if in response to Weiler's criticism of having to respect constitutional orders, the Court refrained from taking any position in the debate between domestic Courts concerning the very validity of the law in question and the meaning of the crucifix[29] and even went as far as denying its own legitimacy to examine the

---

[27] *Lautsi* v. *Italy*, Concurring opinion of Judge Bonello, p. 39.

[28] *Lautsi* v. *Italy*, Grand Chamber, at para. 75.

[29] *Ibid.*

educational curriculum. In sharp contrast to cases such as *Folgerø*[30] and *Zengin*,[31] where just such an examination was undertaken by the Court, the *Lautsi* judgment underlined that it is 'not for the Court to rule on such questions'.[32] In the judgment the Court referred very little to its own jurisprudence and summarised the striking similarity of the head-covering cases in a very thin paragraph finding the cases 'entirely different'.[33] As a result the Court emerged as a judicial body concerned primarily with the constitutional tradition and the identity of the Member States.

The other remained completely out of focus in favour of the culturally and constitutionally homogeneous identity of the Member States. Whereas the other is called upon by Judge Bonello to question her motivation in opposing the system, the system itself is freed from any obligation for any such self-examination. The assumption that an old decree from another era embodies democratic expression of the constitutional will of the people of Italy fossilised the dominant axiom without reflecting on its own capability for redefinition and regardless of its impact on the other.[34] Rather than rescuing the constitutional system from the force of the homogenising rights empire, it reinforced national micro-universalism blind to difference (Braidotti 2006). The objective of achieving deeper embeddedness in national systems (Helfer 2008) and securing a more differentiated approach depending on the circumstances and agents targeted (Besson 2006), instead of contextualising the position of the other, turned the paradigms of judicial reasoning into preoccupation with sovereignty and competences. The Court elaborated extensively on interpretation of the margin of appreciation, the role of consensus and even more – the role of tradition. The Court also expanded the margin of appreciation to a decision whether or not to perpetuate a tradition, seeing it as a privilege of the Contracting States in 'determining the steps to be taken to ensure compliance with the Convention with due regard to the needs and resources of the community and of individuals'.[35]

As Adorno and Horkheimer warned, the project of Enlightenment to liberate people from the structures of authority has the tragic quality of developing new universalisms replacing the old. This is equally true of human rights and striving for recognition: these become no more than established myths replacing old myths, eventually leading to totalitarian approaches (Horkheimer and Adorno 1944). The original force of human rights, lying in their potential to relieve injustice, becomes lost. The utopian call of law for justice, embedded in the ideal of protecting the individual from oppression, becomes secondary. Positivisation of law takes over and strips human rights of their utopian goals (Douzinas 2000).

---

[30]   *Folgerø and others* v. *Norway*, European Court of Human Rights, Judgment, Application No. 15472/02, 29 June 2007.

[31]   *Hasan and Eylem Zengin* v. *Turkey*, European Court of Human Rights, Judgment, Application No. 1448/04, 9 October 2007.

[32]   *Ibid.*, para. 62.

[33]   *Ibid.*

[34]   *Lautsi* v. *Italy*, Grand Chamber, Dissenting Opinion of Judges Maliverni and Kalaydjieva, para. 1.

[35]   *Ibid.*

The judgments in the cases concerning religious symbols are characterised by increasingly positivistic interpretation, almost reversing the utopian call of rights for justice. It is not the religious or non-religious individual that is protected from the domination of the system, but the systems that become protected from the individual. In Douzinas's words:

> Experience tells us, however, that when the fear of the other … becomes their institutional logic, human rights lose their protective value against the state … positivised human rights and legalised desire, based on the fear of the other, coincide and their world and the self-creating potential of existential freedom is distinguished.
>
> (Douzinas 2000, 376)

Pandora's jar appears to be empty even of hope when fear of the other strongly dominates human rights jurisprudence. And this fear in combination with positivistic and legitimacy-driven interpretation embody the symptoms of the end of rights: symptoms occurring despite the best efforts aimed at their prevention.

6.5 Beyond hope: disillusionment with law's objectivity and the universal nature of critique

Regulation of religious symbols in Europe once more exposes disillusionment with the objectivity of the law and its underlying principles. Contra the hopes of positivists, law can never become an objective system separated neatly from the structures of power. Whether it is constitutional law or human rights law, law has a natural tendency to become a system of power based on a total system of explanation and justification (Douzinas, Warrington and McVeigh 1993). Eventually, rights themselves become mere fetishes in which the other, far from being saved from injustice, perversely becomes the one to shoulder the blame for it.

The tale of religious symbols illustrates two distinct cases of the other embedded in their very different respective legal systems. It discloses the sad truth that the discourse of religious pluralism remains nothing more than another totalising grand narrative, an empty fetish of human rights systems. A narrative in which the other remains insulated, subsequently detached and eventually contrasted with the legal system's dominant power erected on society's dominant axioms. Religious pluralism as an ideal, as a utopian call for the justice of the other, remains no more than a facade which may be exploited for the purpose of detaching the other and turning her into a dissident.

This Pandora's tale of religious symbols may also serve as a warning to the critics themselves. Critique that is blind to difference and homogenises the other into preconceived universalisms may, instead of the post-modern task of bringing out the consequences of grand narratives for legal subjects (Douzinas, Warrington and McVeigh 1993), itself become a grand narrative. This critique, like law, risks becoming a totalising power that will further foster the disempowerment and insulation of those who appeal for recognition. In a fixed system of static universals the other remains other, on the margin, out of sight, silenced or ridiculed in the name of grand narratives appealing to difference and pluralism. Whether by law or by law's attempt to respond to the critique of injustice, the other remains always vulnerable. The grand narrative of pluralism is applied *in abstracto* in combination with the task of securing or relieving equally abstract secularism. Others applying for protection in the cases concerning religious symbols were eventually required to be religiously neutral and to adjust to the dominant system. Meanwhile public institutions were allowed to display secular or religious symbolism (albeit labelled 'passive') as if they were human rights bearers. The reversal of entitlement to display symbols based on their confounded classification into 'passive' or 'proselytising' signifies no more than the fear of the one who does not fit the preconceived notion of a static consensus.

In this picture the other remains a Pandora standing helplessly in front of the jar of ills and worries and is assigned the blame for their release. This Pandora's tale warns us that law may never be able to serve justice. Perhaps violence must always lie at its very core (Derrida 1992; Sarat 2001).

References

Adorno, Theodor W. 1951. *Minima Moralia: Reflections on a Damaged Life*. Verso.
Annicchino, Pasquale. 2011. 'Winning the Battle by Losing the War: The Lautsi Case and the Holy Alliance between American Conservative Evangelicals, the Russian Orthodox Church and the Vatican to Reshape European Identity.' *Religion and Human Rights* 6(3): 213–19.
Arendt, Hannah. 1958. *The Human Condition*, 2nd edn. University of Chicago Press.
Baines, Cynthia DeBula. 1996. 'L'Affaire des Foulards: Discrimination, or the Price of a Secular Public Education System.' *Vanderbilt Journal of Transnational Law* 29: 303–27.
Benhabib, Seyla. 2004. *The Rights of Others: Aliens, Residents, and Citizens*. Cambridge University Press.
Benhabib, Seyla. 2010. 'The Return of Political Theology: The Scarf Affair in Comparative Constitutional Perspective in France, Germany and Turkey.' *Philosophy & Social Criticism* 36(3–4): 451–71.
Besson, Samantha. 2006. 'The European Union and Human Rights: Towards a Post-National Human Rights Institution?' *Human Rights Law Review* 6(2): 323–60.
Braidotti, Rosi. 2006. 'The Becoming-Minoritarian of Europe.' In *Deleuze and the Contemporary World*, ed. I. Buchanan and A. Parr, 79–94. Edinburgh University Press.
Calo, Zachary R. 2011. 'Pluralism, Secularism and the European Court of Human Rights.' *Journal of Law and Religion* 26 (February): 101–20.
Cumming-Bruce, Nick and Steven Erlanger. 2009. 'Swiss Ban Building of Minarets on Mosques.' *New York Times*, 30 November, sec. International / Europe.
Deleuze, Gilles and Felix Guattari. 1980. *A Thousand Plateaus: Capitalism and Schizophrenia*. Continuum.

Derrida, Jacques. 1992. 'Force of Law: The Mystical Foundation of Authority.' In *Deconstruction and the Possibility of Justice*, ed. Drucilla Cornell, Michel Rosenfeld and David Gray Carlson, 3–67. Routledge.

Douzinas, Costas. 2000. *The End of Human Rights: Critical Legal Thought at the Turn of the Century*. Hart Publishing.

Douzinas, Costas. 2007. *Human Rights and Empire: The Political Philosophy of Cosmopolitanism*. Routledge.

Douzinas, Costas, Ronnie Warrington and Shaun McVeigh. 1993. *Postmodern Jurisprudence: The Law of Text in the Texts of Law*. Routledge.

Evans, Carolyn. 2001. *Freedom of Religion under the European Convention on Human Rights*. Oxford University Press.

Evans, Carolyn. 2006. 'The Islamic Scarf in the European Court of Human Rights.' *Melbourne Journal of International Law* 7: 52–73.

Freedman, Jane. 2004. 'Secularism as a Barrier to Integration? The French Dilemma.' *International Migration* 42(3): 5–27.

Gey, Steven G. 2005. 'Free Will, Religious Liberty, and a Partial Defense of the French Approach to Religious Expression in Public Schools.' *Houston Law Review* 42: 1–8-.

Gozdecka, Dorota A. and Amy R. Jackson. 2011. 'Caught between Different Legal Pluralisms: Women Who Wear Islamic Dress as the Religious "Other" in European Rights Discourses.' *Journal of Legal Pluralism and Unofficial Law* 64: 91–120.

Gunn, T. Jeremy. 2004. 'Religious Freedom and Laïcité: A Comparison of the United States and France.' *Brigham Young University Law Review* 2004: 419–506.

Gunn, T. Jeremy. 2005a. 'Fearful Symbols: The Islamic Headscarf and the European Court of Human Rights.' Strasbourg Consortium: Freedom of Conscience and Religion at the European Court of Human Rights.

Gunn, T. Jeremy. 2005b. 'French Secularism as Utopia and Myth.' *Houston Law Review* 42: 81–102.

Habermas, Jürgen. 1991. *The Structural Transformation of the Public Sphere: An Inquiry into a Category of Bourgois Society*. MIT Press.

Habermas, Jürgen. 2000. *The Inclusion of the Other: Studies in Political Theory*, ed. Ciaran P. Cronin and Pablo De Greiff, repr. MIT Press.

Helfer, Laurence R. 2008. 'Redesigning the European Court of Human Rights: Embeddedness as a Deep Structural Principle of the European Human Rights Regime.' *European Journal of International Law* 19(1): 125–59.

Horkheimer, Max and Theodor W. Adorno. 1944. *Dialectic of Enlightenment: Philosophical Fragments*. Stanford University Press.

Joppke, C. 2007. 'State Neutrality and Islamic Headscarf Laws in France and Germany.' *Theory and Society* 36(4): 313–42.

Levinas, Emmanuel. 1994. *Outside the Subject*. Stanford University Press.

Luxemburg, Rosa. 1918. *The Russian Revolution and Leninism or Marxism?* University of Michigan Press.

Lyotard, Jean-François. 1984. *The Postmodern Condition: A Report on Knowledge*. Theory and History of Literature 10. Manchester University Press.

Lyotard, Jean-François. 1988. *The Differend: Phrases in Dispute*. Theory and History of Literature 46. University of Minnesota Press.

Marshall, Jill. 2008. 'Women's Right to Autonomy and Identity in European Human Rights Law: Manifesting One's Religion.' *Res Publica* 14(3): 177–92.

McGoldrick, Dominic. 2006. *Human Rights and Religion: The Islamic Headscarf Debate in Europe.* Hart Publishing.

Meerschaut, Karen and Serge Gutwirth. 2008. 'Legal Pluralism and Islam in the Scales of the European Court of Human Rights: The Limits of Categorical Balancing.' In *Conflicts between Fundamental Rights*, ed. E. Brems, 431–65. Intersentia.

Motha, Stewart. 2007. 'Veiled Women and the Affect of Religion in Democracy.' *Journal of Law and Society* 34(1): 139–62.

Nanwani, Shaira 2011. 'The Burqa Ban: An Unreasonable Limitation on Religious Freedom or a Justifiable Restriction.' *Emory International Law Review* 25: 1431–76.

Phipps, William E. 1988. 'Eve and Pandora Contrasted.' *Theology Today* 45(1): 34–48.

Rawls, John. 2005. *Political Liberalism: Expanded Edition.* Columbia University Press.

Rebouche, Rachel. 2008. 'The Substance of Substantive Equality: Gender Equality and Turkey's Headscarf Debate.' *American University International Law Review* 24: 711–37.

Sarat, Austin. 2001. *Law, Violence, and the Possibility of Justice.* Princeton University Press.

Saunders, David. 2009. 'France on the Knife-Edge of Religion: Commemorating the Centenary of the Law of 9 December 1905 on the Separation of Church and State.' In *Secularism, Religion and Multicultural Citizenship*, ed. Geoffrey Brahm Levey and Tariq Modood, 56–81. Cambridge University Press.

Simmons, William Paul. 2011. *Human Rights Law and the Marginalized Other.* Cambridge University Press.

Taylor, Charles. 2003. *Modern Social Imaginaries.* Duke University Press.

Vakulenko, Anastasia. 2007. '"Islamic Headscarves" and the European Convention on Human Rights: An Intersectional Perspective.' *Social & Legal Studies* 16(2): 183–99.

Weiler, Joseph H. H. 2010. 'Lautsi: Crucifix in the Classroom Redux.' *European Journal of International Law/Journal Européen de Droit International* 21(1): 1–6.

Wing, Adrienne Katherine and Monica Nigh Smith. 2006. 'Critical Race Feminism Lifts the Veil? Muslim Women, France, and the Headscarf Ban.' *UC Davis Law Review* 39: 743–85.

Chapter 7

Religions and reproductive rights

Freedom changed to stone?

'My gallant Perseus, tell me by what craft, what courage, you secured the snake-tressed head.' And Agenorides told him of the place that lies, a stronghold safe below the mountain mass of icy Atlas… over rough hillsides of ruined woods he reached the Gorgones' lands, and everywhere in fields and by the road he saw the shapes of men and beasts, all changed to stone by glancing at Medusa's face.

Ovid, *Metamorphoses*, 4

The last of the myths of inclusion illustrates how reversal of the logic of rights from instruments of emancipation to instruments of power may be cemented with the help of the identity principle. The story of human rights in the context of religious pluralism and reproductive rights bears a striking resemblance to the story of the mythical Medusa. Once a beautiful maiden with wonderful tresses, Medusa was changed into one of the Gorgons in the aftermath of an unwanted affair with Poseidon in Athena's temple. Punished for her beauty and the assault on her by the God of the sea, she was transformed into a monstrous creature with snakes on her head and a deadly gaze. Beholders of Medusa's face, human or beast, were instantly turned to stone. In the story below, human rights appear like Medusa, assaulted by a possessive community to preserve established cultural power. By examining the intersections between religion and reproductive rights, this story illustrates that once rights become privileges used for the maintenance of cultural power they restrain the appeals of those struggling for emancipation from recognised and established normativities. Becoming transformed into a rigid mechanism protecting dominant normativities, like Medusa they begin turning their beholders into stone. When the emancipatory potential of rights is assaulted in favour of seeing rights as the privilege of an established community unified around religion or secularism seen as the identity principle, the difference is erased in favour of homogeneity. When that interpretation takes over the logic of rights, both religious pluralism and appeals to reproductive rights and gender equality are ignored. Instead, entitlements stemming from rights are shifted to the community, allowing it to suppress all contradiction. As a result, the landscape is no longer diverse and pluralistic but homogeneous, as around the Gorgon, surrounded by figures of stone.

7.1 Medusa's many suitors: the irresistible appeal of rights and the contest of rights principles

In many accounts of the myth, Athena's severe punishment directed at Medusa was brought on by jealousy over her beauty and seductive hair. Indeed, Medusa's beauty was so appealing that she attracted many suitors in contention for her favours, including the possessive Poseidon. Just as in the myth, rights have proved increasingly attractive to diverse claimants in legal conflicts. Their irresistible appeal has resulted in monopolising multiple legal arguments that have been framed as rights claims. As Douzinas (Douzinas 2000) and Rorty (Rorty 1998) before him have insisted, we live in a culture of rights and their appeal attracts many conflicting sides of legal arguments:

> The conflict itself is evidence of the absence or collapse of any immanent or shared value structure. In the absence of a meta-principle external to the conflict which could act as an arbiter, the importation of rights discourse is likely to strengthen the resolve of the parties and make them less amenable to negotiation or compromise, as it removes the fight from the terrain of warring interests into that of allegedly absolute truths and uncompromising entitlements.... The use of rights discourse to describe normatively the conflict or a set of claims is a limited way of narrativising the situation.
>
> (Douzinas 2000, 251)

Sometimes the attractiveness of rights, just like Medusa's beautiful locks, appeals to suitors whose arguments, despite the appeal to rights, are based on their established interests rather than emancipation claims. When both sides of a legal argument appeal to rights to protect their established privileges, the conflict may result in creation of general statements about rights that describe any claim as a rights claim and bring nothing more than a decrease in sympathy for the suffering (Douzinas 2000, 253). After all, when everything is a matter of rights and everyone has a claim to them, rights become equally valid claims for those in power and those marginalised. Levinas warned against this conceptualisation of rights and envisioned that rights must change into power claims when approached as incontestable features of autonomy and privileges of the self instead of duties to alterity. As a consequence of using rights to protect entitlements, justice becomes no more than a battle of autonomies that must eventually be resolved in favour of the powerful. As will be illustrated in later chapters, in 'The Rights of Man and the Rights of the Other' Levinas explicitly envisioned such conflict fuelled by equating a person with an object in a constant comparison of entitlements (Levinas 1994). In that perpetual conflict, the peace that rights have to offer is uncertain or, as Levinas calls it, 'precarious' (Levinas 1994, 96). In this precariousness the possibility of justice dissolves in the eventuality of prioritising political necessities. Such a contest of entitlements is visible in the area of reproductive rights. While feminist arguments are frequently conceptualised as aligned with secularism against religion, religion is most often seen as an abject other (Hawthorne 2014). But, as the studies below show, the area of reproductive rights proves to be inhabited by far less clear divisions than those between secularism and religion, indeed touching upon the very understanding of subject and community. The conflict of the claims involved repeatedly emerges in such dramatic events as those recently recorded in Ireland, where the death of Savita Halappanavar,[1] a mandatory legal injunction against a rape victim to give birth by Caesarean section,[2] or more recently a legal suit to allow a brain-dead pregnant woman to be taken off life support, have revived interest in the reasoning underpinning penalisation of abortion and reproductive choices. The appeal to the right to privacy is frequently juxtaposed with the appeal to either the right to freedom of religion or to the perceived right to life of a foetus. Intersections of reproductive rights and religion in legal conflict concerning regulation of access to IVF, preimplantation diagnostics or even access to contraceptives are frequently centred on the previously mentioned identity principle and protecting the entitlements of the community unified around that principle. That principle allows community to hijack the self-affirming logic of the self to validate its own existence and expel all that it does not tolerate. As Adorno would have it:

> It is precisely the insatiable identity principle that perpetuates antagonism by suppressing contradiction. What tolerates nothing that is not like itself thwarts the reconcilement for which it mistakes itself.
>
> (Adorno 1973, 142–3)

Whereas without a doubt many if not the majority of people will give the religious or philosophical aspect an important role in their reproductive choices, religious difference and its role in these choices is rarely recognised. Instead, the complexities are often reduced to perceived dichotomies between feminism and religion or the community and the other. In European terms, women's rights, just like religious pluralism, have been proclaimed as the foundation of democracy in Europe. Both the European Union and the Council of Europe have focused strongly on the principle of gender equality. But little in the ECHR deals with gender equality except for Article 14 forbidding discrimination on the grounds of sex. In contrast to this modest emphasis, the EU in its legal instruments elevated gender equality to the level of a fundamental principle as early as the Treaty of Amsterdam[3] and issued a number of directives that have spurred rich ECJ case-law. This body of law comprises an enormous number of norms and rules concerning diverse aspects of gender equality, primarily as regards employment.[4] But little in these refers to reproductive choices in terms of access to the

---

[1] 'Savita Halappanavar's death may stir Ireland to change over abortion', *Guardian*, 18 November 2012.
[2] 'Woman denied abortion in Ireland "became pregnant after rape"', *Guardian*, 18 August 2014.
[3] The Treaty of Amsterdam, 2 October 1997, Amsterdam, Official Journal of the European Communities C 340/1, Article 13.
[4] For example, Directive 2006/54/EC on the implementation of the principle of equal opportunities and equal treatment of men and women in matters of employment and occupation (recast),

means of planning a family. Some reproductive rights in Europe, in the countries that have ratified it, stem from the Convention on the Elimination of All Forms of Discrimination against Women (CEDAW)[5] rather than regional European documents. CEDAW explicitly includes provisions on reproduction and challenges traditional family patterns by introducing the legal obligation to assure equality of men and women in all aspects of life, including family planning. CEDAW stipulates that women ought to have the possibility of deciding on the number and spacing of their children and have access to the information, education and means to enable them to exercise these rights. Firm commitment to the idea of reproductive rights as a necessary corollary of gender equality was expressly reaffirmed during the world summits in Cairo in 1994 and Beijing 1995. The Beijing Platform for Action specifies that 'The explicit recognition and reaffirmation of the right of all women to control all aspects of their health, in particular their own fertility, is basic to their empowerment.'[6]

Against this strong commitment expressed in CEDAW and international declarations, the European legal sphere appears to be sparsely populated in terms of specific references to reproductive rights or the possibility of deciding about having children. Despite commitment to gender equality, reproductive rights in Europe were for long not embraced by any common policy, even though some feminist scholars have argued that without the right to reproductive choice other economic or social rights have only limited power to advance the well-being of women (Freedman and Isaacs 1993). As for the EU, it was only as late as 2002, two years before the 2004 accession of a new group of ten countries, that the EU and the European Parliamentary Committee on Women's Rights and Equal Opportunities adopted a Report on sexual and reproductive health and rights. The so-called Van Lancker report[7] called for a common resolution on reproductive matters, but adoption of an actual resolution specific to this area never followed. The Report considered all relevant international documents and actions and the state of disparities in sexual and reproductive health and rights within the EU, especially in matters relating to women's access to health services, contraception and abortion. It found the policies and disparities in approaches rather significant and called for common action that would urge governments to engage in efforts to provide contraceptives at low cost or free of charge for less privileged groups in society, promote sexual education in a gender-sensitive way and with special attention to the problem of STDs, ensuring counselling for pregnant women and making abortion legal, safe and accessible to all.

Directive 75/117/EEC on equal pay, Directive 86/378/EC on the implementation of the principle of equal treatment for men and women in occupational social security schemes.

5   UN General Assembly, Convention on the Elimination of All Forms of Discrimination Against Women, 18 December 1979, United Nations, Treaty Series, vol. 1249, p. 13. All the EU Member States have ratified CEDAW, though not all without reservations.

6   United Nations, Beijing Declaration and Platform of Action, adopted at the Fourth World Conference on Women, 27 October 1995, A/CONF.177/20, 1995, para 17.

7   Sexual and Reproductive Health and Rights, Van Lancker Report, Speech 02/316, European Parliament, 2 July 2002.

As far as the Council of Europe is concerned, 2004 brought adoption of a Resolution[8] and Recommendation[9] concerning reproductive rights. Observing the enormous disparity of standards between Member States in matters of reproductive health, the documents encouraged development of a comprehensive European strategy for the promotion of reproductive health and rights. In 2008, facing the difficult question of abortion, the Council of Europe adopted a Report[10] and Resolution[11] calling countries which maintain an abortion ban to decriminalise abortion, guarantee effective exercise of the right to abortion and adopt appropriate strategies to promote sexual and reproductive health and rights as well as access to contraception in order to prevent unwanted pregnancies and abortions. The Report and Resolution underlined that abortion is not a family planning method and should be avoided; moreover, the ban on abortion does not result in fewer abortions but leads to clandestine abortions and abortion tourism, which are costly and endanger women's lives and health. The necessity of further commitment to reproductive rights inside Europe was finally recognised by the EU when the European Parliament adopted a resolution on the status of fundamental rights in the EU.[12] In terms of women's reproductive rights, the 2009 Resolution recommended withdrawing states' reservations to CEDAW[13] and assuring that women can fully enjoy reproductive rights, access to contraception and avoid high-risk illegal abortions.

While appearing to be fundamental, the idea of reproductive rights as an expression of gender equality is legally as novel as the idea of religious pluralism. It is therefore surprising that while developing nearly in parallel, the principles have so readily been framed as standing in conflict. The latest documents such as the EU Resolution, while not referring to pluralism, stress that invoking customs, tradition or religious considerations to justify any form of discrimination against women, including adoption of any policies that might endanger their lives, is unacceptable in a democratic state based on the principle of gender equality. While juxtaposition of religion and women's rights has been frequent in the context of rights (Okin 1998, 1999) it has equally often been criticised (Gilman 1999; Volpp 2001; Anthias 2002). As illustrated in these critiques, this opposition does not aid the shaping of a constructive relationship between religion and women's rights, relying on a dichotomy of either/or and assumption of supremacy of liberal norms. Furthermore, construction of a conflict between the two is frequent

---

[8] Parliamentary Assembly of the Council of Europe, Resolution 1399 (2004), 'European strategy for the promotion of sexual and reproductive health and rights', 5 October 2004.

[9] Parliamentary Assembly of the Council of Europe, Recommendation 1675 (2004), 'European strategy for the promotion of sexual and reproductive health and rights'.

[10] Parliamentary Assembly of the Council of Europe, Report, 'Access to safe and legal abortion', Doc. 11537 rev., 8 April 2008.

[11] Parliamentary Assembly of the Council of Europe, Resolution 1607 (2008), 'Access to safe and legal abortion in Europe', 16 April 2008.

[12] European Parliament Resolution 2007 (2145) (INI), 'Situation of fundamental rights in the European Union 2004–2008', 14 January 2009.

[13] For instance Malta included a reservation that the Convention would not challenge the Maltese ban on abortion.

in relation to minority or new religions but comparatively rare in relation to traditionally established and dominant religions. In constructing conflict between the two, legal discourse too often seems to rely on established concepts of freedom as a non-questionable privilege of those in control who are 'mature enough for freedom' (Adorno 1973, 221). In contrast, those not mature enough for freedom are presented as guided by backward 'tradition', with the decision on maturity more often than not rooted in the ontological divide between 'us' and 'them'. While established communities of 'us' are presented as mature enough to control freedom, their religion is often presented merely as 'a tradition' and thus rarely in conflict with gender equality. When the claim to freedom concerns the 'immature', the religion of the other is seen as a barbaric attribute limiting women's rights (Brown 2008, 149–75).

Despite the seeming opposition between the two principles, little in the conflict is in fact concerned with gender equality or with religious pluralism. Undeniably, religious groups usually respond to what they perceive as an attack on sacred values so that churches find themselves in the position of 'defenders' of those values (Wald, Silverman and Fridy 2005, 130). And whereas in relatively diverse societies religious resources may be diverse and may give rise to meaningful pluralistic debates, societies where religious or secular identity or ethical tradition is dominant are more likely to treat themselves as 'mature for freedom' and thus capable of using tradition to create a sense of identity. The problematic appropriation of rights happens when fixed tradition becomes a key player in creation of an identity principle. In those circumstances the appeal to difference might in fact refer to secularism, while religion might be presented as neutral and 'mature' tradition. In those circumstances, claims by the other to reproductive rights are presented as irrational, sometimes radical and endangering the core of the community. As observed by Butler in the slightly different but not dissimilar context of same-sex marriage, a challenge to established traditions is frequently seen as an attack on 'culture' (Butler 2004, 110). When such a perception dominates, Butler observes that:

> The debates center not only on the questions of what culture is and who should be admitted but also on how the subjects of culture should be reproduced. They also concern the status of the state, and in particular its power to confer or withdraw recognition for forms of sexual alliance.
>
> (Butler 2004, 110)

Reproduction is strongly linked with forms of sexual alliance and, not surprisingly, control of the state often resorts to 'recirculation of religious desires, for redemption, for belonging, for eternity' (Butler 2004, 11). Meanwhile, reproductive choices in a religiously plural society are characterised by claims of emancipation happening alongside multiple axes (Balibar 2013) and the main challenge lies in recognising those axes. Without that realisation, reproductive 'freedom' will always be controlled and subordinated to what Adorno would call 'universalising bourgeois consciousness' (Adorno 1973, 231).

7.2 Poseidon's assault: community appropriating rights

In the contest between suitors, Poseidon, god of the sea, overwhelmed by his desire for Medusa, resorted to his powers to assault her in Athena's temple. Resorting to power and control over women's bodies is not uncommon for law and, as illustrated below, not uncommon for human rights. Among other forms of legal control over women, their sexuality and reproductive functions continue to be excessively regulated (Karpin 1992; Fleishman 2000; Jansen 2007). Examples are numerous: from more radical methods of control, such as abortion bans or control of assisted reproduction, to much milder methods such as requirements of maternity clinic control in order to be eligible for maternity social benefits.[14] In the area of human rights, such control is exhibited in judgments that, instead of engaging in a meaningful examination of the intersections between pluralism and women's motives, appeal to homogeneity and the religious or secular identity of a like-minded population.

The prime example of a country whose regulation in this area is dictated by a strong 'ethical inheritance' is Ireland. Despite legal challenges before the ECtHR and the ECJ, Irish law has for years regulated reproductive choices and penalised abortion. As mentioned above, the 1937 Constitution of the independent Republic was implemented in the spirit of Catholicism, and the preponderance of natural law in interpretation of matters concerning sexuality and private life persisted until the case of *McGee*,[15] involving access of a married woman to contraception. Abortion has always been illegal in Ireland and an explicit ban on abortion was introduced to the Irish Constitution in 1983 by the Eighth Amendment incorporated into the text of the Constitution as Article 40.3.3.[16] The article protects the life of the unborn as an absolute right, with the state under an obligation 'to defend and vindicate that right'. The Highest Court has with time softened the strict interpretation of this provision and since the *X case*[17] of 1992, concerning a 14-year-old girl who was raped by her friend's father and who displayed suicidal tendencies, termination is allowed in cases of real, imminent and substantial risk to the life of the mother, including the risk of death by 'self-destruction', which could be avoided by terminating pregnancy. Further cases such as the *C case*,[18] concerning a suicidal teenage Traveller girl, have further impacted interpretation of the ban and introduced the Thirteenth Amendment to the Constitution, removing restrictions on travelling for an abortion.

---

[14] See e.g. in Finland: Äitiysavustuslaki [Law on maternity grant] 28.5.1993/477, 28 May 1993, para. 2.

[15] *McGee v. the Attorney General* [1974] IR 284; *G v. An Bord Uchtála* [1980] IR 32.

[16] This was introduced by amendment no. 8/1983, 1983. The ban on abortion existed even before but did not enjoy constitutional status and was sanctioned by very old provisions from the time of British rule: Offences Against the Person Act, 1861.

[17] *The Attorney General v. X and Others* [1992] 1 IR 1.

[18] *A and B v. Eastern Health Board, Judge Mary Fahy and C, and the Attorney General* (notice party), [1998] 1 IR 464.

The decisive and undoubtedly historically religiously motivated approach of Ireland to abortion has not been changed by the cases that found their way to the ECtHR and the ECJ. The *Grogan*[19] and *Open Door*[20] cases were considered nearly simultaneously in the years 1991 and 1992, before respectively the ECJ and the ECtHR. *Grogan* arose in the aftermath of the Irish High Court's decision[21] in a case brought by the Society for the Protection of Unborn Children (SPUC) against Open Door Counselling. The question considered the lawfulness of providing information and counselling for women seeking abortion abroad. Open Door Counselling and another organisation named Dublin Well Women were providing a broad range of services for pregnant women, from health tests through information on abortion services in the United Kingdom to occasional arrangements for the procedure for women willing to undergo abortion abroad. The SPUC claimed that the activity of Open Door and Dublin Well Women violated the constitutional protection of the unborn and applied to the High Court to restrain these organisations from distributing information and leaflets. According to the High Court judgment of 1986 and the Supreme Court judgment of 1988, assisting pregnant women in Ireland to travel abroad to obtain abortions, inter alia by informing them of the identity and location of a specific clinic or clinics, was prohibited under Article 40.3.3 of the Irish Constitution. In 1989 Stephen Grogan and the other defendants in the main proceedings who worked with students' associations issuing publications containing information about the availability of legal abortion in the United Kingdom were requested by the SPUC not to publish information of the kind in the academic year 1989/90. The defendants did not reply, and the SPUC then brought proceedings in the High Court for a declaration that distribution of such information was unlawful and for an injunction restraining distribution. In October 1989 the High Court decided to refer certain questions to the ECJ for a preliminary ruling under Article 177 of the then binding version of the EEC Treaty. But not surprisingly, in *SPUC* v. *Grogan*, the ECJ did not focus on the religious aspect of the ban but instead examined abortion as a medical service provided legally in another Member State. The Court approached the question strictly from the free market perspective, refuting moral arguments due to the fact that the case dealt with legal systems in which abortion was provided legally. The judgment underlined that the information provided by Steven Grogan and other organisations was provided free of charge and was not a representation of the economic activity of clinics in the United Kingdom. Relying on the strict economic link, spreading this information should be treated exclusively as freedom of expression, which at that time was considered to fall outside the scope of the ECJ's jurisdiction.

---

[19] *Judgment of the Court of 4 October 1991. – The Society for the Protection of Unborn Children Ireland Ltd* v. *Stephen Grogan and others.* European Court of Justice, Case C-159/90, 4 October 1991.

[20] *Open Door and Dublin Well Woman* v. *Ireland,* European Court of Human Rights, Judgment, Application Nos. 14234/88; 14235/88, 29 October 1992.

[21] *The Attorney General (at the relation of the Society for the Protection of Unborn Children Ireland Ltd)* v. *Open Door Counselling Ltd and Dublin Wellwoman Centre Ltd* [1988] Irish Reports 593).

For these reasons, while abortion was found to be a medical service, the ban on distribution of information was not found illegal under Community law.

But the saga concerning distribution of information was not finished before the ECJ. Not surprisingly, the freedom of expression aspect ultimately found its way to the ECtHR.[22] Open Door Ltd filed a complaint concerning the ban on providing information with, at that time, the European Commission of Human Rights, which was responsible for admissibility and found the case admissible. The Court delivered its judgment in October 1992 and found a violation of the right to freedom of expression embodied in Article 10 of the Convention. The ECtHR refused to examine complaints as to whether Irish law was violating the right to privacy and freedom from discrimination of pregnant women who wished to undergo an abortion but instead focused on the absolute and perpetual restraint on provision of information to pregnant women concerning abortion. The Court found that these restrictions failed to meet the requirement of proportionality or necessity in a democratic society. At the same time, however, the judgment underlined that even if the state's discretion in the field of protection of morals is not unfettered and unreviewable it is none the less subject to a 'wide margin of appreciation'. These judgments, despite not lifting the ban, influenced changes to the Irish Constitution introduced by the Fourteenth Amendment embodied in article 40.3.3 and lifting limitations on providing information on abortion.

Many years on from the saga concerning information on abortion services, the ECtHR was once more faced with the Irish abortion ban in 2010 in the case of *A, B and C* v. *Ireland*.[23] It is in that judgment that the morality of the Irish community was invoked as an identity principle validating rights. The case dealt with the situation of three women in Ireland who suffered complications after travelling to England for an abortion. One of the applicants suffered from cancer. While she did not know she was pregnant she had undergone a series of cancer therapies counter-indicated during pregnancy. When she found out about her pregnancy she decided to travel to England for an abortion but suffered complications and bleeding after the procedure. The other two applicants, although not suffering from cancer, also suffered complications after travelling to England for an abortion. The applicants lodged a complaint under Article 8 about the restrictions on lawful abortion in Ireland, in particular restrictions that prevent abortion for reasons of health and/or well-being. Additionally, one of the applicants complained under the same Article about lack of implementation of Article 40.3.3 of the Constitution. While the ECtHR found a violation in regard to the applicant suffering from cancer, it also conceptualised a community of rights as a homogeneous entity built around moral views. The judgment put excessive focus on the role of the 'profound moral views of the majority of the Irish people'[24] in limiting

---

[22] *Open Door and Dublin Well Woman* v. *Ireland*.

[23] *A, B and C* v. *Ireland*, European Court of Human Rights, Judgment, Application No. 25579/05, 16 December 2010.

[24] *Ibid.*, para. 241.

access to abortion. It found that limitations of access based on protection of those moral views constituted a legitimate aim in a democratic society and struck a fair balance:

> Accordingly, having regard to the right to travel abroad lawfully for an abortion with access to appropriate information and medical care in Ireland, the Court does not consider that the prohibition in Ireland of abortion for health and well-being reasons, based as it is on the profound moral views of the Irish people as to the nature of life (see paragraphs 222–27 above) and as to the consequent protection to be accorded to the right to life of the unborn, exceeds the margin of appreciation accorded in that respect to the Irish State. In such circumstances, the Court finds that the impugned prohibition in Ireland struck a fair balance between the right of the first and second applicants to respect for their private lives and the rights invoked on behalf of the unborn.[25]

Even the fact of growing European consensus on access to abortion was not found sufficient to minimise the state's margin of appreciation in the case of protecting the 'profound moral views' of the majority. To quote the Court:

> In the present case, and contrary to the Government's submission, the Court considers that there is indeed a consensus amongst a substantial majority of the Contracting States of the Council of Europe towards allowing abortion on broader grounds than accorded under Irish law. In particular, the Court notes that the first and second applicants could have obtained an abortion on request (according to certain criteria including gestational limits) in some 30 such States. The first applicant could have obtained an abortion justified on health and well-being grounds in approximately 40 Contracting States and the second applicant could have obtained an abortion justified on well-being grounds in some 35 Contracting States. Only 3 States have more restrictive access to abortion services than Ireland namely, a prohibition on abortion regardless of the risk to the woman's life. Certain States have in recent years extended the grounds on which abortion can be obtained.... Ireland is the only State which allows abortion solely where there is a risk to the life (including self-destruction) of the expectant mother. Given this consensus amongst a substantial majority of the Contracting States, it is not necessary to look further to international trends and views which the first two applicants and certain of the third parties argued also leant in favour of broader access to abortion.
>
> However, the Court does not consider that this consensus decisively narrows the broad margin of appreciation of the State.[26]

---

[25] *Ibid*, para. 241.
[26] *Ibid.*, paras 235–6.

The community of rights was thus defined as a community of the majority united by religious morals forming what McCrea would call an ethical inheritance. As such it was awarded a broad margin of appreciation to decide on the rights of those whose moral views fell outside those narrow confines. Despite international consensus on not criminalising abortion,[27] a homogeneously defined community became both the subject and the guarantor of rights endowed with a strong privilege to decide on the rights of others according to its own identity principle. In this equation, pluralism of religious views and heterogeneity of religion was not given consideration in examining whether the prohibition was necessary in a democratic society. Rather than the frequently criticised secularity, this position was based on a troublesome majoritarian model. First of all, it construed a concept of moral majority empowered with the ability to draft a law on the basis of 'profound views'. Second, it did not conceive of the possibility of otherness and the existence of views that are perhaps equally 'profound' and thus calling for recognition. Third, it empowered the majority with the exclusive right to decide on the shape of the rights of the other on the basis of its own definition of morals that it finds 'profound'. It also failed to recognise the importance of actual religious or ethical choices of women. This understanding of rights resorting to majoritarian ideals compels people, as Douzinas would say, to 'find "essence," common "humanity" in the definition of the spirit of the nation or of the people or the leader' (Douzinas 2013, 59). In these circumstances the community begins to follow traditional values and excludes all that is alien and other. As a consequence, this concept of a community begins to use human rights as tools that help 'submerge the "I" into the "We"' (Douzinas 2013, 59). Whether based on a secular or religious foundation, once the essence of the community is defined by an appeal to universal morals, the other is compelled to comply. Difference becomes erased in favour of majoritarian ideals while pluralism, even in its narrow liberal understanding, becomes replaced by mono-tradition. Neither a religious nor a non-religious other, nor women and their diverse motivation, have any place in such an axiom of majority. Seeing the community exclusively as a matrix of affiliations shaped by historical groups strengthens nothing but the distinction between 'us' and 'them' – those who are able and those who are too deficient to acknowledge those affiliations. Rights in turn become a corrective mechanism for the majoritarian community of 'us' empowered to subordinate otherness and repress difference. Rights in their corrective function aim at adjusting religion and belief to the recognised tradition and the established cultural status quo and refuse to recognise subjects that challenge the prevailing regimes of power.

---

[27] In addition to Ireland, Malta penalises abortion without exception. Article 241 of the Criminal Code bans abortion without any legal exceptions and imposes imprisonment ranging from 18 months to 3 years both for the person administering the procedure and the woman undergoing it. Moreover, Article 243 imposes the same penalty for prescribing medical means which might cause a miscarriage. In addition Poland allows for abortion on very narrow grounds according to Ustawa o planowaniu rodziny, ochronie płodu ludzkiego i warunkach dopuszczalności przerwania ciąży (Law on family planning, protection of the foetus and conditions of legally permitted abortion), 7 January 1993, Article 4a.1.

7.3 Rights equipped with Medusa's gaze: who is the other?

Closed off and homogenised notions of community appear to drive the desire of the state to regulate sexuality and reproduction. The reversal of rights from instruments of emancipation to instruments of correction is driven by an identity principle that often underpins the legal determination of what constitutes 'proper conception' and 'proper pregnancy'. This struggle to determine what a 'proper' pregnancy is has recently been experienced by another country with a comparatively religiously homogeneous population with regulation of reproductive freedom. During the last 20 years, Poland has been preoccupied with diverse legal aspects of reproduction, from regulation of abortion, access to contraception or the most recent discussion on access to IVF (Gozdecka 2012). Most of these discussions were underpinned by a focus on Catholic morality and left pluralism out of the picture. One of the most recent and vocal public debates concerning reproduction took place a few years ago when the Polish government began preparing proposals regulating access to IVF and gamete donorship. With the lack of a special law regulating this area, changes to the 'Law on procurement, storing and transplanting of human cells tissues and organs regulates storing of all human cells and tissues without distinction between gamete cells or human embryos'[28] became a bone of contention regarding the religious composition of society. With specific regulation of the area being required by the pack of bioethical EU directives, Directive 2004/23/EC,[29] Directive 2006/17/EC[30] and Directive 2006/86/EC,[31] which regulate quality and safety for donation, procurement, testing, processing, preservation, storage and distribution of human tissues and cells, legislative efforts aimed at adjusting Polish law to the requirements set in EU law. Yet, none other than the position of religion disrupted efforts in an atmosphere of deep dissonance.

The main legislative initiatives included six proposals, including those allowing for IVF and donorship under severe restrictions such as accessibility of IVF only to married couples,[32] themselves including several, albeit milder restrictions,[33]

---

[28] Ustawa o pobieraniu, przechowywaniu i przeszczepianiu komórek, tkanek i narządów (Law on procurement, storing and transplanting of human cells tissues and organs), Dz. U. z 2005 r. Nr 169, poz. 1411, 1 July 2005.

[29] Directive 2004/23/EC of the European Parliament and of the Council of 31 March 2004 on setting standards of quality and safety for the donation, procurement, testing, processing, preservation, storage and distribution of human tissues and cells.

[30] Commission Directive 2006/17/EC of 8 February 2006 implementing Directive 2004/23/EC of the European Parliament and of the Council as regards certain technical requirements for the donation, procurement and testing of human tissues and cells.

[31] Commission Directive 2006/86/EC of 24 October 2006 implementing Directive 2004/23/EC of the European Parliament and of the Council as regards traceability requirements, notification of serious adverse reactions and events and certain technical requirements for the coding, processing, preservation, storage and distribution of human tissues and cells.

[32] Projekt ustawy o ochronie genomu i embrionu ludzkiego oraz Polskiej Radzie Bioetycznej I zmianie innych ustaw (Draft law on the protection of human genome and embryo and the Polish Bioethical Council), Druk 3467, 28 August 2009.

[33] Projekt ustawy o zmianie ustawy o pobieraniu, przechowywaniu i przeszczepianiu tkanek, komorek i narzadow (Draft law amending the law on procurement, storing and transplanting of human

those proposing a total ban and penalisation of IVF[34] and finally those advocating broad access to the procedure and focusing on adjusting the law to the main requirements of EU law.[35] Surprisingly, given the plethora of proposals, the public debate that took place focused little on the best and safest regulation of this difficult area, the shape of pluralism or ensuring that both religious and non-religious motivations of women and couples were taken into consideration. Instead the discussion revolved around the morality of the procedure itself, with the Catholic Church launching a steady attack against the legality of IVF despite the overwhelming support of society for the procedure.[36] When the first initiatives to ban IVF emerged on the legislative scene the Conference of the Episcopate of Poland issued an official statement, which encouraged MPs to introduce an absolute ban on the procedure:

> When the first initiative to regulate [in vitro fertilisation] is taken, all the members of the Parliament who are concerned with protection of human rights should take all the steps necessary to ban this method absolutely. If, however, such a solution were rejected in the Parliament, it is the ethical duty of members of the Parliament to be active in the legislative process and maximally limit the harmful aspects of this regulation.[37]

In the same statement the episcopate referred to the method as 'evil', 'manipulative' and leading to 'massive production' of human beings.[38] Vigilant of subsequent legislative developments, the episcopate's Groups of Experts issued further statements underlining that:

> The opposition of the Catholic Church to the in vitro method stems from the Christian faith, which is the guide in taking all decisions. God created a

cells, tissues and organs), Druk 3470, 28 August 2009, and Projekt ustawy o prawach i wolnosciach czlowieka w dziedzinie zastosowan biologii I medycyny oraz o utworzeniu Polskiej Rady Bioetycznej (Draft law on human rights and freedoms in biology and medicine and creation of the Polish Bioethical Council), Druk 3468, 28 August 2009.

34 Projekt ustawy o ochronie genomu ludzkiego i embrionu ludzkiego (Draft law on the protection of human genome and embryo), Druk 3466, 18 June 2009; Projekt ustawy o zakazie zaplodnienia pozaustrojowego i manipulacji ludzka informacja genetyczna (Draft law on the ban of in vitro fertilization and manipulation of human genetic material), Druk 3471, 17 February 2010; Projekt ustawy o zmianie ustawy – Kodeks karny (Draft law amending the Penal Code), Druk 2249, 15 June 2009.

35 Projekt ustawy o zmianie ustawy o pobieraniu i przeszczepianiu komorek, tkanek i narzadow (Draft law amending the law on procurement, storing and transplanting of human cells, tissues and organs), Druk 2707, 29 July 2009.

36 CBOS, Public Opinion Research Center, *Polish Public Opinion*, ISSN-1233–7250, July 2010, www. cbos.pl/PL/publikacje/public_opinion/2010/07_2010.pdf, accessed 16 March 2011. According to the study, support for IVF dropped from 77 per cent in the year 2009 to 73 per cent in the year 2010.

37 Episcopate of Poland, 'Oświadczenie Zespołu Ekspertów KEP ds. Bioetycznych w porozumieniu z Prezydium Konferencji Episkopatu Polski' (Statement of the Group of Experts on Bioethical Issues of the Conference of the Episcopate of Poland in cooperation with the Central Board of the Conference of the Episcopate of Poland), 22 December 2008, para. 5, translation by the author.

38 *Ibid.*, para. 4.

woman and a man to create life in the act of marital love and only by them themselves. During the in vitro procedure, human dignity is infringed, since conception does not happen in the act of love, but as a result of an experimental technical procedure. The procedure resembles 'production of human beings'.[39]

These perceptions of the nature of IVF are consistent with the position of the Vatican expressed in the encyclical *Evangelium vitae*[40] or the instruction *Donum vitae*[41] and are hardly surprising. In a pluralistic society with a healthy 'competition for worldviews' (Nisbet 2005) these statements could be read as an advancement of religious pluralism. When pluralism is measured *in abstracto* through the religious versus secular dichotomy, religion is frequently viewed as a static, marginalised and non-changeable other. In this understanding the involvement of religious bodies in public discussion can only be seen as a positive factor, boosting rather than restraining religious pluralism. However, when the dominant religious or secular normativity is taken as a measure of the identity principle it might be necessary to reconceptualise who the other is and imagine that multiple others can exist both within and outside religions. When the process of recognition and emancipation ceases to be seen as static and focused on a one-dimensional axis of religion versus secularism, an entirely new dynamic emerges. In this dynamic of many coexisting axes of emancipation, religion, especially when understood institutionally, can cement the static shape of a consensus as strongly as any other force in society. When religious or secular normativity becomes the core of the community, striving for pluralism requires a stronger commitment to difference. In different contexts this difference must be measured differently. An example of the identity principle was strongly expressed in another statement by the Polish episcopate claiming that theories that an embryo is not yet a human being are not based on science and thus equivalent to an ideology[42] that ought to be banned regardless of a person's religious or ethical convictions. The episcopate's expert groups justified the necessity of the ban by reference to the Catholic understanding of natural law, according to which it should be 'natural' to oppose procedures producing a number of human embryos that will not be used and eventually experimented on or destroyed. When religious normativity founds the identity principle, then religion, equally strongly as secularism, mutates into a force calling for erasure of difference and defying the goals of pluralism and inclusion. Depending on the basis of

---

[39] Episcopate of Poland, 'Oświadczenie Zespołu Ekspertów KEP ds. Bioetycznych w porozumieniu z Prezydium Konferencji Episkopatu Polski' (Statement of the Group of Experts on Bioethical Issues of the Conference of the Episcopate of Poland in cooperation with the Central Board of the Conference of the Episcopate of Poland), 24 March 2010, paras 4–5, translation by the author.

[40] John Paul II, *Encyclical letter Evangelium vitae*, no. 1995.03.25, 1995.

[41] Congregation for the Doctrine of the Faith, *Donum vitae*, Instruction on respect for human life in its origin, 1987.

[42] Episcopate of Poland, 'Oświadczenie Zespołu Ekspertów KEP', paras 4–5, translation by the author.

the identity principle, religious or secular, the axis of emancipation may become reversed in comparison to the traditionally conceived axis. When dominant religious normativity founds the identity principle it is not the dominant religion that ought to be emancipated to enter the public sphere or included in a pluralistic public sphere and it is no longer an adherent of the dominant religion, whose right to dissent must be guaranteed to secure pluralism. In this case the direction of emancipation and struggle for recognition of difference is entirely reversed and requires recognition of the possibility of dissent from religion. In the Polish case the voice of differently religious others, including those within the church, became muffled and eventually silenced in the battle between religion and 'secularism'. This approach mistranslated the depth of the religious and ethical picture and replaced the richness of religious difference with a black or white dichotomy of religion and secularism. The Polish debate became too polarised and did not conclude with the adoption of new legislation that would subordinate rights to the identity principle.

Regrettably though, rights have been used as instruments curtailing difference and securing the identity principle in another case concerning 'proper pregnancies'. In the case of *S.H.* v. *Austria*[43] the ECtHR dealt with a ban on certain forms of artificial procreation, selectively chosen in Austrian legislation primarily due to their controversial moral nature. Austrian legislation on donation of gametes allowed only for sperm donation but forbade donation of ova. The applicants, who suffered from a specific type of infertility which would require the use of donated ova, complained against the ban, arguing that it constituted a limitation on the right to privacy and was unnecessary in a democratic society. The identity principle took over the reasoning, beginning from the government's defence that Member States had the right to balance rights with the 'specific social and cultural needs and traditions of their countries'.[44] In the first instance, the Chamber judgment of the ECtHR focused on the discriminatory impact of the provisions on couples suffering from these particular types of infertility and found the provisions to be in breach of Article 8 of the ECHR. But the case found its way to the Grand Chamber, which reversed the judgment and in its reluctance to cross the boundary of local morals emphasised that its 'task is not to substitute itself for the competent national authorities in determining the most appropriate policy for regulating matters of artificial procreation'.[45] The judgment subsequently focused on the national authorities' mandate 'to give an opinion, not only on the "exact content of the requirements of morals" in their country'.[46] These local morals sustaining established 'cultural needs'[47] acquired the privilege of protected boundaries of

---

[43] *S.H. and Others* v. *Austria*, European Court of Human Rights, Judgment, Application No. 57813/00, 3 November 2011.

[44] *S.H. and Others* v. *Austria*, para. 47.

[45] *Ibid.*, para. 92.

[46] *Ibid.*, para. 94.

[47] *Ibid.*, para. 47.

a community. National tradition, whether cultural, moral or religious, became the protected identity principle unifying the community and allowing for exclusion of difference. Those standing outside the confines of self-professed 'cultural needs' were once more excluded from protection of rights. By acknowledging and sanctioning the cultural core as free from contestation, this judgment, just like *A. B. and C. v. Ireland*, cemented dominant cultural, moral and religious normativities. Rights became a privilege of those following the dominant model and once more served as a tool for protecting the community from otherness instead of emancipating otherness from the constraints of established power.

7.4 Fluidity of otherness

At this point critics might say that the approach presented above does not bring anything new to the intersections between reproductive freedom and religion. Thus it is important to demonstrate that the identity principle may be amalgamated around both religious and secular normativities. One controversial area where a potential conflict between religious and moral values and a secular system of education reveals a different other is the area of sex education, touching less directly albeit implicitly upon the sphere of reproductive rights. Many European countries provide sex education as an obligatory part of their school curriculum, stirring objections from religious parents who send their children to state schools. The case of *Kjeldsen, Busk Madsen and Pedersen v. Denmark*[48] brought before the ECtHR concerned practising Christian parents who protested against their children's participation in sex education classes in Denmark. The parents argued that there was a violation of Article 2, Protocol 1 securing their right to educate their children in conformity with their beliefs. Interestingly, while the Court referred explicitly to the principle of pluralism underlining that: 'the second sentence of Article 2 (P1-2) aims in short at safeguarding the possibility of pluralism in education which possibility is essential for the preservation of a "democratic society" as conceived by the Convention', it excluded otherness on grounds of practicality. The judgment underlined that allowing for extensive exemption systems from an integrated school curriculum is not covered by Article 2, Protocol 1, emphasising that with such an exemption, institutionalised teaching 'ran the risk of proving impracticable'. The Court accepted that various instructions might encroach on the religious-philosophical sphere but found the availability of private confessional schools, where children can learn about these topics in a manner compliant with their creed, a sufficient method of balancing religious and secular interests. This relatively early argumentation of the Court in regard to exemptions is different, for instance, from that employed in *Folgerø*[49] regarding the preponderance of Christianity in the Norwegian school curriculum, where the Court found a

[48] *Kjeldsen, Busk Madsen and Pedersen v. Denmark*, European Court of Human Rights, Judgment, Application Nos. 5095/71, 5920/72, 5926/72, 7 December 1976.
[49] *Folgerø and Others v. Norway*, European Court of Human Rights, Judgment, Application No. 15472/02, 29 June 2007.

violation of Article 2 of Protocol 1. In *Folgerø* the Court insisted that the possibility of exemption from integrated teaching on Christianity embedded in a variety of subjects was necessary in a democratic society. Given that integrated religious teaching is not that strikingly different from integrated sex education, the emphasis on practicality raises suspicion when it comes to recognition of difference. The burden placed on the school system to organise the exemption is comparable in the case of both subjects, yet the reading of pluralism follows a secular direction consistent with the perception of religion in Denmark as a secularised form of identity rather than an active religious conviction. Such an active conviction was found to be standing outside the acceptable paradigm of inclusion and thus left unrecognised. As the Danish example illustrates, the other is not the other a priori and is always the one not represented in the dominant normativity. Otherness is not fixable. It is instead a category of exclusion construed in opposition to the majoritarian normativity. The face of the other changes depending on the context, the composition of society and the pathways allowing the other to realise her religious or non-religious life goals. As the Deleuzian fluid understanding of the minority–majority dynamic would have it:

> The notion of minority is very complex, with musical, literary, linguistic, as well as juridical and political, references. The opposition between minority and majority is not simply quantitative. Majority implies a constant, of expression or content, serving as a standard measure by which to evaluate it. Let us suppose that the constant or standard is the average adult-white-heterosexual-European-male speaking a standard language (Joyce's or Ezra Pound's Ulysses). It is obvious that 'man' holds the majority, even if he is less numerous than mosquitoes, children, women, blacks, peasants, homosexuals, etc. That is because he appears twice, once in the constant and again in the variable from which the constant is extracted. Majority assumes a state of power and domination, not the other way around. It assumes the standard measure, not the other way around.
>
> (Deleuze and Guattari 1980)

Devising a one-size-fits-all ideal model of recognition of religious difference is thus not possible a priori because it will depend on who is represented twice. Whereas freedom of religion, or in the cases above protection of private life, are not unconditional rights and can in practice be restricted on multiple grounds, a problem in their interpretation arises when restrictions exclude the other on the ground of her otherness. When the other is placed in the position of a dissident excluded from protection of rights on the mere grounds of her difference, rights appropriate power to represent and reinforce dominant religious or secular tradition and establish them as protected norms and standards. In Iris Marion Young's words:

> The dominant group reinforces its position by bringing the other groups under the measure of its dominant norms .... Since only the dominant

groups' cultural expression receive wide dissemination, their cultural expressions become normal, or the universal, and thereby the unremarkable. Given the normality of its own cultural expressions and identity, the dominant group constructs the differences which some groups exhibit as lack and negation. These groups become marked as Other.

(Young 1990, 59)

7.5 The birth of Pegasus? A different conceptualisation of rights

So far the diagnosis of the state of rights and their principles appears dark, and the intersections of reproductive rights and pluralism appear to lead to an irreconcilable conflict of claims leading to erasure of heterogeneity. As in the myth, rights, like Medusa after her transformation, become a merciless monster. In the myth the unfortunate maiden is finally defeated by resourceful Perseus, who, holding a mirror, succeeds in beheading the Gorgon. Despite Medusa's gloomy faith her death is followed by the birth of an unimaginably beautiful creature. Pegasus, a winged horse emerging from Medusa's severed neck, is a harbinger of hope and renewal. The reader overwhelmed with the state of rights presented in this volume might ask whether this final myth of rights also harbours any hope. And like the myth the latest jurisprudence of the ECtHR appears to make a stronger gesture towards otherness. In the case of *Costa and Pavan* v. *Italy*[50] the Court dealt with another idea related to reproduction, namely prohibition of a preimplantation genetic diagnostic (PGD) in Italy. This led the applicant in the case to undergo an abortion legally allowed on the grounds of a specific genetic disease. While examining whether this interference with the applicant's right was legitimate the Court was not simply persuaded by the argument of protection of legally established morals that the Member State appealed to. The State argued that the ban was necessary to prevent the risk of eugenic selection and secure freedom of conscience of the medical professions. The ECtHR, unlike in the cases analysed above, strongly affirmed that whereas 'PGD raises sensitive moral and ethical questions, the Court notes that the solutions reached by the legislature are not beyond the scrutiny of the Court'.[51] It therefore examined the consistency of Italian legislation and found that allowing abortion rather than PGD not only lacked consistency but also interfered with the right to privacy and put a disproportionate burden on the applicant, whose 'anxiety' and 'painful decisions' related to carrying a foetus with a serious genetic disease could not simply be underestimated.[52]

---

[50] *Costa and Pavan* v. *Italy*, European Court of Human Rights, Judgment, Application No. 54270/10, 28 August 2012.

[51] *Ibid.*, para. 61.

[52] *Ibid.*, para. 59.

The change in judicial reasoning and closer balancing of the interests and the impact of discriminatory provisions in this case contextualises the other and:

> requires us to view each other and every rational being as an individual with a concrete history, identity and affective-emotional constitution. In assuming this standpoint, we abstract from what constitutes our commonality and focus on individuality. We seek to comprehend the needs of the other, his or her motivations, what she searches for and what s/he desires.... Our differences in this case complement rather than exclude one another.
>
> (Benhabib 1992, 159)

This more nuanced standpoint not only allows interrogation of the original violence of the legal system's institutions (Simmons 2011, 124) but also allows for inclusive rather than exclusive applications of the notion of community and its changing identity. The applicants in these cases were not viewed as simply infringing the legally established consensus on controversial cultural issues. Their different values and experiences were not simply excluded a priori as foreign to their respective communities but instead heard as legitimate voices modifying the fluid boundaries of the cultural community and affecting the shape of pluralism.

When interpretation of rights avoids this delicate balancing it risks defining otherness from its outside and imposing the experience and interpretation of life represented by dominant normativity. This might lead to a reversal of the logic of rights where Levinasian bad peace becomes a reality and rights serve as privileges in the battle of autonomies. In this battle of autonomies, freedom of religion, religious pluralism or reproductive freedom will eventually be interpreted in favour of the majority, leading to control of both women and those whose convictions slip the confines of majoritarian tradition. The question remains whether rights could be rethought in favour of the other not only in singular cases like *Costa* v. *Pavan*. If the emancipatory potential of rights could be restored, the task of the theorist consists in offering a roadmap for the application of fluid categories in determining who the other is. Part III will engage in efforts at reconstruction of rights focusing on the dynamic between minority, majority, emancipation and freedom.

References

Adorno, Theodor W. 1973. *Negative Dialectics*. Routledge.
Anthias, Floya. 2002. 'Beyond Feminism and Multiculturalism: Locating Difference and the Politics of Location.' *Women's Studies International Forum* 25(3): 275–86.
Balibar, Etienne. 2013. 'On the Politics of Human Rights.' *Constellations* 20(1): 18–26.
Benhabib, Seyla. 1992. *Situating the Self: Gender, Community, and Postmodernism in Contemporary Ethics*. Routledge.
Brown, Wendy. 2008. *Regulating Aversion: Tolerance in the Age of Identity and Empire*. Princeton University Press.
Butler, Judith. 2004. *Undoing Gender*. Routledge.

Deleuze, Gilles and Felix Guattari. 1980. *A Thousand Plateaus: Capitalism and Schizophrenia.* Continuum.

Douzinas, Costas. 2000. *The End of Human Rights: Critical Legal Thought at the Turn of the Century.* Hart Publishing.

Douzinas, Costas. 2013. 'The Paradoxes of Human Rights.' *Constellations* 20(1): 51–67.

Fleishman, Rishona. 2000. 'The Battle against Reproductive Rights: The Impact of the Catholic Church on Abortion Law in Both International and Domestic Areas.' *Emory International Law Review* 14: 277–314.

Freedman, Lynn P. and Stephen L. Isaacs. 1993. 'Human Rights and Reproductive Choice.' *Studies in Family Planning* 24(1): 18–30.

Gilman, Sander L. 1999. ' "Barbaric" Rituals?' In *Is Multiculturalism Bad for Women?*, ed. Joshua Cohen, Matthew Howard and Martha C. Nussbaum, 53–8. Princeton University Press.

Gozdecka, Dorota A. 2012. 'The Polish Catholic Church and the Regulation of IVF in Poland: Polarised Political Discourses and the Battle over "Proper" Reproduction.' *Feminists@ Law* 2(1).

Hawthorne, Sian Melvill. 2014. 'Entangled Subjects: Feminism, Religion, and the Obligation to Alterity.' In *The Sage Handbook of Feminist Theory*, ed. Mary Evans, Clare Hemming, Marsha Henry, Hazel Johnstone, Sumi Madhok and Sadie Wearing, 114–30. Sage Publications.

Jansen, Yakare-Oule. 2007. 'The Right to Freely Have Sex – Beyond Biology: Reproductive Rights and Sexual Self-Determination.' *Akron Law Review* 40: 311–38.

Karpin, Isabel. 1992. 'Legislating the Female Body: Reproductive Technology and the Reconstructed Woman.' *Columbia Journal of Gender and Law* 3: 325–48.

Levinas, Emmanuel. 1994. *Outside the Subject.* Stanford University Press.

Nisbet, Matthew C. 2005. 'The Competition for Worldviews: Values, Information, and Public Support for Stem Cell Research.' *International Journal of Public Opinion Research* 17(1): 90–112.

Okin, Susan Moller. 1998. 'Feminism, Women's Human Rights, and Cultural Differences.' *Hypatia* 13(2): 32–52.

Okin, Susan Moller. 1999. 'Is Multiculturalism Bad for Women?' In *Is Multiculturalism Bad for Women?*, ed. Joshua Cohen, Matthew Howard and Martha C. Nussbaum, 7–26. Princeton University Press.

Rorty, Richard. 1998. 'Human Rights, Rationality, and Sentimentality.' In *Truth and Progress*, vol. 3, 167–85. Cambridge University Press.

Simmons, William Paul. 2011. *Human Rights Law and the Marginalized Other.* Cambridge University Press.

Volpp, Leti. 2001. 'Feminism versus Multiculturalism.' *Columbia Law Review* 101(5): 1181–218.

Wald, Kenneth D., Adam L. Silverman and Kevin S. Fridy. 2005. 'Making Sense of Religion in Political Life.' *Annual Review of Political Science* 8(1): 121–43.

Young, Iris Marion. 1990. *Justice and the Politics of Difference.* Princeton University Press.

Part III

Religious pluralism, human rights and the dissident

As ridiculous as it may sound … each universal ideological notion is always hegemonized by some particular content which colours its very universality and accounts for its efficiency.
Slavoj Žižek, 'Multiculturalism, or, the Cultural Logic of Multinational Capitalism.' *New Left Review* (1997): 28–51, at 28

Chapter 8

The hollow paradigms of contemporary debates on law and religion and the failed potential of religious pluralism

As demonstrated in the preceding chapters, the age of pluralism has frequently been but a myth that in practice mutated into forms of controlling religious otherness even more strictly than before. Before pluralism was declared a cornerstone of democracy, it was occasionally embraced broadly, as for instance in the case of *Kokkinakis*,[1] which focused extensively on the necessity of retaining the ability to manifest one's own religion in spite of the prevailing socio-legal context. Once religious pluralism became proudly announced as a principle, it quickly mutated into a regime of cementing rather than disrupting the cultural hegemony of religiously (or non-religiously) dominant groups and their protected normativities. The terms through which religious difference was presented gradually reversed rights entitlements and transformed the religiously different, first into the other and then into an unlawful dissident. This reversal has not been sufficiently addressed due to the predominance of secularism versus religion antinomy in analyses of the relationship between law and religion instead of considerations of religious difference.

Prevailing paradigms recurring in the scholarship and jurisprudence of law and religion have oscillated repetitively between secularism, neutrality and inclusion of religion. But despite their prominence they have not thus far moved beyond the 'religion versus secularism' divide or found any convincing solution to the questions 'is religion hostile to democracy?' or 'is secularism hostile to difference?'. Constantly seeking a static and non-changeable answer that could be applicable to a wide array of contexts and respond to questions related to the position of religion in law, these paradigms have not only proved insufficient in securing more inclusive and more diverse societies but have instead frequently perpetuated underlying problems with discussion of law and religion such as maintenance of dominant normativities. Both advocates and critics of secularism begin their discussion by assuming that the existing system for approaching law and religion is necessarily secular and, further, capable of being receptive to difference. What both critics and advocates who are focused on the religion versus secularism divide seem to forget is that secularism is not an uncontested fact but instead a frame

---

[1] *Kokkinakis* v. *Greece*, European Court of Human Rights, Judgment, Application No. 14307/88, 25 May 1993.

created to present the opposition between civilisation and savagery and between rationality and irrationality. As with all Enlightenment myths, the role of secularist discourse is to present and subordinate the 'irrational' and the 'savage' by reference to universal and totalising notions. What is missing from contemporary analysis of secularism and religion antinomy is debunking the myth of secularism and presenting it as a frame through which reality is subordinated to the dictate of reason. Preoccupation with secularism assumes a rational divide of society and its agents along the lines of the principle. Zucca's recent appeal to secularism captures the core of this presumption:

> The secular state is in a difficult position. It barely copes with diversity and the fact of pluralism. And yet there is no alternative. Economically, this state is dependent upon immigration. Politically, it can hardly create barriers and walls of separation between the West and the rest of the world. Socially the state is unable to keep together its own population, which is increasingly atomized. It does not come as a surprise that religion is not welcome; yet, it keeps knocking at the door with increasingly more difficult demands.
>
> (Zucca 2012, 30)

Both critics and advocates of secularism see religion expelled from the realm of a 'rational' man and attribute it to a barbaric, savage man. The religious savage that is allegedly difficult to accommodate is controlled by his irrationality and opposed to the 'civilised' Western man who controls, subordinates and commands his religion with secularism. The leading assumption of the scholarship of secularism is that 'the West', as Zucca calls it, is fully enlightened and secular and therefore struggling with religion coming from outside. Religion and its prominence in the West are not presented as irrational but instead as non-existent. Despite ample evidence to the contrary, religion in the West is seen as absent or at best rationalised and ordered and neatly separated from politics. The Western rational agent does not have a religion in the same way that his barbaric counterpart has. He is not prone to savagery and thus appears confronted when a 'religion', a feature of the barbaric man, 'keeps knocking at the door'. The paradigm of secularism has taken over the analysis of law and religion in Europe and world-wide. But even those who criticise it frequently approach it in its mythical, enlightened form. Meanwhile, what these analyses miss is that Western man's religious normativites continue to be present even in the most formally secularised countries. This blindness to certain forms of religion and struggle with others can be helpfully explained by reference to the parabolic figure of Odysseus that Adorno and Horkheimer explore in their *Dialectic of Enlightenment* (Horkheimer and Adorno 1944). In their analysis, Odysseus stands in for the image of the rational Western man and his society. And the passage of the book exploring Odysseus' encounter with the sirens provides a helpful tool explaining why some normativities are ignored while others are conceptualised as dangerous others that have to be accommodated in the allegedly secular landscape. Passing by the islands of the sirens, Odysseus plugs the ears of his oarsmen and allows himself to listen to the sirens while being tightly bound to the mast, unable to move and at the mercy of his ship's crew. While knowing that his emotions and temptations exist, Odysseus becomes a part of the ship and is carried by its movement. By becoming a part of the ship, moving forward without noticing his suffering, he is forced to ignore the forces of nature and 'irrationality', embodied in sexual desire and the temptation of the sirens' song. Odysseus' desire is subordinated to the movement of the ship and ignored in its undisturbed journey, symbolising enlightened progress. No matter how great or how irrational Odysseus' feelings are, the movement of the ship and the plugged ears of the oarsmen prevent this 'savage' instinct not only from taking over the course of the ship but also from being heard. The oarsmen do not hear their passenger's cries and thus his irrationality, emotion and pain remain unrecognised. Subsequently, as unrecognised and unheard they appear never to have existed and are known only to Odysseus himself. Like Odysseus' private emotions, the religions of the West, no matter how 'irrational' and 'emotional', are unseen and unheard in the greater illusion of secularism. They are tied to the mast of the ship, and their 'irrational' appeals and cries are muted by the assumption that secularism exists – a steady direction that prevails over the cries of the ship's passengers. If unheard and bound to the mast, any form of Western 'irrationality' becomes ignored in favour of securing movement in a certain direction. The 'irrationality' of the ship's passengers ceases being seen as 'irrational' because it appears tamed and bound to the mast and its appeals are muffled by plugged ears. What follows is that only a stranger, on another ship coming from afar, can be prone to the 'irrationality' of religion. And, while the oarsmen's plugged ears indeed have trouble hearing the cries of the other, the main problem with secularism is not primarily unawareness of the newcomer's cries but the utter disregard and denial of the existence of the 'irrationality' of one's own passenger. The problem with secularism is not whether it is sufficiently receptive to difference. The problem with taking secularism as a framework, or even with its critique, lies in turning a deaf ear to one's own religious 'irrationality' and the presumption that the separation between secular and religious actually exists as a part of objective reality. 'Our' irrationality is muffled by the illusion of secularism with which we analyse contemporary approaches to law and religion, whereas 'their' irrationality is ostentatious and presented as a problem to our muffled ears. But ears that cannot hear cannot be made more inclusive, no matter how hard we try to redefine secularism or how we try to make it more religion-friendly. For that we would first have to unplug our own ears and allow ourselves to admit that perhaps we, too, can be led astray from the course by our 'irrationality'. Such humility would allow us to face the newcomer crying out on another ship more humbly – as a companion in the grand struggle between rationality and desire and as a fellow rather than a foe. But to do that we would need to admit that our religion, although tamed and tied to the mast of our ship, is prone to result in similar 'irrationalities' and to create similarly difficult desires. At this moment, however, the 'enlightened' man has trouble with admitting that he experiences desire in the first place. The necessity of placing a cross in every state school in Italy, the ban on abortion in Ireland or Malta, the Polish Parliament praying for rain during 2006[2] or attempting to ban IVF are not presented as the 'irrationality' of religion in the same way in which the religion of a French woman wearing a burqua is. Like sexual desire, this religious 'irrationality' is purged and purified by rituals resembling marriage that veils desire in 'appropriate' robes of 'tradition'. Desire and sexuality do not openly belong to marriage but are instead veiled and subsumed in tradition and duty. As in an 'enlightened' bourgeois marriage, where desire is pacified and normalised, the secularist paradigm has pacified and subordinated our own irrationality and religion, turning it into nothing more than a 'tradition' or perhaps 'profound moral views' that are justified and normalised and thus far from desire or irrationality. Only when we find our irrationality excessive and overly noticeable under the robes of propriety do we ridicule it by claiming that we must put our earplugs in even more tightly and hide our desire even more deeply in our inner chambers. The enlightened man seems to have a real problem with admitting that he is prone to irrationality in the first place.

8.1 Why has religious pluralism failed to meet its own potential?

Compared to the enlightened illusion of secularism, which mistranslated the reality of existing religious and non-religious normativities in Europe, the new paradigm of religious pluralism sprouted a new promise. As an ideal of inclusion and building ever more religiously diverse societies, it promised to get rid of our enlightened earplugs and admit that we all have different desires, sometimes secular, sometimes religious. As an ideal concept encapsulating ultimate religious diversity, it promised to listen and admit that difference indeed exists both within our societies as well as among them. In an ideally diverse pluralist society, desire and rationality coexist side by side so that difficulties are not related to denying one's desires but accommodating them side by side with the desires of the other. But to the disappointment of those expecting a new, better framework to accommodate difference, this new paradigm has so far failed to live up to its promise. Just like secularism or neutrality, religious pluralism has proved to be susceptible to rigidity and colouring of its meaning with reference to established structures of cultural hegemony. In a secularist paradigm this cultural hegemony was credited as nothing more than 'tradition' and frequently conceptualised terms of inclusion through the secularist paradigm. As illustrated in the case studies in Part II on 'myths of inclusion', pluralism followed the illusions of secularism and developed into an Enlightenment notion dominated by fear. As Adorno and Horkheimer remind us:

> Enlightenment is mythic fear turned radical. The pure immanence of positivism, its ultimate product, is no more than a so to speak universal taboo.

---

[2] Hannah Cleaver, 'Polish MPs pray for rain to save crops', *Telegraph*, 21 July 2006.

Nothing at all may remain outside, because the mere idea of outsideness is the very source of fear.

(Horkheimer and Adorno 1944, 16)

The idea of outsideness permeated the building blocks of religious pluralism, thus for instance turning the applicants in the veiling cases into violators of the very idea of pluralism. By resort to secularist denial, 'their' religion was turned into an 'ostentatious' demonstration contravening a well-recognised 'tradition' while 'ours' was once more presented as merely 'profound moral views' or 'constitutional tradition'. Applicants contesting bans on religious head-covering symbolised the return of unsubordinated religion instigating a fear of the return of irrationality, something that the illusion of Enlightenment does not permit. And since only well-recognised tradition has a place on the inside of this new enlightened paradigm of religious pluralism, an atheist in Italy was also denied her 'ostentatious' claim to freedom of non-religion. Finally sublimated by the appeal to secularity, dominant religious normativity was capable of being presented as simply a form of rationality, against which a secular claim represented the ultimate form of 'irrationality'.

This modification of religious pluralism is not surprising when we bear in mind the shape of the principle discussed in the first chapter. Instead of tackling the question of inclusion, the preoccupation with secularism versus religion has ossified cemented established approaches and approached difference superficially through established liberal paradigms and illusions of secularism. Relying on protecting the established consensus, the approach to otherness did not truly challenge the prism of tolerance. Interpreted at best as neutrality, religious pluralism has frequently obscured the visibility of the face of the other. More often than not the other, instead of being faced, was asked to become faceless. The attempt to interpret religious pluralism in a neutral or secularist fashion did not challenge socio-cultural imbalances of power. Quite to the contrary, both pluralism and rights became saturated with preserving the consensus of constitutional orders. The age of religious pluralism has developed enslavement to sameness. It has invited thinking of difference but constrained it to recognition of difference contained in the boundaries of the known, comfortable and predictable. Both with and without religious pluralism at its foundation, freedom of religion has more often than not subordinated difference to homogeneity. This, however, is not all that surprising when we keep in mind the liberal fundamentals lying behind contemporary conceptions of rights and recognition.

Both the interpretation of pluralism through existing spectacles of secularism and the resulting tendency of rights to subordinate difference to the dictate of sameness can be traced back to the centrality of liberal principles permeating the idea of rights and justice. The shape of the principle of pluralism has relied heavily on the model of religious coexistence based on the idea of reaching reasonable and static consensus. It has also eventually expanded into including certain forms of dialogue encapsulated in a theory of communicative action and deliberative models and some forms of multicultural adjustment.

When we examine the principle we are almost at once reminded of John Rawls's *A Theory of Justice* (Rawls 1999) and *Political Liberalism* (Rawls 2005). Examining these works, we encounter a similar approach focused primarily on the problem how the democratic conception of a state can be reconciled with what Rawls calls 'comprehensive religious, political and philosophical doctrines'. Rawls attempts to create a template in which citizens who share different sincere beliefs based on their religious, political or philosophical doctrines can create a society that can agree to be bound by common rules of political life. The model of pluralism envisioned in recommendations and judgments has focused on such basic assumptions of political liberalism as the central role of justice as fairness and the idea of citizens as free and equal. Rawls takes as the underpinning for his theory a model of a society which is characterised by diversity and pluralism. He calls such diversity 'a permanent feature of the public culture of democracy' (Rawls 2005, 36). This vision of pluralism and diversity applies to what he calls comprehensive religious doctrines and, in connection to them, to individual conceptions of the good. Rawls ascertains that all members of a society can be characterised by certain common features. These features include, first of all, regarding themselves as self-authenticated sources of valid claims concerning life and, second, having their own conception of the good. And, finally, the last feature is the capability of taking responsibility for their life goals that might be and often are connected with these conceptions and claims. As a natural consequence of this diversity and everybody's conviction of the validity of their own claims, the conceptions of members of society collide and clash with one another. In a Rawlsian model of pluralism, all members of society, all their conceptions of the good, all their comprehensive doctrines and other features are envisioned as equal. In all the above-mentioned features, citizens must be treated as equals, and the development of the entire theory of political liberalism is meant to sustain this conception of equality as the ideal to achieve and maintain. In *A Theory of Justice* and *Political Liberalism*, concepts such as liberty or equality are considered as inherent to and inseparable from the conception of a democracy. Citizens cannot be treated as unequal due to their particular comprehensive doctrine. The equality of all members of society is the underpinning of all democratic liberal ideas that lays a foundation for systems of rights.

But despite an assumption of equality, other requirements put forward by Rawls for maintaining the liberal democratic model concern doctrines and citizens themselves. In Rawlsian theory, these necessary characteristics are reasonableness and rationality. Reasonableness and rationality apply both to citizens as well as religious, political and philosophical doctrines. Reasonable persons are those who are ready to propose principles and standards as fair terms of cooperation and abide by them willingly if others do the same. Thus the reasonable is a social element which requires reciprocity. Unreasonableness, on the other hand, is characterised by an unwillingness to honour or propose any general terms of cooperation. In defining what reasonable doctrines are, Rawls remains cautious in order to avoid arbitrariness. He points to certain essential features of doctrines in general. They cover major religious, philosophical and moral aspects of human life in a more or less consistent manner and they organise and characterise recognised values so that they can be compatible with one another and express an intelligible view of the world. Finally, what is essential for doctrines is that they do not remain unchanged over time but evolve slowly in light of what, according to the doctrine, can be seen as good and sufficient reasons. The essence of a doctrine's reasonableness is connected with certain democratic characteristics of the entire society. Reasonable doctrines, in Rawlsian theory, recognise that they are one of many reasonable doctrines that reasonable citizens might affirm. Reasonable doctrines recognise that their claims may be of no meaning or value to other reasonable citizens adhering to other reasonable doctrines. Thus what determines a doctrine's reasonableness is the recognition that even in a situation of having political power, those adhering to the doctrine will not attempt to prevent other citizens from affirming their own reasonable views. This self-limitation of doctrines makes room for reasonable pluralism. Reasonable pluralism, according to Rawls, differs from ordinary pluralism in such a way that in ordinary pluralism comprehensive doctrines would suppress, if they could, the liberty of thought of others. In reasonable pluralism they acknowledge other views even if they do not believe in them.

But the Rawlsian model puts the burden of sustaining pluralism on citizens and doctrines themselves and relies heavily on the logic of tolerance. Assuming equality, it also embeds inequality through the judgment on who is rational and who is not. The European model of religious pluralism as illustrated in the chapters above has heavily employed these theoretical assumptions and frequently used criteria of reasonable and rational citizens and doctrines that can build a democracy. The interpretative recommendations of the CoE deeply discourage and condemn fundamentalisms that are seen as unreasonable and excluded from public discussion due to the very fact of their unreasonableness. It is in fact the unreasonableness of a doctrine that has been used as justification for refusal of equal treatment when compared to other doctrines. The primary problem with facing religious difference is that the idea of reasonable doctrines is essentially based on the understanding of Western and primarily Christian religions. As illustrated by emerging case-law, liberal premises have led to an automatic labelling of different conceptions as 'fundamentalist' as the *Dahlab* and *Şahin* cases have illustrated. As Nuotio reminds us:

> A person whose beliefs are strange to us might be measured with a false yardstick if we do not take this fact into account. A person with irrational beliefs might even be regarded as insane and lacking the capacity to be a reasonable person.
>
> (Nuotio 2008, 24)

Thus even at the outset the cornerstones of liberalism fail to solve the problem of how citizens with different, and often mutually incompatible, comprehensive doctrines can coexist together in a just, democratic society.

The problems of recognition are exacerbated by a constructivist vision of justice based on what Rawls calls 'an overlapping consensus' which remains essentially secular. This consensus is an agreement between reasonable citizens to create, follow and accept agreed principles of political justice and settle for themselves how these principles relate to their comprehensive doctrines. This consensus creates a certain common core, where political agreement overlaps with citizens' conceptions. This overlapping consensus is the foundation of public reason, a feature of Kantianism to which Rawls is undoubtedly indebted. Consensus includes agreement on the conception of the society and citizens, principles of justice and basic rights. And it is based on the idea of reciprocity, which means that all citizens agree to follow this political agreement in order to create a society based on equality and liberty and they expect others to be bound by the same rules. This model puts excessive emphasis on the idea of social coherence and peaceful coexistence as a political value of what Rawls calls a 'well-ordered' society. This well-ordered society's overlapping consensus must be so deep as to reach a common core of ideas on society, a fair system of cooperation and of citizens as reasonable, rational, free and equal. It must also be so broad as to cover the principles and values of a political conception of justice as fairness. And it is only in this consensus that we can seek justification of the presumption that political and doctrinal issues are separated from one another. As Rawls maintains, the focal points of the religious and the political spheres are different. Whereas religious values represent concern over supreme values, the political values of a constitutional democracy concentrate on the conception of a just society of equal citizens, which allows different conceptions to flourish in that society. Without citizens' support for public reason and without them honouring the political conception of justice and reciprocity, divisions and hostilities between doctrines are bound to exist. Harmony and concord depend on citizens' willingness and devotion to realise the ideal of public justice. In this model, only a common idea of justice, including the shape of rights and social rules, as distinguished from doctrinal arguments, can form the foundation of a just and well-ordered society. In this constructivist vision rights are thus subordinated to consensus and, as we have observed, so are principles such as religious pluralism.

The idea of consensus permeates the construction of religious pluralism and, in an effort to make the principle of pluralism more inclusive, recommendations have referred to the idea of deliberation that could ensure that the shape of consensus is not static. This idea is based on Habermasian ideas of communicative action and communicative freedom. In the Habermasian model, subjects commit themselves to a consensus built in the process of reciprocally taking positions and recognising each other's valid claims (Habermas 1998, 119). In this process, claims that can form the foundation of a consensus must be mutually recognisable and acceptable (Habermas 1998, 119). In terms of rights, the Habermasian model assumes that the foundation of rights lies in politically autonomous elaboration of 'the right to the greatest possible measure of equal individual liberties' (Habermas 1998, 122). Ideally these rights ought to include equal opportunities to participate in deliberative processes generating and legitimating law, including rights. This signifies exercise of political autonomy. The attempt to rescue consensus from static rigidity is noteworthy, but suffers from a failure to recognise that in a consensus the agents can also agree on the terms of discussion in the sense of agreeing to include some but exclude others from participation. While in terms of securing legitimacy of rights the Habermasian model acknowledges that rights can only be accepted if the participants in the discussion agree to their shape, safeguards for ensuring that everyone can indeed participate are considerably weaker.

To ensure among other things that everyone's capacity to participate and take part in the discussion on pluralism is secured, development of religious pluralism has frequently resorted to yet another liberal principle also focused on the role of autonomy as the foundation of rights and pluralism. While all liberal models underline the principle of autonomy, it has been extensively relied on by Joseph Raz in his idea of pluralism. The centrality of autonomy is related to freedom of choice, including the choice to participate in democratic processes. Raz is concerned with limits on the legitimate exercise of authority that will not endanger autonomy and choices of variety of acceptable moral options (Raz 1986, 398). Subsequently, pluralism is entrenched precisely in the availability of choice and preservation of that availability for different moral conceptions. Raz in fact assumes that the value of autonomy automatically leads to pluralism of views (Raz 1986, 381).

But as we have already observed in Part II, these ideal assumptions appear to fail when the other appeals for recognition of her rights. Either she has not been treated as an autonomous agent capable of choice, or her participation in creating overarching approaches has been limited or, in the worst-case scenario, she has been accused of irrationality. All the ideal tools have been interpreted as belonging to the already recognised members of society, thus rendering religious pluralism a principle of inclusion of the similar. The degree of sufficient similarity was, on the other hand, measured through comparison to the known and reference to the logic of tolerance. Through tolerance, the boundaries of acceptable and unacceptable difference were cut strictly to fit only those whose beliefs were not deemed too radical. The centrality of tolerance has placed a double standard at the heart of human rights. Eventually in the tolerant, rationalised, secular world full of autonomous rational and reasonable agents, religious pluralism began to signify a precarious form of recognition dependent on the judgment of worthiness issued by looking into the mirror to find a model of the acceptable other. This acceptable other could only be found rational if her belief were close enough to one's own perfectly legitimate 'tradition'. In all other circumstance she has been considered too radical and too 'unreasonable' to fit the existing consensus. Inclusion was undone by reference to the liberal tools devised to secure it. This comfortable idea of pluralism based on looking into the mirror rather than into the face of the other has ossified already established and immutable static legal orders determining the shape of human rights. There, legal orders were judged democratic without examination as to whether the other had first of all opportunities to exercise her rights but more importantly whether she had opportunities to affect the shape of rights in the first place. But as we have seen, the other was in fact rarely in the picture at all, replaced with the image of the self. The next deconstructive and reconstructive chapter will attempt to illustrate what prompted the undoing of liberal principles and how these developments could be prevented.

References

Habermas, Jürgen. 1998. *Between Facts and Norms: Contributions to a Discourse Theory of Law and Democracy*. MIT Press.

Horkheimer, Max and Theodor W. Adorno. 1944. *Dialectic of Enlightenment: Philosophical Fragments*. Stanford University Press.

Nuotio, Kimmo. 2008. 'Criminal Law and Cultural Sensitivity.' *Retfaerd* 31 (1/120): 18–44.

Rawls, John. 1999. *A Theory of Justice*, rev. edn. Belknap Press of Harvard University Press.

Rawls, John. 2005. *Political Liberalism: Expanded Edition*. Columbia University Press.

Raz, Joseph. 1986. *The Morality of Freedom*. Oxford University Press.

Zucca, Lorenzo. 2012. *A Secular Europe: Law and Religion in the European Constitutional Landscape*. Oxford University Press.

Chapter 9

Repairing the utopia of rights

Sources of reconstruction

Together with a pessimistic diagnosis of the state of religious pluralism comes a pessimistic but not unique diagnosis of the current state of human rights (Douzinas 2000a; Žižek 2005; Simmons 2011). When viewed in combination with diagnoses of the current approaches to diversity (Parekh 2002; Lentin and Titley 2011; Gozdecka, Ercan and Kmak 2014) the picture of the role of rights in recognition of difference appears overwhelmingly gloomy. It reminds us of the damned from Doré's engraving, cast down and sealed in hell without a possibility of recourse to justice. In this process some of them have been demonised and turned into symbols of a devilish threat to law and order. As seen in Parts I and II above, little in the current construction of rights prevents such an outcome from recurring over and over again when the other appeals for recognition among the established. It is in fact the very centrality of an autonomous self, constitutive of liberal concepts of rights and justice that draws everything around towards the centre of itself, claiming more and more territory and erasing difference despite the best attempts at securing the opposite outcome. Faced with this picture, the reader might legitimately ask what else could possibly be done? After all, multiple reconstructions of the rights of the other have often inevitably led no further than to simply reshaping limitations of liberal approaches to rights and pushing these limitations a little further away. As mentioned at the outset, this volume finds even those diagnoses and efforts immensely valuable for their casting more light on the other, who in other circumstances could so easily be overlooked. Theorists who do not wish to push the limitations of liberalism further often conclude in an unappeasably negative manner, suggesting that rights cannot in fact stand for much else than instruments of abuse and domination (Žižek 2005), especially in multicultural types of discourse (Žižek 1997). Others, by contrast, wish to reconstruct rights to serve the justice of the other by arriving at a mystical place of utopia (Douzinas 2000a; Simmons 2011). To attempt to push liberal limitations further than simply stating that the other has to be seen and faced, we must fix our gaze in the direction of utopia – necessary for the azimuth of reconstruction. The intention of the reconstruction offered below is a rethinking of human rights so that they might escape the traps of liberalism and negative tendencies of enlightened illusions and allow them to regain their force as instruments preventing abuses of power. While the account offered below might appear radical, it is necessary to pave the path of thinking about human rights differently than as a simple extension of legal rights. By conceptualising rights differently, the reconstruction proposed below aims at freeing the utopian call of rights for justice (Douzinas 2000a; Douzinas 2000b) from conceptualisations of interests and privileges that underpin contemporary constructions of human rights and return them to the dominated, the homeless and the dispossessed. If such a reconstruction does not happen, a 'man is repressed and a mockery [is] made of the rights of man, and the promise of an ultimate return to the rights of man is postponed indefinitely' (Levinas 1994, 96).

Having recurred repeatedly throughout the text, four sources of this reconstruction seem apparent. The four main pillars will be based on the theories of Theodor Adorno, Emmanuel Levinas, Jean-François Lyotard and Gilles Deleuze. Coming from different schools, these thinkers are not easily put in the same bag. While each of them has been preoccupied with difference, heterogeneity and preventing the totalising effects of ontological thinking, nevertheless their individual approaches differ greatly. Indeed, in terms of certain concepts, these differences are so grave that mixing their doctrines could lead to philosophical conundrums requiring a far more skilled philosophical reconstruction than this author is capable of (Williams 2005; May 2007; Reynolds and Roffe 2006; Smith 2007). But difficulty does not mean impossibility, and, as demonstrated below, a first-generation Frankfurt School thinker, a phenomenologist, a post-modernist and a poststructuralist metaphysician can be reconciled at least in some respects when we strictly have in mind the problems pointed out in this volume. While placing Adorno next to Lyotard is less controversial (Dews 1986) and even Lyotard himself has examined Adorno's contribution to setting a threshold to post-modernity (Lyotard 1974), placing Levinas, a phenomenologist and philosopher of transcendence, next to Deleuze, a fierce defender of immanence and severe critic of phenomenology, requires a few more words of explanation. But first, to begin the reconstruction we require a starting point based on a viable theoretical deconstruction that offers abstraction going beyond an empirical analysis of the mechanisms of exclusion provided in the parts above. To find such a departure point on our path towards utopian reconstruction, we will first focus on the theories of Adorno and Lyotard. These two theorists provide us with the theoretical tools necessary for diagnosis of where we are before taking any further steps. While diverse in their approaches, these scholars share a suspicion of static ontological categories and totalising traps involved in modelling the other on the self. Three of them also share a preoccupation with Hegelian and phenomenological accounts, allowing them to rethink the role of the self and the place of unity versus difference.

Adorno, a prominent German critic of mass culture and modernity, has been slowly received in the anglophone world and, before Iris Marion Young's work on difference, rarely considered in this context. His slow reception was followed by accusations of being an overly pessimistic bored intellectual (Editors 1974; Jarvis 1998). His *Negative Dialectic* (Adorno 1973) in particular has been seen as no more than a grand-scale negative critique. But Adorno, beginning with his work with

Horkheimer in the *Dialectic of Enlightenment* (Horkheimer and Adorno 1944), paved a steady way for the post-modern project long before it became a philosophical trend. In their opening phrase 'the wholly enlightened earth radiates under the sign of disaster triumphant' (Horkheimer and Adorno 1944, 1) Adorno and Horkheimer encapsulated the tragic consequences of modernity and its inevitable destination, leading only straight to the concentration camps of Auschwitz. For Adorno, the enlightened project is underpinned by illusions of rationality and progress which disguise the true nature of domination. Meanwhile, rationality has proved to be irrational and without reform Enlightenment cannot become anything but a new totality, a myth or even a 'fetish' (Adorno 1951, para. 99). This myth, under the auspices of progress, constrains the true nature of freedom and leads naturally to new abuses and disasters. This tool of Adorno's philosophy has already been used in analysing the myth of secularism, disguising power imbalances on the scene of law and religion. But beyond this, Adorno has engaged in a comprehensive project of tackling the problems of ontology involved in defining freedom. His magnum opus *Negative Dialectic* is an uncompromising assessment of the relationship between freedom and identity. As an avid reader, and critic, of Hegel, in his work Adorno offers a new form of dialectical thinking going beyond the tired triad of *thesis + antithesis = synthesis*. In his new dialectical approach, Adorno rejects positive affirmation and focuses on the negations and the splits within negations. In his dialectical manner, Adorno illustrates the correlation between the freedom and unfreedom of a bourgeois subject and the split between the universal and particular. In doing so, he fiercely criticises the links between identity and structures of domination. Adorno disputes whether identity, freedom or subjectivity could be achieved in a positive, affirmative way. When focusing on identity, he insists that it has been used negatively by linking with unity and imposing identity upon objects. Such imposition results in denial of differences and diversity. This process, according to Adorno, stems from societal formations. In his rejection of the affirmative character of the traditional dialectical method, he therefore embraces non-identity as a concept split between identity and non-identity. And it is just that reaching out towards the concepts of unfreedom and non-identity that can inform our analysis further. As a powerful deconstructive strategy, Adorno's focus on the violence of identity towards non-identity and ignorance of unfreedom in affirmations of freedom will serve as a background for analysing where contemporary rights regimes stand.

But, as with any starting point, the current situation of rights cannot be truly illuminated when we realise where it leads further and where it prevents us from going if we carry on along the same path without changing course. And it is here that Jean-François Lyotard's analyses provide valuable insights. Lyotard, a French philosopher who first used the word 'post-modernity' in his *The Postmodern Condition: A Report on Knowledge* (Lyotard 1984), was initially an avid reader of Husserl's and Merleau-Ponty's phenomenological writings and, like Adorno, a critic of Hegel. His initial adventure with phenomenology led him to consider a way between subjectivity and objectivity that could mark a step forward from

the critical agenda formulated by Marxism. Eventually examining phenomenological accounts to undermine structuralism and foundationalism, he rejected
their further use for materialist models of politics. To find a third way, Lyotard
moved towards analyses of discourse and the place of difference and multiplicity
therein. And it is through theory of discourse that Lyotard reimagined law, politics and justice. As a mere collection of stories, all law and justice are created by
discursive practices and their structures rely on meta-narratives. The main target
of Lyotard's critique became the idea of the historical development of knowledge towards Enlightenment and subsequent totalisation of all knowledge, a suspicion he inherited from Adorno. In this suspicion of meta-narratives, he called
them grand narratives and critiqued their ability to provide criteria for universal
judgment. Arguing for a system that would give up such universal criteria, his
post-modern project advocated imagining the possibility of the coexistence of
multiple judgments and the idea of justice based not on singularity but instead
on multiplicity. Focusing on language, Lyotard examined not only the condition
of knowledge but also ideas of justice and consensus. Moving from *The Postmodern
Condition* to *The Differend* (Lyotard 1988), his analysis examined how injustice is
reproduced in the context of language. He presents the mechanism of silencing
the victims of injustice, illustrating that in addition to literal silencing of the victims of injustice, further injustice might be perpetuated and maintained by presenting these victims through such terms of discourse as are unable to address the
very injustice suffered. He calls such silencing occurring with the use of language
a differend. The *differend* happens when what the phrase refers to (the referent) is
presented by the addressor in such a way that the addressee (the victim) cannot
identify with it. As a consequence of such deep dissonance the victim of injustice
eventually becomes turned into a perpetrator and the perceived coherence of the
system can be retained.

While the analyses of both Adorno and Lyotard followed different theoretical
paths, they illustrate the tragic qualities of mega-narratives and share a suspicion
towards foundationalism, universalism and the dangers of totalising structures.
And it is this suspicion that can provide us with invaluable insights on the current state of rights and their approach to recognition of difference. While helpful in deconstructing the dangers involved in current developments in the arena
of human rights, both theories prove impotent in providing tools for surmount-
ing these obstacles. Adorno's drive towards non-identity does not envision how
non-identity could really be approached to become the focal point for challenging the totalising effects of identity. Meanwhile Lyotard, while envisioning justice based on multiple narratives and plural terms of judgments, appears to fail
to provide tools that might be helpful in envisioning justice and politics after the
death of grand narratives – an absence likely dictated by reluctance to create
another grand narrative. While the ideas of Adorno and Lyotard are crucial for
an understanding of the challenges confronting human rights today, the difficulties they identified require further conceptualisations, allowing a vision of human
rights that could be more receptive to difference. Despite sharing a reluctance

towards replacing one structure with another, this volume will none the less encourage going beyond the *cul-de-sac* in which no reconstruction is ever possible simply because of the dangers of reinventing a new foundationalism. While discouraging creation of a new universal model, an analysis based on a combination of Levinasian *otherwise* and Deleuzian *becoming* will be offered as a flexible roadmap towards overcoming the dangers of totalising structures that result in subsuming difference to sameness.

The problems related to totalising homogenisation erasing heterogeneity are partly linked to the traps of ontology illuminated in the previous parts of the volume. To challenge the problems of subjectivity, it is meaningful to look into theories challenging the centrality of the subject and the centrality of autonomy. If non-identity is to be approached and justice based on multiplicity brought closer, then we need to begin envisioning a way of transcending beyond the self and imagining a more heteronomous account of rights. Therefore, and as others have attempted previously (Douzinas 2000a; Simmons 2011), we will begin the reconstruction by examining the fundamentals of the thought of Emmanuel Levinas.

Levinas, a French thinker of Lithuanian Jewish descent, was unsurprisingly a student of Husserl and Merleau-Ponty and a reader of Hegel, a background that he shared with both Adorno and Lyotard. Unlike them, however, he followed the Husserlian phenomenological path and engaged in reconsidering the ethical relationship with the other. Engaging in counter-ontological critique, Levinas developed a theory of transcending beyond the ego of the self. In *Totality and Infinity* (Levinas 1969) and *Otherwise than Being* (Levinas 1981), he approached the themes of being, otherness and transcendence, treating them primarily as an ethical affair. The source of this ethical affair is the encounter with the other, who can be 'a widow, an orphan or a stranger' (Levinas 1969, 244). In this encounter, the face of the other plays a crucial role. There is something in the face of the other that for Levinas displaces the centrality of the ego. When standing face to face with the other, the self dissolves and transcends itself. In other words, Levinasian transcendence arises in a lived and factual moment of ethical encounter. It is the face of the other that calls the self to responsibility in the moment of encounter. The specificity of the face of the other breaks the boundaries of the ego and calls the self to that responsibility. That responsibility on the other hand is infinite. While the self can approach the other in this ethical relationship, it can never truly reach the other. Proximity is the closest relationship that the self and the other can enjoy. In other words, the other must remain absolutely other, it cannot be taken hostage by the ego of the self. The two can never fully merge, and thus the other can never be reduced to the same through imposition of neutral terms that allow the self to comprehend the other. This means that the other, just like our responsibility, is thus also infinite. Levinas attempts to escape the ontological traps by placing ethics before ontology. Responsibility for the other comes first and is the primary duty of the subject that allows him or her to break away from the confines of totality. The other cannot be judged or chiselled to the expectations of the self. Instead, she must be faced and taken responsibility for. The same applies to rights, which

Levinas believes should be founded on the idea of infinite responsibility transcending the boundary of rights as a privilege (Levinas 1994). As illustrated by Bettina Bergo, Levinasian transcendence is a somewhat peculiar notion of transcendence (Bergo 2005). It is a transcendence-in-immanence examining the possibilities to go beyond one's own immanence in the actual moment of encounter. But Levinasian theory also encounters further difficulties. According to Levinas, responsibility arises when a third person enters the encounter. Unfortunately, his theory does not sufficiently address the possibility of encountering multiple others in the presence of multiple third persons. When there are many others, who are those we have responsibility for? That central difficulty has led some to suggest that Levinasian theory is no more than theology in philosophical disguise (Badiou 2001).

To go beyond this impasse, we will therefore turn towards the Deleuzian notion of becoming. Despite his preoccupation with difference, Deleuze stands in striking contrast to the foregoing thinkers and his analyses feature analyses of Hume and Spinoza rather than Hegel and Husserl. In trying to break away from Hegelians and phenomenologists, he re-examined the potential of Kantian thought for creating (and yet failing to do so) pure immanence. In trying to criticise the shortcomings of Kantianism, he sought to develop his theory of pure immanence and univocity as the underpinning of his philosophy of difference. While creating a pure plane of immanence and situating difference therein, he did not entirely avoid the traps of transcendence (May 2007) but certainly reversed the prioritisation of ethics over ontology that we observed in Levinas. In that aspect, Deleuze remained closer to Lyotard rather than Levinas (Williams 2005). In his effort to conceptualise difference within that framework, Deleuze separated difference from identity. In *Difference and Repetition* (Deleuze 1995), Deleuze detaches difference from four main conceptualisations of it, including Aristotelian, Platonian, Hegelian and Leibnizian. As Williams argues, for Deleuze: 'Difference is the condition for changes in actual things and actual things are the condition for the expression of difference as something that can be determined' (Williams 2003, 56). Therefore Deleuze seeks respect for difference without identity. At the same time he builds his new ontology that is suspicious of thinking in terms and concepts. In this new ontology he subordinates *being* to what he calls *becoming*. *The Anti-Oedipus* (Deleuze and Guattari 2004) and *A Thousand Plateaus* (Deleuze and Guattari 1980), his works jointly co-authored with Felix Guattari, develop this concept among the vast array of new terminology contesting existing ontological categories. Becoming signifies the process in which, as Žižek reminds us, becoming is privileged over being: 'the pure becoming-without-being means that one should sidestep the present – it never "actually occurs," it is "always forthcoming and already past" ' (Žižek 2004, 9). Braidotti reminds us that the radical immanence of the subject is embodied in the subject's perpetual becoming (Braidotti 1997, 68). In other words, the subject is in constant process of anti-essentialist transformations. Becoming is a minoritarian affair and Deleuze further explores becoming minoritarian in his *Kafka: Toward a Minor Literature* (Deleuze 1986). Becoming minoritarian is a confrontation and reconfiguration of the majoritarian standard and an ever 'ongoing process of non-coincidence with the standard, however reconfigured' (Patton 2005, 407).

Despite deep differences between Levinas and Deleuze, some of which appear irreconcilable and require a far more in-depth study than this volume allows, the rethinking of rights at the service of the other will borrow Sarah Cooper's notion of *Otherwise than Becoming* (Cooper 2002). In this acrobatic effort it will attempt to push Levinasian limitations and replace being with becoming in an effort to respond to the question: Who is the other in the presence of the third person? While the priority of infinite responsibility towards the other will be retained, the replacement of being with becoming will allow for preventing the justice of rights from constantly redeveloping and protecting majoritarian standards. This effort will be made by examining the notion of emancipation in the contemporary diverse world in the hope of preserving the emancipatory potential of human rights in contrast to the ossifying potential of legal rights.

References

Adorno, Theodor W. 1951. *Minima Moralia: Reflections on a Damaged Life*. Verso.

Adorno, Theodor W. 1973. *Negative Dialectics*. Routledge.

Badiou, Alain. 2001. *Ethics: An Essay on the Understanding of Evil*. Verso.

Bergo, Bettina. 2005. 'Ontology, Transcendence, and Immanence in Emmanuel Levinas's Philosophy.' *Research in Phenomenology* 35(1): 141–80.

Braidotti, Rosi. 1997. 'Meta(l)morphoses.' *Theory, Culture & Society* 14(2): 67–80.

Cooper, Sarah. 2002. 'Otherwise than Becoming: Jean Rouch and the Ethics of Les Maîtres fous.' *French Studies* 56(4): 483–94.

Deleuze, Gilles. 1986. *Kafka: Toward a Minor Literature*. University of Minnesota Press.

Deleuze, Gilles. 1995. *Difference and Repetition*, trans. Paul Patton. Columbia University Press.

Deleuze, Gilles and Felix Guattari. 1980. *A Thousand Plateaus: Capitalism and Schizophrenia*. Continuum.

Deleuze, Gilles and Felix Guattari. 2004. *Anti-Oedipus*. A&C Black.

Dews, Peter. 1986. 'Adorno, Post-structuralism and the Critique of Identity.' *New Left Review* 157(1): 28–44.

Douzinas, Costas. 2000a. *The End of Human Rights: Critical Legal Thought at the Turn of the Century*. Hart Publishing.

Douzinas, Costas. 2000b. 'Human Rights and Postmodern Utopia.' *Law and Critique* 11(2): 219–40.

Editors. 1974. 'Introduction to Adorno.' *Telos* 19: 2–6.

Gozdecka, Dorota A., Selen A. Ercan and Magdalena Kmak. 2014. 'From Multiculturalism to Post-Multiculturalism: Trends and Paradoxes.' *Journal of Sociology* 50(1): 51–64.

Horkheimer, Max and Theodor W. Adorno. 1944. *Dialectic of Enlightenment: Philosophical Fragments*. Stanford University Press.

Jarvis, Simon. 1998. *Adorno: A Critical Introduction*. Psychology Press.

Lentin, Alana and Gavan Titley. 2011. *The Crises of Multiculturalism: Racism in a Neoliberal Age*. Zed Books.

Levinas, Emmanuel. 1969. *Totality and Infinity: An Essay on Exteriority*. Duquesne University Press.

Levinas, Emmanuel. 1981. *Otherwise than Being, or Beyond Essence*. Springer.

Levinas, Emmanuel. 1994. *Outside the Subject*. Stanford University Press.

Lyotard, Jean-François. 1974. 'Adorno as the Devil.' *Telos* 19: 127–37.

Lyotard, Jean-François. 1984. *The Postmodern Condition: A Report on Knowledge*. Theory and History of Literature 10. Manchester University Press.

Lyotard, Jean-François. 1988. *The Differend: Phrases in Dispute*. Theory and History of Literature 46. University of Minnesota Press.

May, Todd. 2007. *Reconsidering Difference: Nancy, Derrida, Levinas, Deleuze*. Pennsylvania State University Press.

Parekh, Bhikhu C. 2002. *Rethinking Multiculturalism: Cultural Diversity and Political Theory*. Harvard University Press.

Patton, P. 2005. 'Deleuze and Democracy.' *Contemporary Political Theory* 4(4): 400–13.

Reynolds, Jack and Jon Roffe. 2006. 'Deleuze and Merleau-Ponty: Immanence, Univocity and Phenomenology.' *Journal of the British Society for Phenomenology* 37(3): 228–51.

Simmons, William Paul. 2011. *Human Rights Law and the Marginalized Other*. Cambridge University Press.

Smith, Daniel W. 2007. 'Deleuze and the Question of Desire: Toward an Immanent Theory of Ethics.' *Parrhesia* 2: 66–78.

Williams, James. 2003. *Gilles Deleuze's 'Difference and Repetition': A Critical Introduction and Guide*. Edinburgh University Press.

Williams, James. 2005. *The Transversal Thought of Gilles Deleuze: Encounters and Influences*. Clinamen Press.

Žižek, Slavoj. 1997. 'Multiculturalism, Or, the Cultural Logic of Multinational Capitalism.' *New Left Review* 1(225): 28–51.

Žižek, Slavoj. 2004. *Organs without Bodies: Deleuze and Consequences*. Psychology Press.

Žižek, Slavoj. 2005. 'Against Human Rights.' *New Left Review* 34: 115–31.

Chapter 10

Human rights and the dissident

10.1 Stationary consensus of rights and freedom trapped by identity

Despite promising construction and models relying on equality, discourse and autonomy, liberal recognition models all too frequently fail to be receptive to the idea of difference. The key problem of liberal models is their limited receptivity to changing circumstances and varying axes of emancipation. Whether in the symbol of reasonable consensus or in communicative action, the shape of freedom in liberal models turns out to be pre-given and predictable and all too frequently hijacked by identity. It is a freedom already achieved, dispensed in its recognisable forms to those who already have a voice. It is freedom of the known that does violence to heterogeneity by making consensus its ultimate end goal. By attempting to achieve a static consensus, these models fix the position of the known and recognisable and their focus on difference is superficial. As Lyotard reminded us in *Postmodern Condition*, when we base a system on consensus its static qualities necessarily do violence to heterogeneity (Lyotard 1984, 73). The foundationalism of consensus is reinforced by the fact that it is considered the ultimate end of discussion rather than, as Lyotard suggested, being a particular stage of discussion (Lyotard 1984, 65–6). As Seyla Benhabib argues, Lyotard attempted to convince us that we must arrive at an idea of justice that is not linked to consensus (Benhabib 1984, 111). Wary of being caught in the meta-narratives of the subject, Lyotard challenged the static nature of consensus and offered polytheism of values as a basis of a temporary social contract (Rorty 1985; Benhabib 1984). Lyotardian objections to consensus readily apply to contemporary diagnoses of religious pluralism as a human rights principle. When rights and their principles are primarily driven by the idea of securing consensus, then otherness must be violated because the very idea of heterogeneity undermines the image of the predictability of consensus. As the interpretation of religious pluralism has illustrated, even those principles of rights that seem to be striving for heterogeneity turn into rigidity when they focus on sameness for the sake of preserving the idea of consensus synonymous with a static order. Lyotard's idea of more fluid justice is crucial for injecting pluralism into an immutable and ordered vision of pluralism and rescuing rights from the staleness of discussion-ending consensus. The focus on sameness for the preservation of consensus is perpetuated by expelling difference to the outskirts of the established societal agreement. An established and already-achieved consensus has no place for dissent. Instead, homogeneity takes over and draws the boundaries of everything by analogy to the self. Modelling the freedom of others on the freedom of oneself becomes a safeguard preventing new values and new principles from disrupting the consensus understood as the end of discussion. When such modelling takes place, no matter how strongly entrenched and how profoundly emphasised, rights by virtue of their link to freedom become mere tools for maintaining the order of existing consensus and all its underlying power balances, including those that are cultural and religious. When used for such conservationist efforts, human rights and the principles lying at their foundations become grand narratives constantly recurring in judgments and scholarly reasoning but stripped of their emancipatory meaning. As grand narratives they can be assigned and attributed any meaning that can sustain the existing consensus while perpetuating an illusion of progress and Enlightenment. Unfortunately, instead of tools of emancipation human rights have turned into grand narratives manifesting a type of self-certainty which 'artificially erases the traces of otherness and imagines self as identical with itself' (Douzinas 2000, 271).

This erasure happens due to the aforementioned modelling of freedoms of others on well-recognised freedom and to seeing human rights as privileges of subjects. Critiques of the conception of the subject of rights based on Cartesian and Kantian theories have engaged multiple research (Douzinas 2000; Benhabib 2004; Rancière 2004; Žižek 2005) and reiterating these general objections could fill the pages of another lengthy volume. The interesting aspect we observed in the example of freedom of religion is the pairing of the logic of subjectivity with the logic of identity and eventual expansion of the identity principle to the entire community. This mechanism was analysed by Adorno, who maintained that identity is an essentially coercive instrument which drives the desire to bring everything to sameness and subordinate the particular to the universal. He went so far as to call identity a 'primal form of ideology' (Adorno 1973, 148) that can be used for the purposes of domination. It is the logic and principle of identity that Adorno sees as an instrument leading to the conquest of the other by the subject. It is that logic that drives the definitional struggles of the subject to find its essence. Essentialism eventually subordinates the other to the self and erases the particular in favour of the universal, eventually allowing the majority to hijack human rights for the constant effort of preserving the existing consensus. But as contemporary rights case-law illustrates, mutation from the privilege of a subject to an instrument of power happens when a given community at a given time appropriates the logic of identity to define itself by self-referential, homogeneous and exclusionary definitions. While a communitarian critique has been born out of the critique of individualism of the subject and the relationship between the self and the other (Cornell 1986), it has frequently ignored the capacity of a community to exclude otherness. The self-referential community mirrors the ontological hunger of the subject when it is seen as an aggregative extension of the subject. In *Otherwise than Being*, Levinas, in exploring the qualities of the subject, observed that self-interested subjects regroup themselves into totalising systems. Subjects that do not form a meaningful relationship with the other form arrangements and orders and cannot be separated from these structures:

> But the clarity comes from a certain arrangement which orders the entities or the moments and the *esse ipsum* of these entities into a system, assembling them. Being's appearing cannot be separated from a certain conjunction of elements in a structure, a lining up of structures in which being carries on – from their simultaneity, that is, their copresence.
>
> (Levinas 1981, 133)

When such an aggregative structure develops a self-understanding and self-evaluation positioning itself *vis-à-vis* the other, it necessarily draws the limits of the self by excluding otherness. This exclusion happens by reference to the perceived essence of the subject, namely its identity. As Adorno reminds us, the problem of ontological struggles of the subject lies in taking identity as the goal of self-identification and assuming that the formula 'it is' is the ultimate form of identification:

> But definition also approaches that which the object itself is as nonidentical: in placing its mark on the object, definition seeks to be marked by the object. Nonidentity is the secret *telos* of identification. It is the part that can be salvaged; the mistake in traditional thinking is that identity is taken for the goal. The force that shatters the appearance of identity is the force of thinking: the use of 'it is' undermines the form of that appearance, which remains inalienable just the same.
>
> (Adorno 1973, 149)

When identity becomes the end goal, it shares the qualities of a consensus in becoming just another rigid structure that disables conceiving of the possibility of salvaging non-identity. When it becomes a source of such structural foundationalism, the principle of identity begins spreading and imposes an obligation on the particular to become identical with the total. We have so far seen how tradition and legal definitions have been used by rights regimes to impose the identity principle and coupled with an expectation to conform to the dominant normativity. As a result of these expectations, 'nonidentical individuals and performances become commensurable and identical' (Adorno 1973, 146). When the identity-imposing mechanism takes over, the mechanisms used by the self to draw the boundaries between itself and the other are exported to the boundaries of the imagined community that becomes a quasi-extension of the self. In that configuration, dominant communities begin to impose their cultural standards, as Young has reminded us in her analyses (Young 1990). As illustrated in previous chapters, the jurisprudence of rights too often acts as a system drawing the limits of the community and excluding the other in the very same way as the self excludes everything that is not identical with the self. When the identity principle seen as the end goal takes over the logic of rights, then rights begin to exclude otherness at the outset. The justice of rights based on self-referential definitions will always serve the purpose of incorporating the particular into the universal, thus disabling the possibility of emancipation. A narrow reading of community and its 'identity' parallels the egoistic need to reaffirm one's authenticity by an individual (Taylor 1992, 50). Whereas in the act of self-definition individualism 'forgets that every person is a world and comes into existence in common with others' (Douzinas 2013, 59), reliance on a self-referential definition of community compels the other to merge into the common essence. By assuming self-referential and exclusionary definitions, the community can erase the 'individuality and concrete identity of the Other' (Benhabib 1992, 158), or in Adorno's terms erase non-identity. Instead, the community constructs otherness in opposition to the community's own characteristics and expels every identity that does not fall within the self-definition.

As observed here, aggregation of subjects of rights into a community of rights becomes a new totalising structure, and the state's employment of rights in the name of a concrete community will 'interpret and apply them, if at all, according to local legal procedures and moral principles, making the universal the handmaiden of the particular' (Douzinas 2013, 60). Reference to particular national, cultural or religious groups is sustained by presenting their traditions as uniform and united in dominant normative standards. Such employment of the notion of a community leads to what Balibar calls absolutisation of the community (Balibar 2013, 24). In an absolutised community, rights become merely competing claims prone to be employed in the interest of prevailing models and serving no more than rejection of the possibility of resistance (Balibar 2013, 24–5). When the concept of 'community' is employed to suppress multiplicity in the name of cultural, religious or moral essence, the appeal to community does not alleviate but aggravates the problems perpetuated by the centrality of the subject. A 'community' that submerges difference into a homogeneity whose central aim is to protect itself from otherness represents merely an extension of an egoistic self. It appropriates power and employs rights in defence of the homogeneity of the 'community', curtailing the possibility of emancipation and resistance. As a consequence, rights mutate and result in a reversal of their original idea: from emancipation to domination and from liberation to exclusion and fear.

10.2 The dissident and her asymmetric relationship with rights

While expelling otherness, the community inadvertently creates a dissident. A dissident is the other placed far outside the boundary of a community and who has been singled out primarily because of her difference. When a community egoistically appropriates rights to maintain its static foundational consensus, its privileges expand, placing the dissident ever further away from that boundary. Eventually a dissident is placed directly in opposition to the community. She not only fails to be seen as a part of it but is instead conceptualised as the antithesis of, and a danger to, the community itself. As the case-law analysed here has illustrated, statically fixed rights and their principles, such as pluralism, fail to protect those who are depicted as 'dissidents'. In the process of creating a 'dissident', the other placed *vis-à-vis* the community eventually grows to symbolise the antithesis of the entire legal system, including the legalised human rights that are seen as its extension. Despite this perception, her culpability often lies in the mere act of contestation of the status quo and a plea to recognise her difference. But when this difference is turned into a fundamental flaw that renders the other an 'unlawful' dissident, she easily slips off the scales of justice. She is prevented from contesting injustice by mechanisms of the *différend* in which rights seen as an extension of the law become interpreted in a way protectionist of established structures. Rather than being instruments which the dissident can use for contestation, they become the very reason why she cannot contest her injustice. When such a 'bridge' is thrown over the waters of dissent, the dissident is skilfully deprived of her argument and the coherence of the system can be restored in the name of rights. As the diverse studies presented here have shown, the other can be different in different settings and the mechanisms for creating otherness might rely on slightly different techniques. It might be a Muslim woman choosing veiling in a secular narrative, a religiously devoted Dane in a setting where religious normativity is primarily cultural or an atheist Italian immersed in a religiously inspired tradition. Nonetheless, as the examples selected in this study have shown, the dissident is first singled out for her qualities, then subsequently placed on the outside of the community and distanced from it, until her difference turned into a threat to the community itself. In this process, rights mutate into a defence used by the community against the dissident that can easily 'exclude and stratify the less desirable' (Lentin and Titley 2011, 206). To allow for such distancing and such an appropriation of rights in a *différend* type of argument, rights claims that challenge traditional approaches to cultural issues, such as the widely reported headscarf cases, frequently rely on a perception of a conflict of values between communities and dissident identities. The famous *Dahlab* v. *Switzerland* formulation made the conflict abundantly clear by underlining that:

> It … appears difficult to reconcile the wearing of an Islamic headscarf with the message of tolerance, respect for others and, above all, equality and non-discrimination that all teachers in a democratic society must convey to their pupils.[1]

Perception of a conflict fuels the resurgence of a homogeneously defined community and its undisturbed capacity to preserve its 'essence'. As a consequence,

[1] *Dahlab* v. *Switzerland*, European Court of Human Rights, Decision, Application No. 42393/98, 15 February 2001, para. 1.

the relation between the dissident and rights changes into asymmetry. A claimant challenging the cultural status quo is positioned *vis-à-vis* a legal system that includes legalised rights. When placed in opposition to rights and their principles, 'the deep roots of strife and domination' are concealed and the conflict is presented in terms of 'law and rights themselves' (Douzinas 2013, 61). Being placed in opposition to legalised rights, a dissident faces them as a sphere beyond contestation. In such a static consensus, rights as legal instruments shape the asymmetric relationship between the community and those excluded. Whereas the dissident must always justify why they wish to do something different from the majority, the majoritarian system in question is freed from that expectation (Simmons 2011, 70–1). In extreme cases, the possibility of contestation is dismissed by reference to the very existence of legal regulation. Where there is law, consensus cements everything, preventing any possibility of contestation. As a consequence, dissidents challenging the essence of a community are no longer perceived as fighting for recognition of their rights claims. Instead, they symbolise an attempt to bring down the fundamentals of the entire legal and constitutional system. Such framing was visible for instance in the case of *Şefika Köse*,[2] where an attempt by the applicants to appeal to rights was silenced by presenting them as subjects disobedient to law. While assessing the proportionality of the means used by the institution regulating wearing of the headscarf in the case, the Court reiterated that it was 'sufficient to note that both the parents and the pupils were informed of the consequences of not obeying the rules'.[3] The mere existence of law, regardless of its form or receptiveness to difference, precluded the possibility of contestation. What follows from such a framing of the dissident is to further attribute her with qualities of a perpetrator attempting to sanction her own illegal actions by appeal to rights. The formulation in *Dahlab* v. *Switzerland* attempted to silence contestation of existing structures by underlining that it was the very act of dissent that contravened the foundational principles of the legal system in question. The mere act of asserting freedom of religion by wearing a headscarf was seen as 'difficult to reconcile' with 'tolerance, respect for others and, above all, equality and non-discrimination'.[4] The dissident in question was presented as a mere illegal intruder contravening the values of the state, the community of the 'good' and indeed rights themselves.

Surprisingly, dissidents can be presented as employing egoism to achieve the same goal. Judge Bonello made this abundantly clear in his concurring opinion in *Lautsi* v. *Italy* by reproaching the applicant for her appeal to rights. Rather than lawful contestation, the claim brought before an international Court signified an attack on law, culture and tradition:

---

[2] *Şefika Köse and 93 Others* v. *Turkey*, European Court of Human Rights, Decision, Application No. 26625/02, 24 January 2006.

[3] *Ibid.*, para. B.

[4] *Dahlab* v. *Switzerland*, para. 1.

May it please Ms Lautsi, in her own name and on behalf of secularism, not to enlist the services of this Court to ensure the suppression of the Italian school calendar, another Christian-cultural heritage that has survived the centuries without any evidence of irreparable harm to the progress of freedom, emancipation, democracy and civilisation.[5]

While exploiting the very critique of the egoism of the self, the judgment failed to examine that the boundaries of the self were in this case shifted to the imagined homogeneous community. The *differend* was constructed by depriving the applicant of her contestation claim through a statement undermining the legitimacy of her appeal to rights. Statements such as Judge Bonello's refrain from engaging with marginalisation by existing 'tradition' and reinforce the position of the established community by reference to the identity principle. Accepting a wide margin of appreciation free from external scrutiny in matters such as perpetuating particular 'identity-links'[6] sanctioned this egoistic expulsion of otherness in the name of an imagined community. When the logic of a *differend* is used for preservation of the system, the dissident is placed in an asymmetric relationship to rights. She is not only deprived of any possibility of contestation but also placed *vis-à-vis* the quasi-right of communities to exclude the less desirable.

10.3 Emancipation in contemporary diverse societies?

As we have seen in previous chapters, human rights have been used for the totalising purposes of protecting a system and disabling the possibility of emancipation. Having abandoned their utopian goal of disrupting the order, they have been used, instead of for emancipation, as an extension of the existing order of the law. As Costas Douzinas has warned:

> Not only have human rights been hijacked by governments and international committees and their early connection with the utopianism of radical natural law has been severed, but utopia also is not doing so well. It would not be inaccurate to say that our epoch has witnessed the demise of utopian hopes and that, additionally, the utopian motif has been suspended even in critical thought.
>
> (Douzinas 2000, 338)

As we have observed, in complex contemporary socio-cultural landscapes using rights for a conservationist purpose might turn them into tools for preserving existing socio-cultural structures. In the post-revolutionary era fraught with contradictory directions and claims of emancipation, appeal to difference risks

---

[5] *Lautsi* v. *Italy*, European Court of Human Rights, Grand Chamber Judgment, Application No. 30814/06, 18 March 2011, Dissenting opinion of Judge Bonello, *Lautsi* v. *Italy*, para. 1.6.

[6] *Lautsi* v. *Italy*, Grand Chamber, para. 67.

being seen as a defence of a rebel without a cause. But difference still requires recognition, and the contemporary appeal to difference must also recognise the existence of diverse axes of emancipation, as Balibar would call them. To recognise who has this access, a traditional inquiry into emancipation would normally start from a lengthy passage investigating the essence of freedom and its relationship with rights. After all, rights are most often conceptualised as originating in the concept of freedom and protecting nothing but freedom. Therefore a traditional inquiry would investigate and systematise Western philosophical tradition from Aristotle, through Leibniz to Kant and beyond. But a preoccupation with coupling freedom and autonomy would inevitably proliferate problems related to the centrality of the self and its self-interest. And inquiries by many prominent philosophers and theorists appear to have thoroughly explored this field of inquiry, leaving as many questions open as answered. If we strive to define freedom we risk, as with the notion of justice, creating and replicating models and structures that will confine freedom to a static notion eventually reversing its purpose and resulting only in appropriating freedom for the purpose of defending the known. Therefore, for an understanding of emancipation and its axes we could instead use Adorno's dialectical method and turn our eyes towards unfreedom. In fact, the origins of the concept of freedom lie nowhere but in unfreedom itself. According to Hansen:

> The oldest and throughout antiquity most common meaning of *eleutheros* is being free as opposed to being a slave (*doulos*). It is the only meaning attested in the Homeric poems, and if a Greek in antiquity was asked what *eleutheria* was, the presumption is that first of all he would think of the opposition between *eleutheria* and *douleia* and say that a free person (*eleutheros*) was his own master by contrast with a slave (*doulos*) who was the possession of his master (*despotes*).
>
> (Hansen 2010, 1)

In his critique of the Kantian theory of freedom, Adorno frequently turns to the concept of unfreedom, showing that seeking a common formula for freedom restricts it and eventually denies it. First, Adorno finds an ideal of absolute individual freedom to be nonsensical and argues that freedom understood as each individual decision separated from its context and separating the individual from society results in 'the fallacy of absolute, pure being-in-itself' (Adorno 1973, 213). At the same time, he argues further, a 'bombastic' appeal for freedom and increased reference to freedom by the subject, or the community as an extension of subjects, ascribes greater responsibility to the subject. Yet in practice, according to Adorno, no bourgeois society has ever endowed a subject with such freedom (Adorno 1973, 221). This is partly because anything opposed to the subject will be submerged by abstraction to the subject (Adorno 1973, 248). Preoccupied with Kantian notions of freedom, Adorno directs his critique at causality as a function of subjective reason and claims that it is in fact causality without *causa* relying heavily on nothing other than the law. He deeply disagrees with Kant, arguing that his theory leaves an 'intolerable mortgage' on post-Kantianism: 'that freedom without law is not freedom' (Adorno 1973, 248). In this form, freedom is no more than a plea for order and consistency which eventually annexes all non-identity (Adorno 1973, 250). The appeal to freedom becomes exploited for the purpose of 'detestation of anarchy' (Adorno 1973, 250). When freedom is used as a defence from anarchy it becomes inextricably linked with the established order and ceases to exist. As Adorno has demonstrated, freedom and unfreedom exist in a dialectical and dynamic relationship, while emancipation is always inspired by the counter-image of suffering. But if freedom is treated as if it has already been achieved and can be maintained, it only deceives and perpetuates static structures. Emancipation and the struggle for freedom must instead be understood as a constant battle and a process progressing from the direction of unfreedom to the direction of freedom. As Derrida argued in the case of justice:

> It is … because of this always excessive haste of interpretation getting ahead of itself, because of this structural urgency and precipitation of justice that the latter has no horizon of expectation (regulative or messianic). But for this very reason, it *may* have an *avenir*, a 'to-come,' which I rigorously distinguish from the future that can always reproduce the present. Justice remains, is yet, to come, *à venir*, it has an, it is *à-venir*, the very dimension of events irreducibly to come.… 'Perhaps,' one must always say perhaps for justice.
>
> (Derrida 1992, 27)

Just as an established state of justice cannot exist, an established state of freedom cannot exist. Freedom is not an achieved state and a full state of freedom can never come about. Absolute freedom will annihilate itself by generating new conditions of unfreedom. Freedom as an absolute and universal ideal is an inherently enlightened illusion and as such shares all the qualities of Enlightenment, leading only to subordinating everything to the structures serving and maintaining existing hegemonies. Once declared as achieved, freedom becomes violence that perpetuates itself through creation and maintenance of meanings that enslave and oppress. In the static state of 'freedom achieved' there are no emancipatory movements and no renegotiations. The image of freedom is known, predictable and constructed by analogy to norms that have become dominant. Dominant normativities are therefore comfortable since they do not require new efforts at renegotiation. When freedom is treated as established, it is easy to dismiss new claims for renegotiation by saying that these will violate existing achieved 'freedom'. Wearing a veil violates freedom as a democratic principle, says the ECtHR. What it conveniently forgets is that under this interpretation freedom signifies a universalistic system of hegemonic meanings imagining what freedom of religion should entail. The particular instance of unfreedom is dismissed not because it lacks emancipatory potential, but because it discomforts the majority. Dismissed by appeal to an imagined but in fact enslaving freedom, it dismisses the applicants' call for a particular way of achieving freedom that would disrupt the established cultural order. The freedom that the ECtHR refers to is not in fact freedom but an established and easily recognisable system. Despite not being the main inspiration for this book, Rosa Luxemburg's writings on the Russian revolution contain an important fragment focusing on the problematic transition between freedom and unfreedom and more importantly the transient line between minority and freedom. As quoted already once before, Luxemburg asserted that:

> Freedom is always and exclusively freedom for the one who thinks differently. Not because of any fanatical concept of 'justice' but because all that is instructive, wholesome and purifying in political freedom depends on this essential characteristic, and its effectiveness vanishes when 'freedom' becomes a special privilege.
>
> (Luxemburg 1918, 69)

What Luxemburg calls freedom is precisely the moment of emancipation that we are seeking to define. That moment is captured in contestation and dissent or what she sees as the ability to think differently. This ability is extinguished as soon as it is achieved and becomes established as a privilege. Following the revolutionary heritage of Luxemburg's writings we could conceptualise every contestation as an emancipatory and revolutionary moment belonging only to those who think differently. Otherwise, what we call 'freedom' will always result in acknowledging the existing privilege of the stronger, the more powerful or the better represented.

What follows the emancipatory function of human rights must be understood as a drive to shake off the shackles of unfreedom, marginalisation or oppression of those who think differently against those whose established privileges of freedom generate their unfreedom. The essence of rights cannot reside in freedom, because freedom is only a temporary moment, constantly threatened and extinguished by societal conditions. Freedom will degenerate once achieved because it cannot be fixed. Once freedom is fixed it mutates into an order generating new forms of unfreedom. Therefore, to remain emancipatory tools human rights must be seen not as an entitlement for protecting established and existing freedom but a vehicle on the road from unfreedom towards greater freedom. And because freedom, like justice, can never be arrived at, neither can human rights ever 'arrive' at their destination. Emancipation is a constant process of shaking off unfreedom and pursuing a freedom as yet unachieved. What follows from the transitory role of human rights in the struggle for emancipation is the impossibility of there ever existing an established state of human rights seen as privileges. As emancipatory tools, human rights can only be employed in anticipation of a freedom that is always on the horizon. They can only be transitory vehicles enabling the journey from unfreedom towards greater freedom – a journey that ends as soon as one freedom is recognised and begins anew in a new form, in a new contestation, in a new challenge to emancipate from a new, unknown form of unfreedom. The emancipatory direction of rights may change as soon as one freedom is achieved, only to drive the desire to emancipate from a new and yet unknown form of unfreedom. If human rights are to serve the utopian call for justice, they cannot be tools alleviating the fear of impermanence and anarchy nor can they be objects that could be possessed. Instead of the right to 'have rights' as a form of privilege, we must think of the right of access to human rights as a form of 'ticket' to board the vehicle of emancipation on the transient journey from unfreedom towards greater freedom.

References

Adorno, Theodor W. 1973. *Negative Dialectics*. Routledge.

Balibar, Etienne. 2013. 'On the Politics of Human Rights.' *Constellations* 20(1): 18–26.

Benhabib, Seyla. 1984. 'Epistemologies of Postmodernism: A Rejoinder to Jean-François Lyotard.' *New German Critique* Autumn (33): 103–26.

Benhabib, Seyla. 1992. *Situating the Self: Gender, Community, and Postmodernism in Contemporary Ethics*. Routledge.

Benhabib, Seyla. 2004. *The Rights of Others: Aliens, Residents, and Citizens*. Cambridge University Press.

Cornell, Drucilla. 1986. 'The Poststructuralist Challenge to the Ideal of Community.' *Cardozo Law Review* 8: 989–1022.

Derrida, Jacques. 1992. 'Force of Law: The Mystical Foundation of Authority.' In *Deconstruction and the Possibility of Justice*, ed. Drucilla Cornell, Michel Rosenfeld and David Gray Carlson, 3–67. Routledge.

Douzinas, Costas. 2000. *The End of Human Rights: Critical Legal Thought at the Turn of the Century*. Hart Publishing.

Douzinas, Costas. 2013. 'The Paradoxes of Human Rights.' *Constellations* 20(1): 51–67.

Hansen, Mogens Herman. 2010. 'Democratic Freedom and the Concept of Freedom in Plato and Aristotle.' *Greek, Roman, and Byzantine Studies* 50(1): 1–27.

Lentin, Alana, and Gavan Titley. 2011. *The Crises of Multiculturalism: Racism in a Neoliberal Age*. Zed Books.

Levinas, Emmanuel. 1981. *Otherwise than Being, or Beyond Essence*. Springer.

Luxemburg, Rosa. 1918. *The Russian Revolution and Leninism or Marxism?* University of Michigan Press.

Lyotard, Jean François. 1984. *The Postmodern Condition: A Report on Knowledge*. Theory and History of Literature 10. Manchester University Press.

Rancière, Jacques. 2004. 'Who Is the Subject of the Rights of Man?' *South Atlantic Quarterly* 103(2): 297–310.

Rorty, Richard. 1985. 'Habermas and Lyotard on Postmodernity.' In *Habermas and Modernity*, ed. Richard J. Bernstein, 161–75. MIT Press.

Simmons, William Paul. 2011. *Human Rights Law and the Marginalized Other*. Cambridge University Press.

Taylor, Charles. 1992. *The Ethics of Authenticity*. Harvard University Press.

Young, Iris Marion. 1990. *Justice and the Politics of Difference*. Princeton University Press.

Žižek, Slavoj. 2005. 'Against Human Rights.' *New Left Review* 34: 115–31.

Chapter 11

Rights beyond structure?

Towards otherwise than becoming

So far we have examined why rights have a potential to mutate from instruments of freedom to instruments of maintaining static order. Implicated in the intricate ontological mechanism of defining freedom, identity and self, they have been used to maintain rather than disrupt existing power hegemonies in the realm of law and religion. They have become an extension of legal regimes and tools for their protection, mutating into empty phrases of legal discourse. Rather than speaking for the disempowered, the marginalised and the oppressed, human rights have been used to justify further marginalisation of the other and protect already established and static 'freedoms' in the name of imagined consensus. To reinstate the original emancipatory drive of human rights and bring them closer to those to whom the appeal to principles such as religious pluralism was a promise of being recognised at long last, we need to think of human rights as other than privileges of the self protected by the legal order. To save the notion of rights and emancipation from the risk of becoming a new constraining order and perpetuating new forms of stagnation, we require methods of navigation between different emancipatory narratives and conceptualising human rights as a counterbalance to the existing legal order. When we see human rights as an instrument of emancipation rather than as a part of positivised law, it is easier to imagine bringing down the divide between law and ethics. When we tie human rights to the existing legal order then we must inevitably end up in the realm of the totalising ontology of law. There is no law without categories, no legal system without totalities and universalism. Albeit there is, as Manderson argues, a space in the heart of law to let ethics in, even in the legal order *sensu stricto* (Manderson 2007, 96–7), human rights require more than just this tiny space to be able to act as a counter-mechanism challenging existing power abuses. When we tie human rights to a revolutionary drive to emancipation, then we can imagine them as instruments of ethics rather than law or at least ethics coming before law.

And it is exactly at this point that turning to Emmanuel Levinas can help us understand human rights differently than they have been understood as a result of their legalisation and positivisation. Drawing on his ethical preoccupation with the ethical encounter with the other, Levinas applied the principles drawn in *Otherwise than Being* (Levinas 1981) and *Totality and Infinity* (Levinas 1969) in his short essay

'The Rights of Man and Rights of the Other' (Levinas 1994). It is therein that his principles of facing and responsibility have been expanded to the realm of justice. Seeking an escape from ontological categories and the realm of being, Levinas sought first of all to conceptualise freedom of the other as entirely different from one's own freedom. In *Otherwise than Being* he remarks:

> The freedom of another could never begin in my freedom, that is, abide in the same present, be contemporary, be representable to me. The responsibility for the other cannot have begun in my commitment, in my decision. The unlimited responsibility in which I find myself comes from the hither side of my freedom, from a 'prior to every memory,' an 'ulterior to every accomplishment,' from the non-present par excellence, the non-original, the anarchical, prior to or beyond essence.
>
> (Levinas 1981, 10)

If emancipation is a drive from unfreedom towards greater freedom and on this journey rights are to be reconceptualised as ethical principles, then this requires us to abandon imagining the freedom of the other as mirrored on what freedom means to me, to us, to those that I recognise in the comfort of the ontological mirror. As Levinas ascertains, the freedom of the other must remain unrepresentable to me and thus needs to transcend my essence. In other words, it requires acceptance prior to ontology. The freedom of the other cannot be an ontological category but instead must be a function of responsibility that comes before my freedom. It stems from the responsibility awoken by the face of the other. It is the nakedness of the face that pierces all order in the world and allows the consciousness to respond ethically (Levinas 2003, 32). This ethical response is encapsulated in responsibility for the other, which disappears when rights are limited by the constraints of the law. This subordination of rights to the law is 'already a way of treating the person as an object by submitting him or her (the unique, the incomparable) to comparison, to thought, to being placed on the famous scales of justice, and thus to calculation' (Levinas 1994, 96). As we have seen, in this calculation the other easily slips off those scales judged by my categories, by what is familiar to me, by what autonomy or reasonableness mean to me. When such an approach is taken, nothing prevents a 'possible war between multiple freedoms, or a conflict between reasonable wills that must be resolved by justice' (Levinas 1994, 96). In other words, Levinas argues that when human rights are subjected to the process of their legalisation they become conceptualised as entitlements of the subject and as such lead to conflicts when two entitlements collide. And as we have observed in this volume, expanding the logic of subjectivity beyond the individual leads to a war for freedom of the collective self and the marginalised that truly does not stand a chance in this comparison. The scales of justice will always be slippery for the other. Thus the effort to reconstruct the emancipatory logic of rights requires that rights be framed as a responsibility before the other. This responsibility would be a responsibility for the other's journey from unfreedom towards freedom that I do not need to model on my own – freedom which in fact I must necessarily fail to grasp. The Levinasian notion of rights holds a promise of curtailing exclusionary battles between different communities and offers a way of conceptualising rights as inclusive mechanisms of responsibility rather than privilege. He elaborates further that my freedom lies in fact in my responsibility alone. It is a freedom in fraternity, as he says, which is reaffirmed in the one-for-the-other that manifests itself to consciousness (Levinas 1994, 98). It is thus responsibility for emancipation rather than establishment of achieved freedom that promises effective entry to renegotiation of static and stagnant cultural structures upholding diverse forms of domination. This is the process of rebuilding the ethical potential of human rights. If the idea of freedom as an interest is replaced with the idea of a duty, the set of relevant questions changes. Rather than asking 'Who am I? What is my community?' and 'What interests does the other endanger?', the first consideration presents itself in the question 'What am I answerable for?'. This idea of rights puts the other before the self in an act of inexhaustible responsibility, it is the *Otherwise* part of *Otherwise than Being*. The act of definition, on the other hand, becomes secondary. Rights seen as duties relieve the binary tension between the self and the other and the egoistic community and the other. A community based on answerability instead of drawing limits for itself and its interests appears to offer a more promising basis for retaining the emancipatory potential of human rights. But the Levinasian conception suffers from a central difficulty. For Levinas, the act of ethical responsibility can be fulfilled only in the presence of a third person. As he elaborates:

> This 'thirdness' is different from that of the third man, it is the third party that interrupts the face to face of a welcome of the other man, interrupts the proximity or approach of the neighbour, it is the third man with which justice begins.
>
> (Levinas 1981, 150)

It is the third person that motivates the self to the act of responsibility. But it is precisely the third person that creates the basic difficulty. If it is the third person that motivates the self, then how can we reconcile responsibility for the rights of all the others that become visible in the presence of different third persons? How can responsibility respond to the marginalisation of some, but not all, others? Criticised for an ethical and purely philosophical focus, Levinasian theory on its own may lack the potential for effective translation of answerability into the realm of the political (Badiou 2001; Smith 2009, 68–71). Relying on Levinasian theory on an abstract and general level, ethics offer merely a challenge to modernity that lacks the potential to respond to the demands of real life (Smith 2009, 71). After all, has Levinas foreseen that equal responsibility for the rights of all others can be a source of a war of rights based on a conflict between different responsibilities? Consequently, responsibility as the foundation of rights, just like freedom, may lead to the impossibility of emancipation. If we turn to responsibility alone, we can more easily secure the potential of rights to drive emancipation from unfree-dom towards a new freedom but we are left at square one when it comes to the question: Who is the one to become emancipated – a home-schooling conserva-tive Christian or an atheist calling for educational exemption from teaching of Christianity? Or perhaps a Wiccan claiming recognition of their religion in a state prison? Or perhaps all of them at once? Or perhaps, as suggested below, different others in different settings that can become emancipated only once we know the circumstances of their unfreedom.

If we accept the contention that in contemporary societies, axes of emancipa-tion are diverse and can coexist; and if we acknowledge that when one emanci-patory journey ends, another begins, then it is necessary to propose a dynamic vision of those for whom rights ought to be reconstructed. The other cannot be everyone, nor can the third person, or we risk ending up in the same place that we sought an escape from – the condition of war between different emancipations. And it is here that Levinasian *Otherwise than Being* does not quite transcend the boundaries of Being. The other still remains a static category illuminated by the presence of an opaque third person. When the other remains static, exclusionary 'wars' between statically conceptualised responsibilities will be a natural conse-quence. In fact the self risks once more turning even deeper into the self in the search of an understanding who he or she has responsibility for. That turning risks slipping back to the ego and the ontological trappings of subjectivity. The exist-ence of different others necessitates freeing the being in the Levinasian 'otherwise than being' from rigidity and the danger of ontological slippage. Among diverse axes of emancipation, answering the question of whose rights I have a responsibil-ity for requires a focus on diverse aspects such as the local situation, the cases con-sidered, the type of issue and the choices made by the agents themselves (Balibar 2013, 22). In contemporary society it is not enough to conceptualise the other as a simple numerical minority. As illustrated here by reference to Deleuzian concep-tualisations of minority, a minority is not necessarily those who are less numerous but instead those who are underrepresented in a norm. Deleuze ties the notion of minority to the notion of becoming. He privileges becoming over being and assumes that becoming is always already minoritarian. This tying of minority and becoming is related to the fact that a minority has a possibility of deterritorialis-ing the majoritarian norm (Deleuze 1986) by drawing attention to the conditions that make one standard majoritarian. By such deterritorialisation the minority is imbued with the potentiality of becoming. As Patton explained in his defence of Deleuze's minoritarian politics, Deleuze's becoming-minoritarian refers to the 'potential of individuals or groups to deviate from the standard' (Patton 2005, 407). As he further explains, such an approach relates to the fact that individuals and groups never truly conform to the standard. Deleuze's minoritarian politics speak against ever acquiring a majority. This keeps the notion of minority fluid, dynamic and possible to apply in endless combinations and variations. Becoming is thus 'individual or collective struggles to come to terms with events and intoler-able conditions and to shake loose, to whatever degree possible, from determinants and definitions' (Biehl and Locke 2010, 317). As Williams illustrates, Deleuze and Levinas share certain fundamental ethical concepts when it comes to facing the other, but they differ on one fundamental note. For Levinas, transcendence is possible only with the face and so is responsibility. For Deleuze what matters is not in fact the face as an object but a special relation of movement beyond that which has already been identified (Williams 2005). For Deleuze life is immanent and open to constant new becomings. In their radical new conceptualisation of ontology, Deleuze and Guattari conceive of the notion of rhizome (Deleuze and Guattari 1980, ch. 1). Rhizome promises to rise above contraptions of ontology and go beyond fixing forms and subjects. The Deleuzian ontology of rhizome is anti-foundationalist in envisioning the possibility of constantly new points of growth and change. Rhizome defies structures and is not synonymous with being. It defies rigidities and envisions that points of growth might be stimulated in any part of the rhizomatic structure. Becoming corresponds with rhizomatic ontology – the purpose of both is to resist the rigidity of structures:

> At the same time, something else entirely is going on: not imitation at all but a capture of code, surplus value of code, an increase in valence, a veritable becoming, a becoming-wasp of the orchid and a becoming-orchid of the wasp. Each of these becomings brings about the deterritorialization of one term and the reterritorialization of the other; the two becomings interlink and form relays in a circulation of intensities pushing the deterritorialization ever further. There is neither imitation nor resemblance, only an exploding of two heterogeneous series on the line of flight composed by a common rhizome that can no longer be attributed to or subjugated by anything signifying.
> (Deleuze and Guattari 1980, 10)

The process of deterritorialisation involves constant renegotiation. The becoming minoritarian enjoys the possibility of positioning themself against the majority and deterritorialising the majoritarian standard. Becoming is the potentiality to deviate from existing and recognised models (Deleuze and Guattari 1980, 105) and the privilege of becoming over being is dictated by the necessity to preserve constant new configurations and constant new deterritorialisations. In that process neither the minority nor the majority remains unchanged. It is not being but instead becoming that corresponds to the matrix of contemporary different axes of emancipation. Levinasian responsibility secures an approach to rights as different from privileges while Deleuzian becoming preserves the transformative relation – a movement away from whatever constraints limit the minority. Becoming is more flexible than being because it might refer to one person, one ideal, community or a collective of ideals. When inspired by Deleuze, those for whom we have responsibility are those who are about to become, about to contest and renegotiate. This encompasses endless categories of people, movements or groups that think differently. Contemporary revolutionaries whose rights we are responsible for must be seen in a perpetual state of flux. Their becoming can be initiated in any place and at any point in any of the structures that surround them. Once they grow into a new structure, emancipation takes on a new form; a new point of growth within this structure and a new becoming has to be acknowledged. It might be a woman wearing a veil contesting a norm that constrains veiling, but it might also be a woman in a different structure contesting veiling as a majoritarian standard. It might be both a devout Christian seeking exemption from sex education classes and an atheist seeking recognition of her atheism among majoritarian Catholicism. It will be both a youth enrolling in a new religious movement and one escaping from one. It will be both religion contesting the secular and the secular contesting religion. Replacing being with becoming secures that rights can always remain flexible and always respond to changing social circumstances. As tickets to emancipation, their shape cannot be envisioned a priori. 'Who, where and against what?' must remain open to interpretation. In other words what it means for human rights to secure freedom, is securing a becoming freedom, a process of emancipation, a line of flight or the possibility of breaking free from what is already recognised. The capacity of human rights as emancipatory mechanisms ends when they constrain another emancipation. And sometimes that happens as soon as one emancipation is achieved and begins to constrain another. The emancipated then becomes the majority and a new becoming must be possible. The only limit for rights can lie in preventing a becoming that would forever disable the possibility of a new becoming, an emancipation leading to the emergence of an immutable structure and annihilation of the emancipation of another. This is the only limit standing in the way of our responsibility for becoming. Emancipation cannot be achieved once and for all. There must always be the potential for new emancipatory calls to emerge and for new structures to break. There will always be a changeable other – not a structural subject but a changeable becoming. In the legalised world of human rights, this ethical potential of human rights can step back into application of rights in all those places at the heart of law which leave uncertainty – in phrases such as 'necessity in a democratic society' and in all those other phrases which allow us to debate. It is therein that we first and foremost have to ask: 'Where lies our responsibility?'

The reconstruction provided here is a modest, albeit radical proposal to re-inject emancipatory potential into human rights and bring them closer to those for whom they were originally designed – the weak, the marginalised and the disempowered. I leave it to more prominent philosophical minds to judge the feasibility of this reconstruction and reconcile further philosophical dilemmas which that proposal might raise, for instance those related to reconciling appeals to immanence and transcendence in the writings of thinkers whose arguments I have referred to. I do not wish to present this reconstruction as a universal model of thinking about rights but, rather, as a roadmap to a different way of thinking about human rights. I hope that it may offer a way to secure a less totalising application of principles such as religious pluralism and secure that the hope brought by such principles is reinstated for those who need them the most – those on the margins, those ridiculed and those deemed to be standing too far from majoritarian normativities to enjoy the protection of rights.

References

Badiou, Alain. 2001. *Ethics: An Essay on the Understanding of Evil*. Verso.

Balibar, Etienne. 2013. 'On the Politics of Human Rights.' *Constellations* 20(1): 18–26.

Biehl, João and Peter Locke. 2010. 'Deleuze and the Anthropology of Becoming.' *Current Anthropology* 51(3): 317–51

Deleuze, Gilles. 1986. *Kafka: Toward a Minor Literature*. University of Minnesota Press.

Deleuze, Gilles and Felix Guattari. 1980. *A Thousand Plateaus: Capitalism and Schizophrenia*. Continuum.

Levinas, Emmanuel. 1969. *Totality and Infinity: An Essay on Exteriority*. Duquesne University Press.

Levinas, Emmanuel. 1981. *Otherwise than Being, or Beyond Essence*. Springer.

Levinas, Emmanuel. 1994. *Outside the Subject*. Stanford University Press.

Levinas, Emmanuel. 2003. *Humanism of the Other*. University of Illinois Press.

Manderson, Desmond. 2007. *Proximity, Levinas, and the Soul of Law*. McGill-Queen's University Press.

Patton, Paul. 2005. 'Deleuze and Democracy.' *Contemporary Political Theory* 4(4): 400–13.

Smith, Nick. 2009. 'Questions for a Reluctant Jurisprudence of Alterity.' In *Essays on Levinas and Law: A Mosaic*, ed. Desmond Manderson, 55–75. Palgrave Macmillan.

Williams, James. 2005. *The Transversal Thought of Gilles Deleuze: Encounters and Influences*. Clinamen Press.

Conclusions

The emerging principle of religious pluralism in the human rights discourses in Europe promised to be a gigantic step towards assuring that all believers and non-believers can live according to the dictates of their conscience. For a continent with the memory of religious wars, taking a decisive step in the direction of religious pluralism marked a new promising era of recognition and inclusiveness unknown before. Unfortunately, against this promising benchmark such recent events as the *Charlie Hebdo* shooting or the attack on a Danish synagogue continue to remind us that the era of conflict is not that far behind and that the principle of religious pluralism has perhaps failed to live up to its promise. The envisioned dialogue and equality appear even further on the horizon than before the declaration of the era of pluralism. Frequently the blame for this failure is placed on religious adherents for what is perceived as a non-compromising stance and alleged radicalism. Certainly, this author is not attempting to justify violence in any shape or form and does indeed consider violence a movement disabling all emancipation and dismantling the possibility of pluralism.

However, as this volume has attempted to remind us, the blame for the failure of this most progressive principle should not perhaps be so readily put on these individuals but rather on the construction of the narrative of religious pluralism. Far from challenging the existing structures of cultural power and providing a counterbalance for dominant normativities, the principle of religious pluralism is built on shaky foundations. It dictates the type of newcomers that can be included on the religious scene of Europe, and administers their religious freedom. In such a setting the merely different was eventually turned into the absolutely other, who in due course became synonymous with a dissident intending to bring down the fundamentals of established legal orders.

The crooked foundations of pluralism operated to create a boundary between 'us' and 'them'. It disabled not only recognition but frequently even a dialogue, and infinite reiterations of the mechanism eventually placed 'us' and 'the other' on opposing sides of an uncrossable abyss. As illustrated in this book, this mechanism was readily applied to even those adherents who did not advocate violence or harm. Before they could even access rights, members of new religious movements or those holding more individualised beliefs were defined through the lens of analogy to the well-established and well-known religions and branded as followers of 'sects'. When put in that frame they were not only positioned on the margins and excluded, but assumed to be too 'radical' to enjoy a freedom comparable to that enjoyed by those whose religious or secular normativities were recognised by law. Their difference was turned into otherness before it could even appeal to rights.

But even for those whose religion was not a subject of contestation, religious pluralism has proved to be a narrative disabling rather than enabling emancipation. When appealing to freedom of religion in defence of their religious symbolism, the religiously different are put even further to the margins and pushed even deeper into the ever-narrowing so-called 'private sphere'. They are at the same time told that their religious or secular symbolism is too egoistic or too radical to be recognised. This stands in contrast to the symbolism chosen by public institutions in the name of a 'tradition', legal order or for the comfort of the majority. The other was once more, already at the outset, enframed as a 'radical' trying to bring down the principle of pluralism, while the public institutions were endowed with a quasi-right to select and display whatever symbolism they choose, secular or religious. But the distancing of 'us' and 'them' did not stop there. When the other encroached on the so-called 'ethical inheritance' of the majority, she was truly shown her place in this new vision of pluralism. She was silenced and chastised in the name of 'profound moral views' that disabled any possibility of contestation of the existing secular or religious normativities.

In such a vision of pluralism, human rights – such as freedom of religion – became no more than tools to maintain consensus. This consensus disabled the possibility of emancipation and renegotiation and served as a defence of already established freedoms. The rights in their appeal to consensus annexed the principle of identity and protected established freedom at all costs. Any attempt to emancipate from the constraints of the imagined 'us' was rebuffed with an appeal to the collective identity. Consequently, human rights instead of being tools of contestation became tools maintaining established orders. Instead of being tools contesting existing structures, they mutated into even more solid and rigid structures. In these structures no emancipation and no renegotiation was ever possible. Focused on 'us' and employing strategies used by the subject to reify its own boundaries against the 'other', we grew further and further apart. Eventually the other could no longer even identify with the narratives we employed for the purpose of defending 'our' solid structures. The appeal to rights was turned into our privilege and removed from the hands of the other. Rights became 'our' moral structure and served to make the boundaries between 'us' and 'them' even clearer.

In such a version of rights and pluralism no renegotiations and no emancipation is ever possible. When freedom is turned into stone, the scales of justice are impossibly weighted and the other slides off, unable to even phrase her appeal. 'We' on the other hand can sleep 'peacefully', undisturbed by newcomers, new renegotiations and new religions. Or can we?

This book advocates against such a rigid version of freedom and pluralism and against further distancing between self and the other. To inject pluralism into pluralism and bring back emancipatory potential of human rights, rights must be reconceptualised and infused with their original revolutionary logic. As argued here this can only happen through proximity and the traversing of these established and ossified boundaries. The appeal to human rights can only be meaningful if we treat them as responsibility rather than privilege, and if we accept the other as a constantly changing subject. Not in fact the subject that we imagine her to be, but instead an entity in a constant process of change; an entity we cannot quite imagine; an apparition in the process of becoming who faces us primarily to discomfort us and renegotiate both herself and ourselves. In this encounter nothing can stay rigid and we all must emerge anew.

This radical version of rights and pluralism is a challenge to the fear of anarchy and impermanence that fuels the need for preserving existing orders. But radical pluralism is also imbued with a promise. A promise to restart a dialogue of renegotiations where the other is not reduced to what we imagine her to be or what we allow her to be. If this step does not happen, those branded 'too radical' before they even became radical will indeed keep radicalising. We risk being faced with more *Charlie Hebdo*-like events and more spectacles of terror. As boundaries between 'us' and 'them' continue growing, they risk making the abyss of disagreements too broad to be bridged. Eventually, the gap may become too wide for peaceful renegotiations to be possible. Instead, the fear of anarchy will paradoxically close the imaginary 'us' and 'them' in our respective structures that bind so tightly that renegotiations can only happen by confrontation. Breeding nothing but violence, the fear of anarchy can lead only to a different form of anarchy. Holding tightly to our structures we risk recreating the boundaries of heaven and hell, as depicted on the cover of this book. In the biblical story the distance between the two grew so big and insurmountable that they could only come together in an apocalyptic confrontation. A promise of radical pluralism is not a guarantee or security against such a turn of events. It is merely a hope that another way is not only possible but indeed necessary.

Index

References such as '178–9' indicate (not necessarily continuous) discussion of a topic across a range of pages. Wherever possible in the case of topics with many references, these have either been divided into sub-topics or only the most significant discussions of the topic are listed. Because the entire work is about the 'pluralism', the use of this term (and certain others which occur constantly throughout the book) as an entry point has been minimized. Information will be found under the corresponding detailed topics.

Treaty on the Functioning of the
European Union, *see* TFEU
Turkey 29, 36, 69, 101, 112, 162

unfreedom 27, 32, 36, 151, 164–7,
169, 171
United Kingdom 27, 48, 54, 90, 124
unity 7, 33, 39, 150–1
unreasonable doctrines 15–16, 56
unreasonableness 144–5, *see also*
reasonableness
utopia of rights 149–55

values 3, 5–6, 13–16, 19–20, 40, 104,
145–7, 161–2

Vatican 65–9, 130
veiling 22, 53, 107, 161
victims 44, 95, 99, 101, 103, 152
violence 4, 56, 62, 151, 157, 165, 175, 177

war 6, 56, 86, 169–71; religious 1, 175
Williams, J 150, 154, 172
Wingrove case 27–8
women 59–60, 100, 107, 119–21, 123–5,
127, 129–30, 173; Muslim 15, 22;
pregnant 120, 124–5
worship 42–3, 53, 66, 81–2, 88, 90
worthiness 34, 82, 86, 94–5, 147

Zucca, L 1, 8, 52, 69, 140

For Product Safety Concerns and Information please contact our EU
representative GPSR@taylorandfrancis.com
Taylor & Francis Verlag GmbH, Kaufingerstraße 24, 80331 München, Germany